A Pain in the Bum

The picture of the butterfly, taken on my phone had an uplifting effect on me. I took it on a visit to Yorkshire Lavender while waiting for the results of the initial tests. My mum loved butterflies and my gran's favourite perfume was lavender and the thought came into my mind that I would soon have the confirmation that I did have cancer, but that I had the genes of these two strong women and they would help me to get through it.

A Pain in the Bum

THE MEANDERINGS OF A HEALTHY WOMAN

Copyright and Ordering

First Printing: 2021
ISBN: 9798590032099

Published by Swinton Writers in t'Critchley Hub
Age UK Critchley Community Hub
75 Chorley Road
Swinton
Manchester
M27 4AF
United Kingdom

Email: switchswinton@gmail.com

Ordering Information:
Available through Amazon and good book distributors or directly from author at veromum@ymail.com

Contents

Acknowledgements

In August 2013, thanks to the NHS Cancer Screening Programme, I discovered that I had Bowel Cancer. My cancer journey fortunately ended when I walked out of hospital cured. Many people have a much sadder ride.

I was so very fortunate, not to have to face this alone, whenever I began to feel overwhelmed, the rock who is my husband was by my side. My children and grandchildren lifted my spirits by being positive about the whole thing and my siblings and friends with their black humour gave me the best medicine.

My gratitude to all the medical staff at Christie of Salford and Royal Bolton Hospital, using their skills and NHS Resources, they took away the cancer and gave me back a future. We should never be unappreciative of our health service.

Before I went into hospital, a friend bought me a note book and I decided to keep a diary to help me keep track of my treatment. Following successful treatment, I thought I might turn my diary into a book, but lacking any knowledge of how to go about that, and still working long hours as a childminder, the idea was shelved. During the COVID lockdown in 2020, a friend suggested that I join SWit'CH Swinton writing group, which, due to the pandemic was meeting each week on Zoom. Thank you to Rosemary for introducing me to the club and Judith, Chris, Chris, Sylvia, Bill, Stella and Paul for their kind editing, encouragement and friendship.

This writing club has given me enjoyment and something to look forward to each week. I've made friends, discovered a talent for writing* and been encouraged to finish and publish my book.

Here it is.

*Some of my other reminiscences have been included in the SWit'CH anthology 'Memries Unlocked'.

1 - Diagnosis

I wasn't surprised when the results of the screening came back as abnormal (after all I have never even tried to be normal).

A couple of years ago I had visited to the doctor because of blood in my poo. After a quick examination he assured me that it was caused by hemorrhoids. I accepted his diagnoses but had a niggling doubt that he had only just "looked" - no blood samples, I could be pooing blood from two different sources.

Shortly afterwards I spotted a 6 bedroomed house and knew I had to have it. I did not know what I was letting myself in for. A broker who had assured me that he could get me a mortgage let me down - after I had put in a successful bid. The council who had sold it to me (it had been a children's home), informed me that I had to prove it had been suitably advertised for use as a children's home, or they wouldn't give us permission to live in it? For goodness sake, they had sold it to me, didn't they know whether it had been suitably advertised? The house had been vandalized and set on fire, and had all the copper pipes stolen, which in turn meant that the dining room ceiling had collapsed, when the water from the tanks had come through. The kitchen had been trashed and the bedrooms were decorated in varying colours of wood chip. On top of that we couldn't get a buyer for our original house, so had no way to pay anyone.

Two years later with the help and generosity of my lovely family (always knew being the eldest child of 8 would come in useful), and hours and hours of hard work, we had our dream house. Not in a salubrious area, it is in the middle of a council estate, in a suburb of Salford, but it was my castle. The builder and plasterer (both a bit disappointed that they hadn't spotted the potential) had encouraged us to bring the house up to spec and very generously waited for payment for nearly a year for our house to sell. This was the first house that Paolo and I, had bought together and we both poured our heart and souls into it. We worked like slaves every spare minute and gave anyone that came to visit a guided tour.

As the house began to take shape and we began to have time to think about the rest of our lives, the niggling doubt about the blood in the toilet began to tap away in my brain again, augmented with bit of a change in bowel habits when I would sometimes have to rush to the toilet. All in all I was pleased when the screening test (sent to everyone over 60 years of age) popped through my door. (In the same post came my bus pass and a report from Ofsted confirming our *Outstanding* status.) I knew it would come back as abnormal and happily provided them with a second one. I couldn't believe it when they asked me if I wanted to have a Colonoscopy (camera up the bum for uninitiated) and told me to go away and think about it carefully. Why would I provide the smears on the test and then not take it any further. I replied that I didn't need time to think and would they make the arrangements ASAP PLEASE.

Strangely enough we had taken two weeks holiday from our jobs as childminders to go to Italy but for some reason I had made excuses not to go, otherwise I wouldn't have received the results for another 2 weeks. I had the Colonoscopy the following Wednesday before which I had to drink a huge amount of laxative powder in water until I was passing clear fluid instead of poo to clear out the colon.

It was fascinating watching the images on the screen as the camera moved around the colon (reminded me of the pigs belly my mam used to eat in vinegar). I suspected that something was amiss when the nurse suddenly turned the screen out of my view, but I pushed the doubt out of my mind. I prayed desperately for the results to come back clear so that I could go home and live happily ever after without the niggling doubts.

I began to feel a little nervous when I seemed to be waiting for the discharge notes longer than any of the other people, who were having their cups of tea and then strolling off with their transport home, while Paolo and I made small talk and individually worried, pretending to each other that this was a normal day and we would be going home and reassuring our children that I was a perfectly healthy hypochondriac.

The bombshell was dropped and arrangements were made for MRI and CT scans and we went home to tell the children and the rest of our family and friends that I had a tumour in the Rectum.

My children already knew of the abnormal test results and that I was going for a colonoscopy, so I knew they would be hanging on to their mobile phones waiting for the results and I also knew that this was not the sort of news you could send a quick text about. I called on Helen first. As I walked through the front door she called a breezy" Hi" from upstairs, I started to climb the stairs and she began to come down saying "How did it go mum, do you want a brew?" I shook my head at her and motioned for her to go back into the bedroom - I didn't want Jamie 9 or Lily 5 to witness the emotion that I knew would follow. Helen's face registered the terror she was feeling and I hated myself for putting her through this. I told her the facts that I knew up to now and that I was not going to question "Why me?" I had 62 years of good health, perhaps it was my turn. For me it was important to face the worst, so that anything else would be a good result. Helen likes to be in charge and protested to me through her tears that we would all get through this, that I was not to mention any other result but getting better. I promised I would do my best and we held each other and sobbed for a few minutes, dried our tears and pretended that everything was normal. I went back downstairs and chatted to Jamie about his 10th birthday coming up on 26th August. Later I see Robert, Helen's husband he is also very upset. He says that when his mum died he didn't know how he was going to stop hurting but that he had always imagined that I would live forever, he reiterated Helen's words and said that getting better was my only option. No pressure then!.

Next I went to see Rachael, my little star, she has had so much shit happen to her over the last few years including the death by cancer of her son's other nanna a couple of years ago, ironically at the age of 62, but she keeps on keeping on, with a shrug of her shoulders and a lovely kind heart. She stood silently listening to me, fighting away the tears and smiling through her gulps. We hugged each other gently, as if we each were made of eggshells and she told me that I was strong and would fight it. I felt helpless as I left her on her own, no partner to comfort her. I felt sad at leaving her on her own to deal with this awful news, knowing that she would go away and cry by herself. "Yes I will mum" she said,

"But only for a little while, then I will have a nice warm bath and a cup of tea and I will be fine" this is a family joke because my kids say that I think this is a cure for anything, and they are probably right.

Then I went to see my eldest son Nathan. He had one grandson on his hip and another pulling at his trouser leg, he has a lot on his plate at the moment with wayward step-daughters. He shook his head mouthing NO NO NO in between gently dealing with his tired grandsons. I felt so proud of him! I could see his fear and anger and sadness in his face, but I knew that he too would deal with this with strength. As I was leaving, his partner Kathryn came downstairs to get ready for her night shift and was talking ten to the dozen. Nathan just looked at her and said, "Mum's got cancer" I excused myself and left him to explain everything and her to comfort him.

I still had to tell Matteo, As I got back home I saw that his car was in the drive and prepared myself on how to tell him. But when I got in he already knew as his dad had told him. I find out later that Paolo had found the strength to put aside his own emotions to tell Matteo about the results. They hugged and Matteo went up to his room to get things straight in his mind. As soon as he left the room, Lauren (Teo's girlfriend) witnessed Paolo collapsing into gut wrenching, howling tears. As I came into the living room, Matteo gave me a hug and we didn't talk for a few minutes, then I made him promise that he would not change any of his plans because of this, he had just decided that university life was not for him and he knew that I was a bit disappointed, but he has always been so mature and his reasons for doing things were always thought out. I feel such sadness for him, he was only 8 when his dad had cancer, 11 years ago and now he is having to deal with it again at this crucial stage of his life. I tell him that I have to have scans to determine the severity of the tumour but hopefully we have caught it early as I have not been feeling ill up to now. We hug and shed a few tears then have a cup of tea and change the subject.

How could I tell Adam? He had started work very early that morning, I knew he would go to the quiz night after work and

6

come home drunk, after all it was Thursday. I couldn't send him a text, nor phone him. He came home in the early hours of the morning and I got up to meet him. "Hi mum" he slurred, "want a cuppa?", I let him make me a drink, biting my lip as he dropped coffee and sugar all over the work surfaces and floor of the kitchen. I considered waiting until the morning to drop my bombshell, but then what if he once again went out before I woke and then was given the news by someone else?. He is forever telling me that I don't tell him anything. Taking the bull by the horns I tell him as slowly as I can about the results from the colonoscopy. He immediately sobers up and begins to cry. He sobs like a baby and asks me questions that I cannot even remember now. Suddenly he gets to grips with it, he puts his arms around me and tells me that this is just a blip in our lives, something to get on with for 6 months, then everything is back to normal. I agree with him and go to bed, surprisingly I sleep like a baby and wake up refreshed.

Paolo told his two sons Patrick and Joseph, they live in Sheffield and London respectively, I heard him gulping away emotion as he told them. For the first time I was glad that they had never called me mum, perhaps that would cushion the sadness for them.

I also phoned my sister and brothers. This was so difficult, listening to the people I love without question, going through the emotions and trying to be brave and sensible for my sake, while I remind them of their own mortality. I walked around the corner to tell my auntie Josie. We have always been close. I know that she really hasn't got over her sister, my mum dying and now I am telling her that perhaps I will die before her too.

2 - Rearranged Holiday

Not going to Italy had its benefits, we went to York and then to Scarborough, for the first time in my life. The weather was lovely and I can't imagine why I have never travelled to this part of the country before, I am excited at the prospect of bringing my grandchildren here. We visit Whitby, where I remember my gran visiting 50 years ago and I start to smell lavender everywhere, which also reminds me of my her. We go to visit Yorkshire Lavender where a butterfly poses for me while I take a photo. My family will vouch that I am the worst photographer in the world; the photos I take have my thumb jutting into the lens or heads missing and always out of focus. The photo of the butterfly is beautiful and perfect. My mum had a thing about butterflies. I say to Paolo, "my mum and gran are here to support me, I am going to get some bad news when we get home" He tells me not to be silly!

We go to Morecambe to stay with friends in their caravan for the weekend. While there, we go to see the Searchers. As we find our seats I mention to my friend Jackie how many old people are in the audience, she says "Veronica, just look in the mirror." They say anorexics look in the mirror and see a fat body. I look and see a 20 something young woman - it works for me.

Also sharing our weekend away are Pat and Terry. Terry is 70 going on 15 and has dementia. He wants to go abroad for a holiday, but Pat tries to make him understand that it is difficult to get Insurance because of his dementia. "Has it come back?", he says, "I'll have to go back to the clinic and get it sorted!" If only it was so simple. Pat has health worries of her own, for the duration of the weekend she has to keep running to the toilet and has stomach pain. She says that she has been to the doctor"s on several occasions but each time he has referred her to the hospital, they have sent her home with pain relief. I tell her that the next time she should refuse to go home until they diagnose her problem. Little did we know then, that Pat's tumour was already more advanced than mine.

3 - The CT and MRI Scans

For a week before the CT scan I had to eat a low residue diet, the exact opposite of the Slimming World diet that I had been following for a couple of weeks. So I gave up the slimming YIPEE. The next day it should have been NIL BY MOUTH for an hour before my appointment, but I didn't read these instructions until half an hour before, as I sat drinking a cup of tea. It didn't matter as I sat waiting for at least half an hour before I was "seen to" and then I had to do another marathon drinking session. The nurse brought me a big jug and a glass and told me to fill the glass every 15 minutes and drink it - I don't understand people who find this difficult. When he returned and I had finished the jug, he gave me another glass to drink just in case. I think he maybe thought Paolo had helped me to drink it. As I lay on the scanner waiting to go through the giant polo mint, the doctor injected a warm liquid into the vein on my arm. She explained that I would feel the warmth circulating through me and I would feel a sensation as if I had wet myself. I felt the sensation but it was much more pleasurable than wetting myself. - I came away with a smile on my face.

For: MRI Pelvis Rectum
On: Friday, 30 August, 2013 at 8.30 am
At: The Royal Bolton Hospital, Magnetic Resonance Imaging Dept.

The MRI Scan lasts for about 10 minutes and is very noisy. The operative popped an ear plug in each ear, the right one of which popped straight back out. I mentioned it but she just said, "It's all right, I am putting these earphones on top, they will squash it back in". But they didn't squash it back in and the noise in my right ear was very loud. I was tempted to reach up and adjust it but was aware of the close quarters of the scanning equipment and had visions of them having to dismantle this million pound piece of equipment to get my trapped arm free.

Your appointment is with Mr J Hobbiss Clinic and will be on:
Thursday 5th September 2013 at 2.30 pm in Minerva Day Outpatients Department

After the scans, we made an appointment to see the surgeon who would have studied the results of the scans, and who would suggest methods of treatment. While waiting in the corridor on the day of the appointment, a bumbling elderly gentleman with a passing resemblance to Benny Hill, mistook a storeroom for an interview room and was corrected by a passing nurse, I laughingly mentioned to Paolo, that if that was the surgeon, I was going home. A few minutes later we were face to face with Benny Hill, AKA Mr. Hobbiss.

As he went slowly through my history, starting at the very beginning when I visited the doctor two years ago, the theme tune of Benny Hill ran through my head as I willed him to cut to the chase.

Mr. Hobbiss explained, that fortunately the scans did not show up any further tumours. I heaved a sigh of relief and looked at Paolo who reached for my hand. Unfortunately he missed my hand and grabbed my knee, which shot up and kicked the desk in front of me, good job I have exceedingly short legs or Benny might have had the smile wiped off his face.

He explained that the treatment he suggested was radiotherapy on 4 days running followed soon after by an operation to cut away the tumour and to fit a stoma bag. The stoma would stay in place for about 3 months. During the operation samples of lymph nodes would be taken and tested to see if the cancer had begun to spread, in which case I would be offered chemotherapy, at some point in the future when I had recovered from the op.

Before he finished the consultation My Hobbiss had to examine me. As his finger went up my backside and I cracked jokes about nip and tuck, I imagined Paolo behind the curtain with his fingers in his ears going LA LA LA . It takes a certain kind of man to listen while another man fingers his wife - and Paolo is definitely not that kind of man. Then when the surgeon told me I had strong muscles (presumably I was squashing his finger) I only just stopped myself saying "Oh you are awful.... but I like you". (You won't get this joke if you are younger than 30) However, the compliment had worked the trick (it doesn't take much) I no longer thought of Mr Hobbiss as a comedy hero, he was obviously a man of experience and good taste, and I could trust him with my life.

10

When I got home (despite recommendations from the cancer nurse not to tell too many people too soon, as I would have to deal with their emotions as well as my own) I sat down to email all my family and friends.

After the initial shock and disbelief, the black humour started. Of course the camera up the arse cannot be mentioned with a straight face, but jokes about burying me in the back garden (after all the house was my pride and joy) and whether it would affect the selling price when the time came.

My brother mentioned that it was like being pregnant really - perfectly healthy but with something growing inside your body.

Strangely enough I remained calm and matter of fact about the whole thing even telling my sister that when she retired she could come and help Paolo with the childminding.   That if I died I wanted to be buried in my wedding dress (did I really think I would still fit in it). I joked with a friend about her praying for me saying that at least if I didn't recover I would go to heaven. Our friend John (The aforementioned builder with the same Salford humour) remarked that he had better get his invoice in (for our new garage) before I popped my clogs.

After afternoon cream tea at a little church one Saturday I decided to visit my mum. After 9 years, I still say the cemetery where she lives, rather that the cemetery where she is buried. My friend came with me and we were laughing irreverently at the things that people leave on the graves, we picked our plots and decided that whichever of us went first, we would find the most inappropriate item to leave on the grave so that someone else could have a laugh at our expense.

First lot of Emails
Here are a few emails and text messages that passed between my family and friends at this time. Firstly from me telling everyone the news:
Hi Everyone,
First, I must apologise to any one of you who didn't know anything about this, it's a brutal way of telling you. But there are so many people who do know and want to be kept up to date, this is the only way I can do it without spending all my time on the phone.
The good news is that it is not as bad as I had begun to imagine,

11

i.e.. I am not riddled with cancer! As far as the scans can see it has not spread to any other organs.

The bad news is that this is not going to be the walk in the park that I had hoped (nip in for surgery, back to work the week after).

1. The tumour is in the rectum so the bit they cut out is the bit that holds everything in. I will need to have a stoma bag for three months then hopefully the procedure will be reversed.

2. I will have to have 4 bouts of radiotherapy and then surgery. I will be in hospital for a week or two after surgery.

3. After surgery the lymph nodes will be examined to see if the cancer has begun to spread, and if so, I will need chemo.

The surgery is major and even though the surgeon advised me that I could keep on childminding, the cancer nurse has told me that I will not be able to lift anything heavier than a 2 Lt. bottle or drive the car for at least 6 weeks.

The surgery is pencilled in for 7th October 2013, if they can arrange the radiotherapy before then. I have to see the radiologist on the 16th September. I'm hoping that in 4 months this will all be behind us and we can carry on. With the help and co-operation of my lovely family and friends there should not be too much disruption for the kids.

Love to you all Veronica xxxx

Before anyone can reply, I continue......

Hi everyone,

I can't sleep, too many questions going round in my brain, also did bugger all yesterday except chat and eat, used no energy at all, so now I am awake. Since 20 heads are better than one here goes.

I will see the cancer nurse on Wednesday and she said to bring a list of questions with me.

Up to now I have thought of these:

1 Is the surgery key hole or not, the surgeon seemed to say both when we spoke to him.

2 Is there anyway I can prepare for surgery i.e gain weight, lose weight exercise?

3 How big is the tumour and and is it at the first stage or second (you would think I would remember what he said about this)

4 After radiotherapy, will I be radioactive i.e. can I come into contact with the kids (the surgeon said I needn't give up work, so I would presume the answer to this is no).

5 Are there alternatives to surgery? I've read an article on Papilon treatment that uses just radio waves

6 Will I still be able to have children? - after all I am only 62, still time to ditch my present toy-boy for a newer model.

If you were in my situation, what questions would you ask -

answers on a postcard please. If anyone receives this email that didn't receive the last one - sorry if you are confused.

Can anyone remind me how to make a group, so that I don't need to keep going down my list of contacts to send this.

To all of you with bad backs, stress, eczema, arthritis etc who are saying "its about time something wiped that smug look off her face" watch this space, I will come out of this healthier, slimmer, more beautiful and 20 years younger (you can do anything with surgery nowadays) and I will be smugger than ever.

Thanks to all of you for your kind words, flowers, jokes,(even the bad ones) hugs and tears - all appreciated

Love Veronica xxx

While I am trying to think of more questions, Paolo appears from behind me with a cup of tea, "Ask them if you can use the Rampant Rabbit instead of the vaginal dilator -WTF!! I turn around to look at him in disbelief and realise that this is his sense of humour, I also spot the smirk on his face I say "your eyes are bigger than your belly Paolo, go drink your tea". As you will notice tea is used for quenching more than one thirst in our house.

Note to anyone that has never got drunk at an Anne Summers Party, the Rampant Rabbit is not a real animal.

First lot of Email Replies
Extra questions and suggestions.....
1. Can I have a disabled badge so I can get parked nearer to the shops when its raining?
2. Can I have a NHS wig even if I don't lose my hair, for when I can't be arsed washing my hair?
3. If I get radio wave treatment, does it restrict what radio station you can listen to?
4. Are you single, with a healthy bank balance, and do you like gardening(cos I have a friend who is single, and her garden needs doing, and she has enough debt for both of you!!) (This is assuming your surgeon is male..... on second thoughts it doesn't matter.... my garden and bank balance are a mess!!)
there will be more questions to follow as I am now being mithered by my grandchildren. Suggestions for lack of sleep.
1. Ring me up I will gladly drop off my ironing.
2. Don't bother with more children.......... said with my fingers in my ears whilst my grandchildren are running around my house, at this early hour on a Sunday morning.... and by the fact that you can forgive your grandchildren more... and children just drive you round the bend!!

13

If love will help, you have it in abundance from me. Love you Lesley xxxx

Hi A questionnaire!! Well, you know how much I love these things so I really can't wait to answer such long winded questions. As honesty is my middle name, you can be assured I will answer with the truth, the whole truth and nothing but the truth at all times.
I'm surprised that you mention that all you did was chat and eat yesterday. This gives the impression that you usually have more exciting things going on in your life, whereas I know and you know, that chatting and eating are what you have spent most of your life doing up to now!!!

Right, here are my answers:

1 As you know, I have a somewhat morbid interest in all things medical and as such I have consulted with my good friend Mr Google and we have together come up with this answer.
I expect they may first try to do the operation via the less invasive procedure of keyhole surgery. Unfortunately, when they discover there is no instrument in the world that will push its way though so many layers of fat, they will surely have to resort to the old fashioned way and get out the big carving knife !! Hope this is some help!
2 There is nothing you can do to prepare yourself for surgery, apart from the obvious......
Write your will, check your life insurance is up to date and write letters to your children.
3 The tumour is massive. By the time they have cut it out, you will have lost 6 inches off your bottom!! Whoop whoop!!!
4 No, as much as I know you would love to have a green radioactive glow around your being, this doesn't actually happen. You cannot go round telling everyone you are a saint...
5. There are many alternatives to surgery, but nothing quite beats the traditional way of cutting the nasty little bugger right out and throwing him in the trash.
6. Fuck off!!! Don't you think there are enough crazy people in the world already ????
Healthier, slimmer, more beautiful and 20 years younger ????? Get real woman!!!!! They are surgeons not fuckin miracle workers!!!!!
Au Revoir my little shit bag!!
Love you lots Xxx

Hi Veronica,
I am glad to hear that although it's not going to be an easy road, there is a light at the end of the tunnel. A time frame to work towards.

If it's okay with you, I would like to come round to see you. Please don't feel obliged to say yes, if it's not okay. I would just like to see how you are doing.

HI,
We are praying for you & your family. Love from Jason, Pat & Peter

Sorry to hear about that. I know you have lots of support around you but if there is any help we can give you only have to say.

All our love. Thinking of you always Janet Kevin Donna & Jennifer. XXXX

Hi
Well at least now you know what you're dealing with. I have no doubt that you will sail with your positive attitude and your great family!

I am definitely only doing 4 days this year so if Paolo needs any help with children I will happily come and help.

You have both always been fantastic with me and my family and now hope fully I can repay you!!

Hope you got Ollie's picture, he was great, went straight into school, no bother! Although trying to get him to understand he is not coming to yours in the morning is proving more difficult.

Love you lots Emma xxxxxxxxx

i Veronica
I'm really sorry to read this news. If there's anything you need or any help, I'm always here. Love Marion and Stan. Xxx

Hi Veronica,
So sorry to hear your news, with your spirit and resilience I'm sure it won't be life changing, just an inconvenience.

Thinking of you and sending positive thoughts, been through it myself, it can be beaten. Looking forward to the healthier, slimmer, more beautiful you, not so much change then.

Love to you all.

Lynn & Colin

I know I've spoke to you in person about most of this but if there's anything we can do, please just let me know. Millie knows that you need an operation and that she must be EXTRA good when you come home as you will be tired and unable to shout! I am super confident that this is all she or any of the other kids will ever need to know. You and Paolo are a fab team and have a great system so I've no doubt that we'll hardly notice a change but if things are ever getting on top of you or you need extra help, remember that I don't work Monday or Friday and would be at school anyway so I'm happy to wait with children or walk them back for you if you need

15

Paolo for anything. See you in the morning xx

Hi Vron have had you in my thoughts (and prayers) very much over the last few days. I am just so sorry that you are having to go through all this. Probably more than a lot of people I can imagine how it feels for you, having gone through it all side-by-side with Anne so recently. The questions sound particularly familiar - we tried to think of all those things too, and wound up not asking half of the things we wanted to know. Things I can remember:
1. Like you we were told keyhole surgery by one doctor, then "oh no, not at all" by another. Turned out to be a 5" incision from her belly button directly south. I rather imagine yours would be similar.
2. Now come on, Veronica - you know nobody is going to tell you to gain weight for surgery! But if you do hear of a pre-surgery chocolate fudgecake and wine diet, I'd like to know in case I have need of it in the future!
After worrying for a week, Anne received a letter telling her about the status of her problem - it might have helped if they'd told her before that as it wasn't as desperate as she had thought. She was a stage 2 (of four),not madly urgent, but just to be sorted as soon as could be arranged. The time frame sounds about the same as yours. Have they told you anything more yet?
4. Going back to work - Anne's documentation said she should take 4-6 weeks off, and four weeks off driving. She has gone back today, just half days, after three weeks. For you, I would say if your eyes aren't glowing green and you don't scare the children, go for it!
5. I have never heard of the Papilon treatment. My friend next door here had radiotherapy last year and she said it was a piece of cake (Probably not chocolate fudge!)
6. And yes, I am sure you will be able to have children. After all, I am Catholic. I believe in miracles.
I will ask Anne is there is anything else she can think of for you to ask.
Take care. Much love, Dorothy xx

Ask him if he knows how lucky he is to have met you, as we all are to have you as a big part of our lives
Love Robert. X

Oh I do love you Veronica, I can't answer your questions but someone else will.
Love and hugs xxx

Just to let you know that you are amazing and so strong ....But it's also ok to fall apart a bit and let us take care of you. You are so loved. The champagne attack is on. We are gonna beat this in style.

16

Love you my sunflower (sometimes disguised as a chrysanthemum) Big hugs xxx

To be honest I've thought is was going to be really bad from the first time I saw the kit test letter in the bathroom, and now I know this, it's really a big relief... It's not perfect of course, but I can't think of anyone more ready for the fight than you mum! I love you so much, and I'm proud of how well you're dealing with this, and how easy you're making things for everybody! You should be the new face for the "keep calm and carry on" posters!! Haha Love you xx

You have always taught me that if you want something you have to fight, and we are all going to fight together to beat this. I love you more that I could ever tell you, without you there would be nothing. Be strong. I cant believe you said you would go to Bolton cause it's easy to get to if you go on your own, you will never be alone. Helen xxx

At some point during this time I decide to write this book, so that afterwards I will be able to remember in which order things happened. I send the first attempt to a couple of friends for some feed back. I apologise now to anyone mentioned before this point as I have probably already remembered things in the wrong order and forgotten some things altogether.

The Replies:

Now Veronica, I've been in training since you said you wanted to do a marathon! I've even located the 'Boothstown Wobble' which takes place in a couple of weeks that might be doable!!! But I can now breathe a sigh of relief.... Writing a book is much more you and I promise I will buy it and read it!! I'm loving the first draft already and not only because it might let me off the marathon but because its ace as are you. I can't get the bloody Benny hill theme tune out of my head!!!
Write the book... You must and I'll take your photo for the back cover!! It will be your bum!!! Or should that be on the front???
You are my inspiration and my soul sister and my best friend. And for that I will do the marathon (mini) as well as buy your book.
Love you Lesley

For the first time since this nightmare began you've made me cry -

10th September 2013 Just realised what a selfish self centred person I am becoming. I am revelling in all this attention and not taking into account the trials and tribulations of the people around me. I am after all not "ill" yet, though I suppose I might be forgiven for moaning after the treatment. I make up my mind not to tell another soul. Half an hour later I have broken the promise to myself when another old friend turns up at my door bringing chocolate. What can I do but make a cup of tea and and retell once more, accounts of the last few weeks and bask in the warm glow of knowing that people love me - and forgetting to ask how she is!

Another example of my selfishness happened on Sunday, as Paolo lay in bed phoning his mum in Switzerland, I went down to make our breakfast, we take it in turns each week to make smoked salmon on toast - even I can manage that without burning anything. As I got downstairs, Adam was going up with two cups of coffee in one hand, a heavy bag on his shoulder and a plate of something in the other hand. As he walked along, the coffee splashed onto the carpet and skirting board, this is a regular occurrence. I yell at him about the mess (I have talked quietly to him about this in the past) then added "I don't want people coming to my funeral and seeing coffee stains everywhere". In my defence it was not premeditated, it popped out of my mouth before being filtered in my brain, but it was unbelievably cruel. When I got back to bed Paolo was so angry with me. He didn't need to say much as I made excuses and tried to convince myself it was justified. Anyway the next day Adam used a tray to carry his drink upstairs, so the unpremeditated cruelty worked. Love is not always kind, but he was the wrong one for me to pick on. He has had to put up with diabetes since he was a little boy of eleven. Without complaint he has tested his blood and injected his insulin, I am ashamed of myself.

On Sunday, Helen takes Jamie and Lily to church, (Arron her eldest son used to play the oboe and sing during the Mass, but now, an A level student, he no longer goes) As she enters the

18

church, a friend comes over and hugs her and asks her how I am, she motions with her eyes that the kids don't know anything, and says that I am fine. This happens a few times. After church, a well-meaning member of the congregation, throws her arms around her and says she is so sorry to hear about her mum's cancer. Jamie gets really upset and asks her "Has nanna got cancer? 'she explains that cancer is just a name and that it is curable so not to worry. Later at home, Helen breaks down, the built up grief, combined with PMT render her a wreck and she cries all afternoon. I am so upset when I learn this. Helen is a strong and tough woman. She is good at her job and very ambitious and creative. She is a loving mum and daughter. But underneath, she is very vulnerable and easily hurt, she reminds me of my mum and I love her with all my heart.

4 - Stoma Bag

I Have an appointment with the cancer nurse on 11th September at 11.00 am (not sure if that is her title or one I have just made up). She gave me a tick list of questions to assess how stressed I was. I'm afraid I failed miserably; I only ticked one box because my head is itchy and she assured me this had nothing to do with the cancer nor the scans. Note to self - dig out the nit comb. I asked her if the operation was by the keyhole surgery or the cut a big hole in your belly method. Aren't I lucky, I am to have both. Whoopee. Four key holes will allow the instruments in to detach the colon from the back of my body, then a cut will be made from my navel down to get to the nitty gritty.

She gave me a delightful demonstration on how to attach and detach a stoma bag, how to empty it and even pictures of the stoma itself. I've spent 62 years blissfully unaware that a stoma is a hole in your body.

Oh yes and Wendy was right, I won't be radioactive and have a green glow around me, pity that, it would have impressed all the Ben Ten fans that I look after.

Once more I keep everyone up to date by email
Been to the hospital today to ask all the questions I couldn't think of last week. Thank you to all my friends - you know who you are - for your imaginative contributions, I didn't ask her any of them, some people don't share our humour. Had a lovely demonstration of how to attach a stoma bag, and how to empty it. All these lovely new experiences for me, that I could relate to the children. No child should start school without knowing how to attach a stoma bag.
The replies
Renee Smith Thinking of you Veronica, wishing u you a speedy recovery x
Calum Macleod Good luck veronica thinking of you x
Wendy Marshall You could demonstrate to everyone using one of the playdoh funfactory machines.I'll stick a picture of you on the front, then I'll push the handle and you can attach the bag. Just off out to buy some brown playdoh. Actually , that's the colour it goes anyway when the kids mixed all the colours!!!!!
Renee Smith Ha ha ur mad Wendy x
Carole Gallagher Love and prayers being sent Veronica for a

speedy recovery - God bless xxxx

Diane Povey They gave me a practice kit! Had to fill it with water and some jelly stuff. Got the hang of the real thing in no time! Get in touch if you want any tips! Xxx

Paula Ward Well it must meet some EYFS aim????? Manual Handling/Physical Development????

Linda Kenny Go girl your humour is unbelievable keep it up love to all xxx

Kaz Critchley Sending you all my love and best wishes for a speedy recovery xx

5 - Grandchildren

Isaac is my youngest grandson and spoilt, I suppose, in many ways, mostly by me. I don't know why I spoil him, somewhere in my brain, I think he is the reincarnation of my mum. When shopping with him (not often) he says "Nanna can I have this", I say "Is it your birthday?, Is it Christmas?, then no you can't have it" . In September I go shopping with him and he says "Nanna can I have this for my birthday (a Brachiosaurus), I say yes OK. He continues, "Nanna can I have this for my birthday" (A playdough recycling truck), I say which one do you want, the Brachiosaurus or the truck" - "both", "you can't have both", "why" - "Its too much" "But Nanna, everyone gets too much for their Birthday". He gets both, I'm such a pushover.

Rachael is organising a birthday party for Isaac at her house, for her friends with small children and his cousins. He is also having a party at my house after school, and I tell him he can invite two school friends.. While shopping in Asda, Rachael thinks she spots David, Isaac's friend from school. She goes up to the child and tells his mum, "My mum is having a party for Isaac after school on 12th September, Is it OK for me to pick David up from school and take him there? The mother looks puzzled but agrees. Then Rachael turns to Isaac and says   "Isaac, come here, your friend David is here" Isaac glances up and says, "That's not David, that's Keith from Nanna's. On relating this to me later Rachael is mortified, I never thought of myself as racist, she says, but I presumed it was David because he was black. I tell her she of course not racist, she just confused two little boys with similar looks, who she doesn't see very often. I see Keith's mum later in the week and we have a laugh about the confusion, she just thought Rachael had got mixed up with names. We all know that Rachael, despite her intelligence and brown hair is sometimes a bit dizzy.

As a birthday surprise, Rachael has bought Isaac a trampoline and Paolo and Matteo have erected it in her back garden. She has closed the curtains each evening so that he doesn't see it. One evening, I phone Rachael and she tells me that Isaac is in bed being very quiet. I say, "he is probably looking out of his window at his surprise". On the morning of his birthday, Rachael says "look what Mummy has bought you, and opens the curtains. He says "Thank you mummy, I saw it through my bedroom window yesterday." Later, the rain stops in time for us to inflate the bouncy castle, two little boys think it is a good idea to get the arrows off the roof by firing all the other arrows up there too, Lily traps her foot on a trike, and Oliver has a tantrum because Isaac won't let him play with the Power Ranger (You don't have to share on your birthday apparently) So all in all a good day.

Isaac also enjoys a trip to Chester zoo with his dad, he is a lucky little boy.

A couple of days later, another lovely day, the sun is shining (just), Robert brings Lily and Jamie round and we watch the kids play in the garden while we drink coffee and put the world to rights. Lily is trying to fly, by jumping off the slide and flapping a sunshade. Jamie is practising hitting a tennis ball until it goes over the fence and then he makes yet another bug den. He is going to be a vet when he grows up he says. Later Nathan arrives with Bailey and Bobby, his grandsons and I buy the kids McDonalds. In the afternoon I drop the kids off with Rachael for Isaac's other party. 12 kids in superhero costumes are tearing round the house including my brother (aged 43 going on 5) dressed in a pink wig. We decide not to stay for the party (busman's holiday) and go to buy some paint and more plants for the garden. We return later (When some of the children have left and the adults have started on the wine) Helen is there and tells us that Arron has been accepted as First Oboe in the Halle Youth Orchestra. My heart feels like bursting with pride. I am so lucky with my family.

6 - Auntie Josie

13th September. Finally I am taking my auntie Josie, to an osteopath. She has not walked straight since having a fall nearly 2 years ago and I have been trying to persuade her to see a therapist. For every question the practitioner asks she has a long story. Instead of the usual 1 hour treatment, Josie gets 90 minutes At one point she starts to talk about a recent appointment at the opticians department at Bolton Hospital. She says, "I couldn't see the doctor, so I have to go back next week". I begin to panic since she has only allowed my sister to drive her there, but then sent her away saying she would catch the bus home. I ask her "Josie, could you not see him because your eyes have deteriorated so much". No you daft bugger, because he was called away to an emergency".

I love my Auntie Jo, she has always been there for me, it was like having two mums. As I was the eldest of eight children, my mum's attention was often diverted to younger children and living in a two-up, two-down, very cold and damp terraced house, there wasn't much privacy so I was very fortunate to have Josie as a refuge, and my cousin Linda was an added bonus.

As we leave the physiotherapist, he asks Josie if she feels OK (waiting for some assurance that his service is acceptable). She replies "I'm alright", He says "hope you have less pain this week-end" and she answers "I'd better had do". I'm sure if she didn't, she would be back there for her money back. I did notice though that as she walked away, she was standing straighter and her walking stick was swinging from her arm.

My optimism for Josie was short lived, her pain continued. Two years on from this she got to a point where she was in too much pain to climb down the stairs from her bedroom. She phoned her friend, who took her to A & E. Once more they X-rayed her hip and said there was no injury and wanted to send her home. Fortunately, Jean her friend argued with them saying that Josie was obviously still in pain, had very poor vision and at 82 needed a care plan before being sent home. While the care plan was being put into place, the hospital decided to do a scan and found that she indeed had a broken hip which she had been walking on for two years.

It was decided that because of her age and health, under local anaesthetic, screws would be put into her hip rather than a full hip replacement. This was not successful, as her osteoporosis caused the bones around the screws to crumble and the screws came out. This was followed eventually by a hip replacement. Around this time, Linda, her daughter took matters into her own hands and organised sheltered accommodation for her mum. At the time this seemed the best thing to do, and Linda put a lot of love and care into decorating the flat to make her mum comfortable. Unfortunately, Josie's mental health had taken a turn for the worse, not helped by the increasing number of pills that she had to take each day and the frequent hospital admissions. She never settled in the flat and in 2016 relocated to a nursing home.

As we sing Happy Birthday to Josie on her 85th Birthday, I look back with nostalgia to how she could talk nine to the dozen on that day with the osteopath. Now she understands everything you say to her, but her words are mixed up in the way a stroke victim talks. The staff at the nursing home thinks she is lovely, but they will never know the sharp tongued, strong woman that she was.

7 - Nostalgia

The builders arrive late in the day with cement to add the floor to the new garage, the kids are fascinated to watch the huge mixer reverse into our drive (I am very worried that it will take the gate off on its way out). It is late in the day and the cement is too wet for them to smooth it off, so John (the builder) has to come back in the evening. (This is an unknown, John drinks beer in the evening, not work - especially Friday). He shouts "Veronica get the red wine out". Now there's a command I can't refuse. We drink the bottle between us, Paolo drinking coffee, because he is taking antibiotics for a tooth infection. We have a great evening swapping stories of our lives in Salford and Paolo's in Switzerland.

John had us roaring with laughter about the time when as a child of 8, he fell on a bottle and cut his hand open. A policeman saw him and dropped him at the Jewish Hospital where they sewed him up and discharged him. He said "How do I get home?", they told him to walk. It was seven miles. He arrived home just as his parents came home from the pub, happily oblivious to the mishap. They asked him why he was still out and where he had been, "To the Jewish Hospital" his dad gave him a crack around the head saying "That's all I need, get to bed". A week later after having the six stitches removed from his hand, the class bully grabbled his hand and twisted his thumb, reopening the wound. He had to return to the hospital to have it stitched again. The next time the bully tried to repeat the trick, John got there first and punched him in the face, he was now the class bully, and revelled in the new status.

We were reminiscing upon our "lovely" childhoods, without Health and Safety, Anti-bullying, Stranger Danger, Where parents didn't worry about being your friend or hurting your feelings if they thought it was for your own good. When corporal punishment was the norm! When it was OK for neighbours to give you a slap for playing knocker-door-run (if they caught you)! When you didn't tell your mum that the teacher had caned you, because she would hit you even harder for misbehaving at school. When children were expected to be seen and not heard. When 8 year olds were considered capable of taking younger brothers and sister to school and to supervise them after school, until working mums came home. (I now pick up two nine year olds from school who are not allowed to leave until the teacher has seen me) How did we ever survive?

My childhood was different. My mam took us to school each day, always pushing a baby in the big coach built Silver Cross Pram and older children holding on. I remember chapped legs being rubbed sore in wellington boots. Occasionally hot baked potatoes in our pockets to keep us warm. She walked the mile to school and back again at 9 o'clock, fed the baby, cleaned the house, did the shopping then walked back to pick us up at 12 to take us home, for a home cooked meal. Back to school again at 1.30 pm and home again to continue housework or maybe have a cup of tea with neighbours, until 3.30 pm when the infants finished school. As each of us went into the Juniors, we finished school half an hour later and so were trusted to walk home alone. I can remember climbing walls, hanging on by fingertips, daring each other to drop down the other side. On Friday evenings, pay day for my dad, we had treats, sweets and comics. But when I was about 9, technology came to our house, mam wanted to watch Princess Alexandra getting married and had worked out that the money usually spent on sweets and comics, would pay the weekly rental for a television. We were all amazed at the black and white characters on the screen, but I personally missed the Friday night comics, and mam was very strict about what we could watch, Coronation Street, when it started was banned for some reason.

As John was leaving he hugged us both so hard he nearly broke my ribs and this brash rough man told me to take care of myself, and told us that he was sure I would be OK (not before trying to add another £500 to his bill though).

8 - Scan Results

Dear Mrs. Scotton
I am writing to inform you that an appointment has been arranged for you to attend the Churchill Unit at the Royal Bolton Hospital which is located at the rear of the main hospital building on Churchill Drive
Your appointment is with Dr N Alam Clinic and will be on: Monday 16th September 2013 at 9.20 am

Dr Alam is the Consultant Radiographer and she is lovely. Unlike all the other medical personnel I had come into contact with, she does not insist that I have not understood, or not accepted, the seriousness of the situation. She breezes through my history and acknowledges that there is more than one way of dealing with things. She tells me that the scans have revealed that I have a couple of gall stones which are not causing any problems at present, a small hiatus hernia (that I already knew about) and some corrosion of the spine, that is apparently appropriate for my age. The good news is that as far as can be determined by the scans, the tumour is in the bowel wall but has not pushed through to any other organ. She does mention that infected lymph nodes may still be found after surgery, when she examines them with a microscope, but for the moment they are planning on a cure. Every so often I find myself with butterflies in my tummy at the thought of the surgery and the treatment, but to be honest, not as much as I normally feel, at the thought of driving somewhere I am not familiar with.

For some reason I have started saying "Thank you God" I didn't realise I was saying it so often until Paolo pointed it out to me. I say thank you when the sun shines, when it rains (it waters the garden), when I get good news at the hospital (I suppose that should be "not quite as bad as it might have been news")

I don't know if I really believe in God. Well not the God with the white beard and long white robe, that the nuns taught us about at St John's. I believe in reincarnation, I hope that when I die it won't just be the end.

I feel sad that most religions have been hi-jacked by power seekers for their own greed. Jesus, Mohamed, Moses and all the other religion makers, got it right with the 10 commandments. If everyone followed them it would be like heaven on earth I would imagine. Most of the religions teach their followers to thank God several times a day. This is a good thing, by concentrating on your good fortune, you can be philosophical about misfortune. That's my sermon for the day.

When I first found out I had cancer, one of my very best friends came to see me in tears. She said "Oh you are so brave, you keep getting knocked down and then you get up again" I asked her what she was talking about, I couldn't remember when I had suffered any misfortune (this could possibly be because I can't usually remember anything further back than yesterday, or because I was half way through a nice bottle of red). The thing is I honestly think that I am very lucky with my life. I've got a lovely house, it hasn't got a swimming pool in the back garden but then the public swimming pool is only a five minute drive away and I don't have to maintain it. The sun doesn't shine every day but then sunshine gets boring and you have all the hassle of putting sun cream on the kids and trying to get them to keep the sun hats on. I have got family and friends that love me, and enough money to keep the wolves from the door, and a job I love (not keen on the paperwork but you can't have everything.) And I have a lovely husband who came into my life when I was least expecting it. He is tolerant, generous and kind to everyone. He tells me I am beautiful and clever (he's good at stretching the truth sometimes), He cooks me delicious food, is creating a lovely garden, and doesn't moan when I say I am nipping out for a few minutes and then don't come home for an hour (gossiping is my hobby and if I meet an old friend...)

While shopping in Tesco, I pick up a new nighty for my stay in hospital and start to think of what else I might need. Apart from childbirth, I have only ever been in hospital once before and that was in 1974. I went in to have a cyst removed from an ovary, but came back from surgery with a drainage tube from an abscess on my appendix. I hated it, I was desperate to get home to my baby, and not only because my boobs were painful without him suckling. Nathan was ten months old, and while I was in hospital, he cut his first tooth, walked his first steps and weaned from my breast milk on to solid food (not the mush I had been trying to tempt him

29

with). I wanted to go home so badly, I never mentioned to the hospital staff that I was feeling really ill. When the nurse told me that the surgeon was doing his rounds and to get into bed to wait for him, I lay down and fell asleep. ten minutes later I was woken by the nurse, and surprisingly felt much better and I was soon to learn the reason. As she pulled back the bedclothes, the smell hit all our nostrils. Instead of stitching me up, the doctor had put some kind of metal clips down my stomach, to close the wound. The wound had become very infected and as I had been napping, it had burst open and the bed was full of the green gunk. Unfortunately this meant another week in hospital and a course of antibiotics. In all, Nathan stayed with my mum for nearly 4 weeks. My brother Carl is only five years older than Nathan, so she had taken it all in her stride. I think Nathan still has the dual personality as my youngest brother, as well as my eldest son.

Tuesday 17th September 9.30 a.m, A Stoma Nurse called Zoe visited me at home, to provide me with a Pre-operative Practice Pack - A step by step guide for patients, and to demonstrate how to use the stoma bag after the ileostomy (a bowel movement is not recommended after surgery to the rectum). In the practice pack is an imitation stoma (a red piece of soft plastic that looked a bit like the top of a bottle of coke) Morform Thickening Agent (to thicken water to resemble faeces), A Disposal bag, some wipes and some guidance leaflets. There are also two DVDs one demonstrating how to apply, empty and remove the stoma bag, and another with stories demonstrating how other people cope living with a stoma. I declined the offer of a practice run, the real thing will be soon enough - How difficult can it be?

A loop ileostomy is created when a loop of the small bowel (ileum) is brought out as a stoma. This allows the colon to heal after part of the colon (due to disease or obstruction) is removed and the two ends of the colon are joined together. This can be a temporary stoma and may be able to be closed or reversed at a later operation

Later in the day I receive a phone call from a nurse at "The Christie in Salford", she invites me to attend the radiology clinic to have another CT scan on Thursday 16th September. This time the scanner is connected to a computer that calculates exactly where the radiotherapy treatment needs to be targeted. I tell her I will be there, forgetting to check if we have any other appointments at that time. I subsequently realise that Paolo has a dentist appointment, but hey, I think cancer overrides a filling.

Neo-adjuvant (pre-operative)radiotherapy for rectal cancer is given before surgery to shrink the tumour, in order to make it easier to remove, and reduce the risk of the cancer coming back

The nurse is chatty and informative and gives me details of where to park, what to expect and how long I am likely to be. This makes it much easier for me to make arrangements for the children in our care (our income). I decide that I will go alone, and leave Paolo to look after the children, I will be back in plenty of time for the afternoon school run. I feel quite cosseted by all these people looking out for me. I don't remember Paolo getting so much information 10 years ago, when he had testicular cancer.

Everyone with cancer is cared for by a Multi-disciplinary team who meet every week to ensure that all the different parts of your treatment are delivered as seamlessly as possible.

The members of this team are: Surgeon; Clinical Oncologist; Diagnostic Radiographer/Radiologist; Pathologist; Colorectal Nurse Specialist; Stoma Nurse Specialist. All these people looking after me, I feel so special. On the other hand, my cancer is keeping them in a job, perhaps they should be grateful to me.

My brother is married to a girl from Thailand. Her aunt is dying from Breast Cancer, she walks around the village with the hole in her chest getting bigger and bigger and the only treatment that is available to her, is the "doctor" who comes around every so often and sells her medicine to reduce the pain. (My brother says it is basically strong whisky with herbs). I thank God (there I go again) every day for the NHS.

After Paolo's cancer, he could not return to working in a restaurant, his weakened muscles needed building up first. He started to volunteer for CALL the cancer charity which provides a listening ear and transport to hospital, amongst other things. He also volunteered for Barnados and at one time as a gardener at

31

Blackleach Country Park. As time went on and he became stronger, he started helping me with the childminding business and was so good at it, that he never returned to the hospitality industry, but registered as a childminder in his own right. This has been a blessing in disguise; he got to spend more time with his children, in particular Matteo our youngest. He taught him to play chess and helped him with his French homework. At the time his illness was horrendous and frightening, but with hindsight it changed our lives for the better in so many ways. I wonder if this tumour that is growing inside me, will bring any bonuses.

As I mentioned I have taken up swimming again. For two years I got up at 6.am, three days a week to swim 30 lengths but I got out of the habit last Christmas when the pool was closed for two weeks. However, with the prospects of an operation looming I have decided to dig out my costume again and attempt to build up my fitness, in the couple of weeks before my op. It was quite heartwarming on my first day back at the pool when first the receptionist smiled and said welcome back, then the pool attendant waved a cheery hello and put out his palms as if to say, "where have you been"? Several of the swimmers made similar comments (making me feel guilty as they all seemed to remember my name - I am rubbish at names!). It was quite a sad experience though, as Gladys and Gordon were not hogging the end lane. When I first started the early morning swim, they were always there before me, I thought they were man and wife, until I found they were neighbours who had lived in the same street for 40 years, whose children had gone to school together, and whose respective partners had died within weeks of each other. Gordon would let himself into Gladys house and wake her with a cup of tea and together they went swimming. They holiday'ed together but Gladys always refused to marry him. At 74 years of age (she could be mistaken for 60) she said she was too old for "all that" and she was my inspiration. Swimming 32 lengths, three times a week, having two jobs - cleaning in a pub and home help, and always laughing and joking. One day Gladys started talking gibberish and her daughter took her to see the doctor. She was riddled with cancer and it had reached her brain. She died within weeks.

Since I have returned to the pool, the urgency to "go" has

disappeared and I wonder whether I would have been so prompt to return the bowel screening kit if it wasn't for this. Anyone who has got one in the kitchen draw, or under a pile of bills to pay, I urge you to dig it out and send it off, IT IS A LIFESAVER.

9 - Independence

Thursday 19th September 2013 10.30 am Feeling very brave, I drive myself to The Christie at Salford for another scan. This one is to pinpoint the positions for the radiotherapy machine (I'm sure it has a technical name). I arrive at 10.10 as I had given myself time to find the place, park etc. I sit down to wait, buy myself a cup of tea and curse because I have forgotten my glasses and my book. At 11.00 I have still not been seen so I go the reception to see if I have been forgotten. The receptionist tells me that my scan isn't until 11.30 a.m. I know that the appointment was definitely 10.30. She asks me if I know the name of the person I spoke to, and unbelievably I remember she was called Paula. At this, the woman sitting next to her looks up and says "thats me, you have to come in an hour earlier to have the drink! Has no-one brought you a jug?" Around about this time something spooky happens, I send a text to Paolo saying that I will be delayed. He replies with "Are you alright?" and I say "Yes I'm just bored, I've forgotten my book!" and he answers again "My heart is with you xx" (soppy Italian) The spooky thing is that I learn later that my texts have not been delivered to Paolo, but his texts to me, while not actually answering mine had slotted in perfectly.

Soon after this a nurse asks me if I want blackcurrant, orange, or lemon flavoured water. I choose lemon - it tastes like liquorice. After the prescribed time I am ushered into the room with the doughnut shaped scanner, positioned carefully, and told to lie as still as possible. A high pitched whine followed by the sound of an airplane taking off, then a noise like dishwasher and finally another high pitched whine is emitted from the doughnut. The scanner operator comes back into the room and makes little tattoos on my tummy then I am free to go. I return to the desk to be told my four radiology treatments will be on 1st, 2nd, 3rd and 4th October followed by the operation on the 7th. I have eleven more days to carry the tumour around. Eleven more days of being overweight (remember my promises to myself that I was going to be slimmer and more beautiful - watch this space).

I have made the decision that I am going to drive myself for all of the radiotherapy sessions. Several people have questioned this decision, saying can't one of your children go with you? Why doesn't Paolo take a day off to take you? Do you want me to go with you? The reason I am doing this is a bit selfish really, because I know that people want to help, they want to cuddle me and wrap me in cotton wool, but sometimes I really like to do thing by myself (probably stemming from being the eldest of 8 children in a family, and rarely getting time to sit quietly in my own company). It is silly for Paolo to drive me to the hospital, which is only about 15 minutes away, and for all the parents to have to arrange alternative childcare, when the treatment is painless and only takes about 10 minutes (so I'm told). Also I am becoming quite paranoid about driving anywhere other than to the supermarket or the school run. Driving to the hospital is my way of squashing this stupid fear - for goodness sake I have been driving over 30 years. After all this is over I mean to drive myself to a different destination each week, if I can face the fear of cancer I should have no trouble.

One evening as I watch Grand Designs on the TV I hear a little tap on the window. It is Jean (my sister's friend) "I've just bought you that book I promised" - I didn't recall her promising me anything - but I thanked her, "and a little pressie from me". I was so touched, it was a lovely box to keep all the pamphlets etc, that I seem to be accumulating daily, a little book for questions, another one for appointments and a third with "My Thoughts" embellished on the front. The box and the books were all decorated with butterflies. Jean was diagnosed with bowel cancer two years ago and has now come out the other side. She tells me that I can phone her any time. So many people have said this to me, I think everyone knows I like to talk. Thank you to all my friends.

A couple of days later, Rachael also arrives bearing gifts, a bag full of new nighties, pyjamas, bed socks and slippers, for use in the hospital and while recovering. It's like getting ready for a holiday.

I've just received a message on my answering machine to phone Peter something undecipherable from Ofsted. I dial the number and am given a choice of buttons to press. Sod that, I will let Peter whateverhisname use Ofsted's time and money to phone me. I have more important things to do, pick up and cuddle my babies, since I won't be able to do that after the 7th October for at least 6 weeks.

My sister has bought tickets for my daughters and me, for Facinating Ada at the Opera House in Manchester. They were intended as an early Christmas Present. The problem is that they are for the performance on 13th October, i.e. six days after my operation. I am asking myself a few questions:

Will I be out of hospital in time?

Will I be fit enough to go?

Will I have got the hang of the Stoma Bag within that time? Will I burst my stitches open when laughing?

My daughters reckon that if they put me in a wheelchair we might get priority seating or at least not have to queue. I'll let you know later.

10 - Love My Job

Four of the kids we look after are starting school, big boys and girls in school uniform. The proud parents post photos on facebook and phone me to tell me they have gone in school without a backward glance. I am so proud, these kids come into our care as babies and leave to go to school three years later and we have helped to prepare them, and given them the confidence to cope with the transition. Why do I not cry when told I have cancer of the rectum and yet blubber all over the place to see these happy little faces?.

One of the older girls comes back to see us. She has just left us to go to High School but comes back so that Paolo can help her bake a cake for her nana who will be 65. (I suspect also to scrounge some of Paolo's home cooking for her tea). Childminding is the best job in the world, job satisfaction jumps up and bites you on the bum when you least expect it.

Later that evening I suddenly feel really tired. I complain to Paolo that every bit of my body is tired and wonder if the cancer is making itself felt. Paolo says "Veronica, you have been up since 6.am, swum 30 lengths, done three lots of washing, been running around after 3 one-year olds and a two year old. Done the school run to two different school, Cleaned up all the tea things and picked up all the toys, then swept out the garage for me to paint" Why would you not feel tired? Go and have a bath and a nice cup of tea! I take his point.

Watching Gino D'Acampo making a frittata on TV on Friday night, I say" that looks lovely, I wouldn't mind that". Saturday evening Paolo comes in from a day's gardening, washes is hands and makes me a frittata, Gino style, complete with white wine and tomato salad. I love you Paolo

On Saturday I get a lovely surprise when one of my old neighbours pays a visit, we chat about our children, then she tells me about a friend of her daughter's who has just learned she has terminal cancer at the age of 31. Life is not fair.

Sunday 22nd September - Lovely lazy day. I put a colour on my hair that is supposed to be dark blonde, but I leave it on too long, so it is brown. My friend Linda drops by to bring me a "Get Well" card, before she goes to Cuba - alright for some! It's the same group of friends that we went on a cruise with, and whom we visit in their caravans. I think I would prefer to go to Cuba with them than have surgery. Then another friend Lesley brings us a home made syrup and ginger cake, delicious, we invite her for dinner. Sorry Linda a card is very nice, but a ginger cake wins hands down.

I tell Lesley about my plan to be well enough to go to see *Fascinating Aida,* and she agrees with Rachael that a wheelchair and an invalid might be a good plan to get us into the best seats. But first I need to get out of the hospital a day early. For a few minutes Lesley and my sister (who is also visiting) try to persuade me that it might not be in my best interest to go out so soon after major surgery, then Lesley decides it might be OK if we all decide not to laugh, at which point we all burst into laughter, I don't think this idea will work. My Auntie Josie phones me to say she is a bit too shaky so will not be coming for dinner, so I go round to see her and persuade her that she will be OK if I collect her in the car. I am a bit worried about her and wonder how I can persuade her to let me go to the doctors with her. We have a lovely roast dinner with wine, followed by ginger cake. Life is good.

Later I email another friend who has had similar surgery, she has now got two belly button holes because she split open her stitches by laughing. Now that would be a talking point - come in and see my two belly buttons - a change from etchings.

I also get an email from a cousin in New Zealand whose daughter has to travel four hours for her radiology, whereas mine is only 15 minutes, another thing to be thankful for. I now have a full week without any hospital appointments, and a night out with friends on Wednesday to look forward to. Adam gives me a book of short stories, I say "Thanks Adam, I will save this for the hospital", He says "That's why I gave you the Lee Child book, but you read it" Books, cake, wine, cards and flowers, it really is like my birthday.

Later, on Facebook, I see a post from Angelo, an old chef friend of

Paolo's, showing off his new Ferrari. Paolo has always wanted a Ferrari, like any other Italian I imagine.
These are the following texts
Veronica Scotton
Just been admiring Angelo's Ferrari in Facebook. Paolo said he would rather have a lovely wife(I think his fingers are crossed). I said "will you still think that when I am wearing a stoma bag" he said I married you for life" didn't quite answer the question there Paolo.
Julie Daley, Calum Macleod, Ysane Morton and 5 others like this.
Michelle Smith We will xxxx
Gary Williams Didn't say he had a lovely wife either
Veronica Scotton So very true xx
Veronica Scotton Master of the double entendre
Lesley Hopwood-Ryan Very funny Gary!!! I think it will add a little to your womanly mystery!!! Can you get glittery ones? Xx
Veronica Scotton Don't do glitter, but I could ask for a bright red one and wear a short kilt

Tuesday 24th September Paolo has taken the kids to the Fun House and left me free for the morning. I have had my hair cut and blowed - first time ever within working hours. I could get used to this.

Wednesday 25th September. I enroll for a course on Child Psychology. 9.30 a.m. - 11.30 a.m. each Wednesday. Something to focus on during the coming weeks. I've always been interested in this subject, I just hope I will have the strength to enjoy it.

In the evening I have a lovely evening with friends, enjoying a meal and a drink or two at Wetherspoons in Walkden. One of my friends has not been inside this pub for years since her son was murdered. The last place he had visited before his death was The Bull which has since been taken over by the conglomerate. But she buried her ghosts just to spend the evening with me before I start my treatment. My friends are the best.

Paolo spends each Wednesday evening keeping company with an elderly lady who has terminal cancer. Last year she organised a fundraising party for CALL using the money she had saved for her funeral. She is donating her body to medical research. He picked us all up on his way home and delivered each of my friends to their homes without question. He is one in a million.

11 - Coming into money

At some point, while reading Martins Money Tips on email, I must have filled in a form to retrieve lost savings/premium bonds. I receive a letter asking me for any other names I have had, so by return post I tell them I have been known as Veronica Williams, Veronica Baines and Veronica Scotton. I get a bit exited and tell Paolo that if I get £100, I will treat the kids to £10 each. Then I get another letter asking me for my signature in each of the names, my imagination begins to run riot. If I get £1,000 I will give them each £100. A further letter asks me for bank details so that the money can be paid into it, bearing in mind, I know I have never left a bank account with any more than £1 and I have only ever had £1 premium bond, I begin to imagine vast amounts of money, with £100,000 the kids could have £10,000. Today I receive a cheque for 24p. Gutted! I think some bored clerk in an office has been playing games with me. Either that or it has been a clever con to get my bank details, Must check my bank account.

Friday 27th September

Glorious day, who would believe it is nearly October? The kids have their snacks in the back garden and then I get all the paints out and we make footprints on a long roll of old wallpaper, loads of mess, loads of fun followed by more fun washing off the paint in a paddling pool filled with warm water and bubbles. After tea I help Paolo to move a huge fence that the builders used, to protect the children while they were building the garage. Paolo has his sensible work boots on, I have sandals - guess which one of us drops the fence on our toes?. In the bath later, I panic thinking that my toe has turned black, fortunately the black washed off, I had not washed them properly after the foot-printing.

Saturday night, I have the strangest dream. I am on the way up to surgery, with the surgeon no less, pushing the bed when a nurse runs up shouting "stop, she has forgotten her nightie" the surgeon says "Right then we will cancel the operation" The nurse replies that the hospital could lend me one, but the surgeon is adamant that if I have forgotten my nightie I cannot be serious about having the operation.

Sunday 29th September My sister Gail and I go to Stafford to see my brother, Ian. I tell him my news to which he replies "Well brace yourself girl, you know that the treatment is worse than the disease". Thanks for that Ian! We have a drive out to a country pub and I have beef stroganoff followed by bread and butter pudding. When I get home Paolo has cooked dinner, roast pork with all the trimmings. I am stuffed. Good job I am not planning a Slimming World visit this week. The next day Ian phones me (a rare occurrence) and says how gutted he is. He tells me that I have a lovely family, fabulous friends and the house of my dreams and I must fight this disease so that I can enjoy it much longer. I feel sad for him. He is three years younger than me, but an old man living a lonely life in a bedsit, relying on benefits. He could have had it all, at 18 years old he was a soldier, tall and handsome, but now he has lost contact with his children and chain-smokes his benefits away. When my mum passed away, she left a letter to all her children, saying how proud she was, of us all and asking us to look after each other. I wonder if I could do more for him? (I excuse myself from doing more because it would never be reciprocated - a ridiculous excuse) I hope my mum is looking down and is still proud and not disappointed.

12 - Radiotherapy

Dear Mrs Scotton
The following appointments have been made for you for your course of radiotherapy:
Date Wednesday 02/10/2013 11.40 am
Venue Salford 1
Action 4 Field Pelvis
Date Wednesday 02/10/2013 11.45 am
venue Salford 1
Action Pre Cone Beam Imaging Scan
Thursday 03/10/2013 01.20 am
Salford 1
4 Field Pelvis
Friday 04/10/2013 04:40 pm

This appointment was received on Wednesday, the day after I had had my first radiotherapy on Tuesday, I think they are struggling to keep up with me

As promised the latest email update

The radiotherapy was a piece of cake. The only stress was not being able to get into the car park, because the code they had given me had been changed. I was back in time for the school run, despite the new 40 mph speed limit on the East Lancs.
This week I have three more trips to Christie Hospital, the stoma nurses are coming to the house to draw on my belly, and another appointment, yet to be arranged, for a pre-op consultation. Just to make sure I am kept busy, I have a Child Psychology Class on Wednesday morning, three toddlers and three schools to pick up from (Paolo helps a little lol)
I'm getting really nervous about Monday now, but I can't back out, the alternative doesn't bare thinking about.
Speak again soon Veronica xxx
And the answers
hi Vron did you see that article on sky news site yesterday ,saying they have a new drug that clears up most malignant melanoma tumours and they reckon it will be used on other cancers when it comes out of trial stage. Finding a car parking space is very stressful bet you were tearing your hair out. Kevin xx

Veronica,
I have been thinking of ways to help you and think one way may be to provide you with a diet of baked beans and sprouts at the

weekend. Ever since you mentioned the surgeons mistake of entering the store cupboard instead of the surgery I have been concerned. My earlier offering of proposed diet is to ensure a little guidance that you could provide him with. You will just need to f**t to give him a clue.... We wouldn't want him going in the wrong 'entry'!!!!
Love you, L xx
Glad everything went well today. Was thinking of you. Take care xxx.
You are a star.
Glad it all went well Vron, you know I worry. All the best with the treatment. I'll keep you in my prayers.
Hi Veronica sorry to hear your news ,you seem to be coping well don't overdo it, I will be thinking of you, hope the belly drawing goes well, stay positive you're doing great, love Gemma

Wednesday 2nd October A bit emotional today as it is 5 years since Paolo's dad disappeared from the face of the earth. We always presumed that he would be found eventually.

Received a phone call from the care team at the hospital to ask if I have had my pre-op assessment. (I think I have slipped through the net here, I later find I should have had this two weeks earlier). They make an appointment for Friday at 11.00 pm at Bolton One. (Same day as the radiotherapy at Salford 1)

In the evening while Paolo is doing his volunteering, visiting the sick, my sister and a couple of friends come round to gossip over a couple of bottles of wine and snacks. I mention about the pre assessment at Bolton One (which I had presumed was an annex on the hospital when Jean tells me that it is a medical building in the centre of Bolton. Good job she was here or I would have been arriving at the wrong place.

Wednesday 2nd October 2013

My keep up email to family and friends
Hi Everyone No ill-effects from radiotherapy yesterday. I woke up early this morning and couldn't get back to sleep so went for my usual 30 lengths. My appointment today was 11.45 so I left my Wednesday Class and arrived at 11.35 am. The receptionist checked in my parking token (correct code today) and waved me through to the waiting area. After waiting ONE HOUR arrrrgh, I walked back to the reception to ask if there was a delay to which she answered "YOU HAVEN'T CHECKED IN". Apparently there is

43

another reception in the waiting area, that I hadn't noticed. I don't know who I am the most mad at, the receptionist for not being specific, or myself for not asking the question earlier.

The Radiology staff couldn't have apologised more and the treatment went ahead without fuss or pain. So glad my tumour is where it is, Paolo had to have radiotherapy on his stomach which made hipm nauseous and sick and (gasp horror) put him off eating. Two down, two to go.

Friday 4th October

I'm absolutely knackered. I had to attend Bolton One, and was bombarded with questions, blood tests and swab tests. I was given so much information about the enhanced recovery program that I thought my brain would explode. A nurse called Darren, with a lovely manner makes four attempts to get blood out of my arm (Scottish ancestors we don't like giving anything away) he tells me he has been doing this job for 27 years, and never before taken four stabs at a patient's arm, to get any blood, always a first time.

The enhanced recovery program is an agreement between patient and hospital. The hospital provides the surgeon and other medical staff and medicine. The patient agrees to get as fit as possible before surgery, drink the liquid build up shakes provided by the hospital, to get up as soon as possible after surgery and to walk 60 metres, twice a day.

Daren asks me "When the staff are waking you up after surgery should they call you Veronica"? I say "Well if they call me Susan I won't know who they are talking to!" I get home in the afternoon and have just enough time to have a sandwich and a cup of tea when it is time for the school run. Then off out I go to Christie in Salford, for the final dose of radiotherapy and another question and answer session with yet another professional. The actual radiotherapy takes only about 10 minutes but I almost fall asleep and would have stayed lying there if it had been allowed. As I get in the car, I realise that I cannot remember one word of the question and answer session.

13 - Looking for Hedgehogs

Two of my grandchildren are staying with us tonight. An early night is needed me thinks.

After Jamie and Lily are tucked up in bed with a DVD, Paolo and I have a takeaway curry, with a cup of tea, not the same without the wine but good enough.

Saturday 5th October

Been up all night with heartburn, for some reason I'm not allowed Gaviscon. I try water and milk, sitting up in bed, walking around the house. I finally go back to bed and go to sleep at about 4.30 a.m. At 7.30 am I am woken by the sound of Lily, waking her brother Jamie. I groan, Paolo goes down to make a brew and I give up on going back to sleep. Lily has a gymnastic lesson so we go there, while Jamie stays at home with his pappy and makes a hedgehog hotel in the back garden. I'm glad I take Lily, I have taken her once before and I always intended to take her again, but time flies. It is lovely to see the difference in her since the last time I came, much more confidence, she's a little chatterbox and I love her to bits.

Later I take Jamie to his guitar lesson and chat to an old friend, while he provides the background music. Then take a birthday card to Mason, my other grandson who is 13 today, they grow up too fast, he is taller than me and getting very handsome.

After dinner comprising bacon butties (come on Paolo you're slipping) we go to visit my brother Kevin, to see if the animal house that Jamie made in his garden has had any visitors, then on to my friend's house whose garden is a jungle, we should definitely find a hedgehog there. We don't find any hedgehogs and Jamie is a little disappointed. Lily instructs him to just pray to God. Jamie sarcastically says "Oh Right, Please God send me some hedgehogs" Lily says "Not like that Jamie this is how to pray" then with a toneless singing voice, unfortunately inherited from me goes on to sing "Dear God bring Jamie a hedgehog, Dear God bring Jamie a hedgehog" After several renditions of this she stops and says "Now we just wait" Jamie and I smile conspiratorially at each other, but I think "Perhaps I should have prayed harder for this chalice to be taken from me. "It must be bad when I start quoting the bible.

In the evening I get really tired, the combination of sleepless night and stressful day on Friday. I decide to go to bed early - 10 o'clock is early for me. As usual the early night doesn't materialise when I decide that I really should practice putting on the stoma bag. Sticking on the imitation Stoma is easy, applying the stoma bag a piece of cake, even emptying out the Morform Thickening Agent is not difficult so why am I collapsed on the bed crying like a baby? After a while I stop blubbering and decide to have a shower to see if the stoma bag continues to stick to me, it does, then I decide to put a dry one on and leave it on for bed to see how that feels. I'd better warn Paolo or he will get a shock when he comes to bed.

The next morning, I am surprised that the fake stoma and bag have not been uncomfortable, and I have slept quite easily in them. I take them off and have a shower - and then realise that I have pulled off the blue cross that the stoma nurse marked on my tummy for the surgeon.

On Sunday we go to church like the prodigal son. I am overwhelmed by the number of people there who know about me and have been praying for me. It is a lovely feeling being part of a community. After church we visit one of our neighbours whose girlfriend has been diagnosed with cervical cancer, but who doesn't want anyone to know. He is suffering in silence because he cannot tell any of his family or friends. (he told us when I told him about my cancer and talking to us is the only time he gets to voice his fears).

We have a lovely Sunday dinner and all our children call to wish me luck and give me hugs and encouragement. They tell me I am amazing and am making it easy for them because I am facing it in my usual no-messing way. I do not tell them that I am beginning to shake in my boots, it would do no good.

At 10.00 pm, Darren the nurse from Bolton One arrives to give me an enema, he tells me to try to keep it in for 20 minutes, then wishes me luck and goes on his way. Paolo lies on the bed next to me to keep me company and tries to encourage me but it's no use, I only manage 17 minutes before I rush to the toilet and explode the contents of my bowel.

14 - The Big Day

The big day is here, we arrive at Bolton Hospital at 7.15 am as instructed and try to book in at Word F6. The receptionist doesn't have my notes. I tell her that Daren (the male nurse with the enema) said I might go straight to E3. I was hoping for E3 ward because there was a possibility that Paolo would be able to stay with me for a while. The receptionist spots a cop-out and sends us up to E3 but my notes are not there, neither do they have an empty bed available. I return to F6 and Paolo is sent packing.

I am asked to sit in a waiting room. Soon I am invited into another room where the anaesthetist comes to check, once more, that they have the right person. He asks me my name, date of birth, address. I am then ushered into another room with an en suite and given another enema. I don't think I last even 10 minutes without Paolo's encouragement but the nurse doesn't batter an eyelid, I think Daren might have been pulling a fast one. The nurse measures my legs and fits flight socks and TED Boots which massage my calves to help prevent clots. Then I lean forward on the bed so that a liquid can be injected into the spinal fluid which numbs and paralyses me from the waist down. It is the strangest sensation when the anaesthetist asks me to lift up my right leg and nothing happens. I am then put to sleep completely and don't know anything more until I wake up at 7.30 in the ward. The operation seems to have been less straightforward than planned and took 5 hours instead of 3, Paolo, Adam and Gail are waiting there for me, I only have a vague memory of that night.

Tuesday 8th October 2013 I wake up on E3 ward very early in the morning and think I am paralysed, I cannot move a muscle but then realise that I am pinned to the bed by wires and tubes. Two wires are attached to the TED boots on my legs, to keep the message going. This apparently helps to prevent clots, which are a danger: after an op, to the over 60, to anyone having cancer treatment and to anyone bedridden I seem to tick all the boxes.

I have a catheter to drain and measure my urine, an Ileostomy bag, a drainage bag on the end of a very long tube which during the next week drives me mad. It wraps around everything and trips

48

me up, it tangles with the catheter and wraps around the trolley that has to accompany me everywhere. The trolley has two drip feeds, one with saline and minerals and the other with antibiotics. I also have an oxygen mask which is soon replaced by a fine tube with little projected tubes that fit up my nose. After a few days the lining of my nose is so dry that I start to find big blood red crows. The cannula is attached to my right hand where the drip is entering my body and the blood pressure monitor is on my left arm monitoring automatically at regular intervals. I also have several sticky things on my body to measure heart rate etc. I have a control in my hand for me to self-administer morphine and another to call for a nurse. I cannot move in the bed without some attachment to my body painfully pulling me back.

Before the end of the day the Blood Pressure Sleeve and boots are taken off and I am able to walk the 60 meters, three times a day pushing the stand with the drip and morphine and carrying the catheter and drainage tube. It sounds like torture but I am up for it, I have decided that I am going to have the quickest recovery EVER and I am on a mission. Little did I know.

15 - Not Going To Plan

Wednesday 9th October After Paolo and Gail have left I realise that the wound where the drainage tube is, has leaked all over the bed. The nurse sticks the plaster around the drainage and offers to make my bed. I go for a wash and blood leaks all over the floor. Once back in bed I listen to snippets of conversation about blood pressure and kidney function and begin to panic. I feel nauseous and the nurse gives me some more pain relief and I eventually fall asleep sitting up.

Thursday 10th October The doctors have done their rounds and prodded my tummy. They decide to put a drain into the stoma, which is still not working. That should make me feel better. The drain in the stoma has no effect. I feel tired and sore. My belly is distended and I feel sick. On the plus side I no longer need the oxygen mask\tubes.

I think my sense of humour has been amputated, I can't think of anything amusing to say.

Thursday evening I drag all the tubes to the toilet to clean my teeth. Can't wait until the drip feed is finished and I can walk around freely. At the toilet I start throwing up, disgusting green and black gunk, because of the tube attached to my arm I cannot reach the alarm. I am crying with frustration and pain. I am sick twice more and the nurse finally hears me. She wants to put a drain up my nose to drain the stomach. I ask her not to, my nose is still sore from the oxygen tubes.

In the middle of the night, I hear a bubbling sound, and I have some pain in my tummy. When I look the stoma has started to fill - YESSS, some good news at last. There was talk of another op to correct a twist in the bowel. I don't have a good night, I am too hot, I smell from the leaks in the drainage tube, my back aches, I feel nauseous, I am scared.

A woman has been brought in to the bed opposite, she is about my age and this is her third lot of cancer and she is being a lot more cheerful. I give myself a shake. Paolo phones me early on Friday morning and tells me he is on the toilet enjoying a poo -

I've created a monster. His natural reaction to illness etc is to cry and moan, but he has learned to be a bit tougher, he makes me laugh and shakes me out of my depression.

The doctors on their round tell me I am making good progress (what do they know?) and say that the catheter and drainage tube can come out this afternoon or tomorrow. I suddenly start to feel better - a light at the end of a tunnel.

The catheter comes out and I walk to the loo. Nothing happens, I can't wee. The nurse tells me that this is normal and not to worry, she unhooks me from the drip feed, I can't tell you how elated I feel, I walk up and down the word, not having this encumbrance of the pole on casters that I have been attached to for the last 4 days.

At visiting time, two of my very best friends and my auntie come to see me, they tell me I am looking well. I explain that it is high blood pressure giving me the healthy glow. But I feel ill, I haven't managed to wee since the tube came out, I have a temperature, I feel sick and my bowels are making strange gurgling noises. Wendy wants to go to ask the nurse for painkillers, I fob her off saying I feel fine, but in the end I ask them to leave. Mr Hobbiss the surgeon comes and tells me that unfortunately I will have to have the catheter re-instated and that if the stoma doesn't start working properly, I will have to have a scan and he may have to re-do the operation (the stoma bit). I feel very despondent, what happened to my plan to be out of hospital in 5 days? I want things to happen quickly, I don't want to wait. I lie on the bed and think of England while the nurse inserts the catheter, I sip an ensure Plus Drink while the rest of the patients tuck into their evening meals (it smells awful anyway). I feel sad.

Paolo arrives 20 minutes late at the evening visiting time, one of the kid's parents had arrived late. He makes light talk about his day and the funny things the kids have said and done and I relax. He tells me I will be fine, just need to let the doctors do their jobs. I begin to cheer up - it's not the end of the word. He gives me a kiss as he goes and says he will see me tomorrow. As he leaves the ward I start being sick again!

The nurses want to put a tube up my nose to draw the bile from my stomach but I have only just had a bit of freedom without the drip and the catheter.

Saturday 13th October starts off well with a shower, I wash my hair and change my nightie - heaven. The catheter is back in so no nickers once more - who's proud? I notice the wee is going darker, I need to get more fluid in but I keep being sick, reluctantly I agree to the stomach tube. The tube wont go up my nose, I have to have the drip reattached, once more I am the prisoner of technology. I still feel very sick.

Paolo phones and tells me about jobs he is doing at home. I phone my cousin Linda to wish her a happy birthday. My mouth is dry, I am beginning to appreciate how ill Paolo must have felt 10 years ago.

In the afternoon Gail, Carl and Shelley (my brother and his partner) brighten my afternoon for an hour.

On Saturday evening Paolo Adam and Patrick come to visit. Just as they arrive I begin to be sick again. I hate people watching me be sick, but I don't want to send them away as they have just got here. The nurse brings me some liquid morphine and the pains decrease. After the visitors leave, I relax watching TV and have the best sleep since I came in here. I wake up several times during the night but I am so relaxed that I am happy to go back to sleep or think happy thoughts.

There is a man in the men's bay further along the ward. He obviously has some learning difficulties because he keeps up the mantra 24/7. At the moment he is repeating "What time is it? What time is it please?" I wonder how the nurses cope and the patients in beds near him.

Sunday. Most of the staff on today are agency. They are very nice. I feel like I need a wee. It's getting uncomfortable, maybe the catheter has pulled away from my bladder, I think I may be slipping back into my moaning head.

I phone Josie to make sure she has something for dinner as she usually comes to our house on Sunday. I tell her that Helen is cooking and she is welcome to go there but she assures me that she has got something in and will be fine. It's nice to chat about things other than hospitals.

I phone my friend Jackie who has just returned from a holiday in Cuba, I ask her how it went. She says never mind my holiday, how are you? I tell her the last thing I want to discuss is catheters and sickness so we have a long conversation about Cuba and about the cruise we went on together a couple of years ago. The phone is a great healer when you are in hospital, it keeps you in touch with the outside word and gives you something to aim for.

Helen, Rachael and Lily visit me in the afternoon. Rachael brings me magazines and dry shampoo. Lily watches X factor on the TV. They are all gorgeous I am so proud. Helen and Rachael discuss going to see Fascinating Ada - Grrr, I should have been going. Robert, Helen's husband is cooking dinner for Paolo, Adam, Helen, Rachael, Arron, Jamie and Lily then tonight he is babysitting while the girls go out. He's lovely, I am proud he is my son-in-law.

The nurse disconnects me from the saline drip and I realise that if I wear my dressing gown, I can hook the urine container on to the pocket and put the wound drain in another pocket it makes things so much easier. I think I may design a gadget and go on Dragons Den when I am better.

Just before visiting I get a huge pain in my stomach and I think once more I am going to give everyone a demonstration of being sick. The nurse gives me some anti-sickness medication just as the Doctor comes to see me. He says they are going to take a scan to see if there is a problem with my bladder and to see if I have a blockage in the bowel that is causing the sickness. Paolo comes on his own in the evening and I am impressed that he has managed to wash and dry my nighties without shrinking them. My Man of Many Talents! Irene a lovely lady in the ward is going home. How Lucky.

Sunday night I can't sleep, I am looking forward to having Rice Krispies (that I usually don't like) I start to shake because I am so hungry, but then in the morning they say clear fluids only

Monday 14th October The lovely Chinese doctor comes to see me and tells me that all the tests are coming back good. I have the Rice Krispies - then I am sick again !!! I have a little cry!

Josie comes at visiting time bless her, she is not in the best of health and has very little eyesight and yet she manages to get on two buses to come to see me three times during my hospitalisation. She tells me that Natasha, her granddaughter and four great-grandchildren are arriving the next day for a visit from the Isle of Sky. She is really looking forward to them coming and apologises for not being able to visit me again. I tell her not to be silly and that I am a bit disappointed that I will not be at home to chat to Natasha. The cannula has been re-instated in my wrist so I can't write without setting the beeper off, in fact I cant do anything without setting it off.

At tea time I have a small portion of potatoes and gravy and keep it down yeah. Its a good day. At visiting time my sister asks one of the doctors if I am allowed to suck boiled sweets and he says I am. That night I go to town on a bag of Werthers, unfortunately I am not very good at sucking sweets, before long I am biting them. I am rewarded with pains in my stomach once more. Why can I never do things in moderation? Robert comes to see me he brings me grapes that I have asked for, I know that I will have to peel each one before eating, but I have all the time in the world. He also brings me buttered malt bread. I thank him but I know that I cannot eat it. Its got dried fruit, wholemeal flour and god knows what else that is on the forbidden list. After he goes, the Soreen starts calling to me. I think I will just lick the butter off. Then I start to nibble at the forbidden fruit. I only eat one slice but it does the trick, my brain starts to work, "Bring me the medicine to stop me being sick, bring me the pain relief." Tuesday the doctors tell me that they plan to remove the drain and the catheter so I should be able to go home in a couple of days, it can't come quick enough!

Various people have asked me this week if the cancer has gone completely, I keep telling them that doctors said the operation was a complete success, I realise that I don't know if that means that all the cancer has been removed so I ask the question and the doctor tells me that yes it has all gone.

There is possibly a problem with the bladder as it is so close to the operation site and I may have to go home with a catheter fastened to my leg - not a pretty sight and the thought of it depresses me for a while particularly because even though I have this drain inserted into the bladder I constantly feel the need to pass water and there is no relief from it.

Arthur, the voice from the next bay is chanting again "Nurse come and help me please, Nurse come and help me please"sometimes he adds "cumon luvie, cumon darlin."

The drain is removed, the length of the pipe inside me must be about 4 foot long, no wonder I have been uncomfortable. The drip is removed, my only attachment is the catheter. I feel almost human. Arthur has stopped shouting, all's well with the world.

An old lady is wheeled into the space next to my bed. She is chatty, seemingly unaffected by the anaesthetic she has been under She has just had her ileostomy reversal. She tells me that when she had the original operation (the one that I have just had), she felt no pain afterwards because she had an injection in her back! I had an injection and anaesthetic and I have been in pain and being sick for 8 days. What's going on?

Wednesday 16th October 2013 I have eaten all my meals (small amounts but what can you expect) had the catheter removed and had a wee. Gail and Mark visit me in the afternoon and Linda and Paolo in the evening. Just posting and answering posts on Facebook and I realise that I have a grin on my face. I'm on the mend.

On Wednesday night an agency nurse is doing the observations in the ward it takes her longer than the regular staff understandably. But the regular nurse usually turns the lights off at about 9 and does the rest by torchlight. This moron leaves the big lights on until midnight. Does she know that there are patients in this ward who have only just come back from surgery and are desperately trying to sleep? Understandably the women in the ward are not happy. The lovely lady who had earlier been complaining that she was in more pain than she had at her earlier surgery is rambling about men in her kitchen. She becomes more lucid and asks the agency nurse to help her to get more comfortable in the bed. The nurse refuses, she says she is not allowed to lift - WHAT?? Why have you not done lifting and handling training, you are working in a surgical ward! How is this old dear with her slippy flight socks supposed to push herself up the bed without help? Another lady is complaining that she is cold, no one comes to help. There are two drips bleeping, I am exhausted, my bladder is complaining. I decide that warm milk is the answer but the nurse informs me that she can't warm it up. I have to make do with cold milk which I don't particularly like, but it does the trick, the periods between my need to pass water increases and I drift off to sleep, only to dream about my son falling down stairs. The lady in the next bed, still slightly delirious I think, suddenly shouts that in TENKO they would treat you better. I can't help laugh. I say "They would shoot you in TENKO", "yes!" she says but they would stop your drip bleeping".

Thursday 17th October Going home today with any luck. Just need my stitches out. I eat breakfast and the doctors come round and say I look well and all the observations are good. They tell me about district nurses, stoma nurses, scans and appointments. I ask them whether the lymph nodes extracted during the operation have been examined through the microscope but they reply "Not Yet!" I refuse to let that little grumbling possibility spoil my going home day. I go for a shower, wash my hair, clean my teeth and change the stoma bag. Then I am so tired I feel I have climbed Mount Everest. I go back to bed, but the ward is so noisy and busy there is no rest. After lunch it's visiting time. Just as Matteo and Lauren arrive the nurse comes to take out the stitches, they should slide out easily but the skin has stared to grow over the bead at the end. I puff and blow for a few seconds and it is all over. I dress quickly, pack my bag, distribute magazines and chocolate to the amazing nurses and I am on my way. At home, I enjoy a cup of tea and chat to Matteo and Adam then tuck myself up in bed for half an hour. When the delicious smell of pasta carbonara filters up the stairs, I go down and enjoy home cooked food for the first time in 10 days. The children and later their parents are pleased to see me and I become a little emotional and I am glad to be tucked back up in bed in my pyjamas.

Friday 18th October I am up showered, and shaved my legs. I don't know whether my legs have gone slimmer and so the hairs are not as spread out or the hair growth has gone into hyperdrive while I have been in hospital. Either way my legs look like they belong to a monkey, or they did, now they look and feel beautiful. I am dressed before 8.30 am and I am feeling energised. My plan is to stay up until after the stoma nurses have been. It's lovely to sit on my own settee and watch 3 x 1 year old's spinning round to get dizzy and then fall down giggling - who shows them how to do that and which developmental category do I enter it in? After delicious carrot soup, I snuggle up with Alfie to watch TV. The stoma nurse phones at 3 to tell me they will call on Monday. Too late to go to bed now. Over meatballs at tea time the children begin to question me about my operation. I briefly tell the kids in language they can understand what my operation was about and show them the stomas bag. They are neither repulsed nor amazed. The general consensus was "oh right" and then back to their evening meal. I love kids. At 7 pm Daren the nurse from Bolton One phones to ask if I am OK, he reminds me that I am still in high risk of clots and tells me to put the pressure socks on and keep doing the leg exercises.

On Saturday I wake up and "post on Facebook"
Ready for a new day. Just got the washing and ironing to do. Then I will clean out the chickens before I do the shopping. - Just kiddingxxx

I am uncomfortable and sore, but after I shower and dress, I feel much better. I decide to tackle the mountain of post that always seems to accumulate even though I usually recycle most immediately it arrives. I buy two different lots of cancer charity raffle tickets (they were in luck - how could I say no at this time) and then walk to the post box at the end of the street. I nearly spend £102 in the Easylife catalogue but the computer won't accept my password - phew... I think the anaesthesia is still clogging my brain. I put some washing in the machine and put shopping away when Paolo arrives from Tesco. Who ever thought that these mundane tasks could help to make me feel "normal".

With stoma bag tucked into my knickers instead of swinging loose from my belly, I can almost believe that the last two weeks have just been a horrible nightmare. I have a long list of food to avoid, but while sorting through the paperwork this morning, I find a brochure about ileostomy that seems to say you can eat everything until you find it upsets you, then remove it from your diet. That sounds like a plan. We have hot cooked chicken on tiger bread with lashings of butter then later for dinner Salmon and Hake in lemon sauce with rice and wild mushrooms and rocket salad. Washed down with a bottle of Sauvignon Blanc. Must admit, I had the hint of indigestion at bedtime, but it was worth it.

For a few years I have been researching my family tree. In the post I discover a brown envelope full of photocopies of old letters Written between my Great Uncle Luc and his French cousins during the WW1. I am engrossed and still reading them at midnight.

My body is used to quite a lot of physical exercise, picking up children and walking and playing with them all day. Now even though I suppose I need rest to heal, I don't seem to be able to sleep very well (the indigestion is not helping). I try drinking milk, I get into the spare bed, then out again. Eventually I turn on the computer and engross myself in it until 5.30 am, surely I must be tired now. At 7.am the alarm wakes me. Paolo goes downstairs and brings tea and salmon on toast, our usual Sunday breakfast and we sit and pour over the old photos and letters.

Eventually we get up and dressed and decide to go for a walk. We walk around Ashton's Field and though I am by now feeling weak and tired it is nice to feel the weather on my face. I send Daren a text asking him what I can take for heart burn and he phones me back immediately saying Gaviscon - WHAT??? I am sure I have read within the mountain of bumf that I cannot take Gaviscon. The cure to my discomfort had been sitting there on my bedside table all night.

We go back home and I take a spoonful of Gaviscon, I get in the spare bed - I had stripped our bed and put the bedding into the wash. I sleep, a lovely restful sleep for two hours and awake ready for the day. Paolo has cooked a pork loin and vegetables. My auntie comes for dinner, then my "nearly" auntie Elsie (she is my cousin"s auntie, but her sons once christened me their nearly

58

cousin, so she is by default my nearly auntie) and my sister arrive. We have a lovely relaxing gossiping couple of hours and I could easily believe that the last fortnight has all been an awful nightmare. Then I touch my stoma bag. No it's all true but the worst is over.

The two glasses of wine I have drunk over the last two days have made the contents of the stoma bag very loose. This makes emptying it much easier but more frequent. Also it can (and is) making me dehydrated because all the food and drink is passing through my body too quickly. I should have been given Loperamide from the hospital but there's been an oversight. I decide to have some blueberry wheats (breakfast cereal) and voila I am cured. Paolo turns the mattress on the bed, we put on the fresh bedding, I have a shower and a couple paracetamols and sleep like a baby until 3.am. When I wake, I am in some discomfort, not exactly pain. I empty the stoma bag, have a drink of water and some more pain relief and lie back down in bed relaxed. Although sleep doesn't come back to me I don't mind, I am home. No wires or tubes or monitors. No nurses to take blood samples or check urine output. No mentally challenged men with loud voices. No bright lights. Just a loving husband lying next to me sleeping peacefully. He doesn't molly coddle me, but cooks delicious, nutritious meals. Takes me out walking to build up my strength and help me sleep He walks upstairs behind me when he thinks I look wobbly (he thinks I haven't noticed this). He doesn't insist I "Take things easy" - I would probably hit him with something, but when I feel tired after only being up an hour and decide to go back to bed, he says "Good Idea, I'll bring you a drink. I love him with my heart and soul.

10 years ago when he had cancer, he was a different kind of patient, I was a different kind of nurse. From beginning to end Paolo was terrified of the cancer. We were younger, poorer and with dependent children. Without Paolo's wage we were in danger of losing our house. I worked and paid bills, cooked meals, drove Matteo to school and after school activities, drove Paolo to Christies. I was afraid that Paolo would not have the strength in his body or character to fight the cancer and frequently bullied him to get up or go for a walk. I encouraged him to spend time with

Matteo (9 years old at the time). Up till that point, because of long working hours and traveling time they had not spend much time together. He taught him to play chess and encouraged him to play clarinet. Christies kept a check on Paolo for ten years after the cancer and he had just had his last check when I was diagnosed, irony!

Monday 21st October I get up at 7 am and have a cup of tea and some more breakfast cereal and go back to bed At 8 o'clock I think I will have a quick shower. I empty the stoma bag and take it off in the shower. I always feel better after putting on a clean bag. I shampoo my hair, turning my face into the lovely hot water imagining I am an advert for invigorating shower gel. Gradually I become aware of water round my ankles. I look down and see the shower tray is blocked and overflowing, the giant nipple that is the short piece of small bowel sticking from my belly is oozing poo. For a second I am transfixed, it looks like something from a B rated SciFi movie. My quick shower turns into a full blown unblocking the drain, cleaning the shower cubicle, mopping the floor session.

I was supposed to go downstairs to keep an eye on the babies while Paolo did the school run, but by the time I eventually emerge he has put on their coats and fastened them into the car. When he comes home he tells me that he met one of our friends who has told him that her sister has lung cancer in both lungs. I imagine little lymph nodes like tadpoles and wonder if any of them are swimming round my body as we speak, choosing where they are going to spawn.

Stop It Veronica It Doesn't Suit You.

While Paolo plays with the three little girls we care for, I go on the computer and sort out my car insurance. My brother Kevin phones and we have a nice leisurely chat, bragging about our indestructibility (who are we kidding?) I make toast and milk for the kids and let them eat it in the living room, the only carpeted room in the house, I rarely allow this treat. Brea gets giddy and spills the milk on the carpet and "posts" toast down the back of the radiator. Lesson learned.

I put on a CD that encourages the kids to "run like a dinosaur" and "fly like an eagle". This is a favourite with the kids that have just left us for school and these little ones soon get the hang of it, they have so much energy and don't seem to get as tired as I do today.

We have lovely vegetable soup for lunch with garlic croutons, my mouth is watering in anticipation as I encourage the girls to eat. But then Paolo - bless him - pours a lovely heart shaped swirl of cream into the top of mine to build me up and profess his love. I only eat a small portion (believe me this is unusual), the soup is too rich and is rising back from my stomach. Memories of the green/black gunk that I kept filling the sick bowls with at the hospital stop me from trying to eat any more. What a waste.

As we finish eating the district nurse arrives - hooray, I've not been abandoned. She admires my house (with childminding in mind) and she fills in my details. I think basically she had just been given my name and told to come and see me. She said that the hole left by the drainage tube would not heal while filled with crud, (Is that a medical term?) she cleans it out and puts on a dressing and tells me to keep it dry. I tell her I can only keep it dry until the next morning's shower.

She leaves me a few spare dressings and tells me to phone the GP and get a prescription for Imodium to bulk up my stoma contents. She also advises me to ask for something to make me sleep but I am not happy about that. I'm sure my sleep patterns will sort themselves out soon. And at the moment if I get tired during the day or evening I can just go to bed. I don't have to get up. Paolo has proved his competence while I have been in hospital so I don't think twice about taking myself off for an hour when I get tired.

I phone the doctors surgery and the receptionist is her usual "helpful" self telling me that "No, the doctor can't write prescriptions for Loperamide or insomnia without seeing you". I say OK then he will have to do a house call. I can almost hear her eyes rolling. She says "Do you normally come into the surgery" I say "Yes, on the very rare occasions I need a doctor, I do" but as I have just had a five hour operation to remove a tumour and have a stoma fitted, I don't want to sit in a room full of sick people. Her attitude changes immediately - Bless - she is only doing her job.

As the kids become noisier after tea, I miss two phone calls. One at 4.45 from Daren and the other at 5.00pm from Dr Hyams.

Daren just turns up with a tape measure to see if my legs have slimmed down to make sure he is supplying me with the correctly sized protecta stockings.

Later Paolo's mum phones from Switzerland and I listen in to the conversation. (Not that I understand more than a few phrases). She tells Paolo that I must be patient as I am not 20 any more. I say "Patient? Is that a french work, I have never heard it before". And as for not being 20, thats only chronologically.

My sister sends me a link on Mumsnet entitled Do You Dunk Your Penis?. If laughter is the best medicine, I shall start training for the marathon. The thread runs and runs and I am nearly wetting myself. As I am reading it, Patrick sends me a text asking how I am. I answer that I am well and then send him the link. I immediately begin to question my sanity. Is this the sort of thing an old stepmother shares with a young professional stepson. He doesn't answer, I worry that he is too shocked - poor lamb he probably doesn't understand that elderly parents still do sex. (Well we reminisce occasionally.).

17 - Getting Back to Normal

Tuesday 22nd October I wake up feeling quite well except for this dull back ache that I realise is not getting better. I had presumed it was being caused by the hospital bed but I have been home for 5 nights now. I eat breakfast, have a strip wash so as not to wet the dressing over the drain hole. Paolo takes a couple of kids to school and says he will drop my car off for MOT and be back in half an hour. He instructs me not to lift the girls under any circumstances. I sit on the floor and help Alexia (20 months) to construct a train track, just as the stoma nurse arrives. She says she will wait until Paolo arrives to look at my stoma. I tell her that I am constantly dry and cannot get enough to drink. She explains that is it a vicious circle The more I drink, the more liquid is the food traveling into the stoma bag. The softer it is the quicker it travels through my body and the less chance for my body to hydrate itself. My backache apparently is my kidneys (or was it liver - whatever!) complaining for lack of liquid. When Paolo arrives she tells me to remove the bag so she can examine the contents, What a delightful job! and tells me it is imperative to get some Loperamide and some dioralyte. The Loperamide to bulk up the stools and the dioralyte to replace some of the salts and minerals that are lacking in my body. After lunch of Pasta soup and white bread, I have a dioralyte and a Loperamide (I know the Loperamide is supposed to be taken before food) then I feel completely bloated. I go for a little lie down (like grandfather in my pocket) and fall asleep for an hour and a half. No wonder I am up all night.

When I wake up I phone Emma my hairdresser and even though she isn't mobile I ask her if she will come to my house and give me a trim as my hair, wild and curly at the best of times is now so dry I'm afraid it may burst into flames like the bush fires in Australia on the news. She says she will come tomorrow in her dinner hour and bring Mary with her to do my nails - aww, you never appreciate how kind people are until something like this happens.

As Paolo goes out for the afternoon school run my sister Gail arrives. I make boiled carrots and mashed potatoes - Paolo will make the sausage when he comes back. The mechanic brings the car back and I pay him, glad that nothing major has to be repaired or replaced on the car. The kids arrive back from school and Alise and Maddie, 9 years olds, give us a rendition of "Its The Hard Knock Life For Us from the Musical Annie that they are learning at school. We clap and cheer then the other kids want some praise: "Watch me do a cartwheel nanna", "I got a new book at school today nanna", My teacher said I was the best helper at school today, I got a sticker" Kids! Don't you love em!

The sausage and mash is lovely comfort food, most of the kids have second helpings. After tea they do their own things. The 9 year olds take themselves up stairs to the spare bedroom to practice their musical. Alexia finds a puddle to sit in two minutes before her grandad comes to collect her. Isaac 5 and Ashton 4, think it is hilariously funny to dip their heads in a play tray full of rain water and then shake their heads vigorously to wet each other even more. Jamie as usual gets the model animals out to construct yet another zoo. Lily, 5, brings sanity to the house when she suggests watching a DVD. I say good idea, everyone put the toys away and I will start the DVD and bring chocolate. Result five minutes later, a relatively tidy house and 8 kids with eyes glued to the screen and mouths stuffed with chocolate. I am not advocating this as good childminding practice, please excuse my lack of energy, I will do better next time.

After the kids have left I realise that despite the Loperamide and dioralyte I am still very thirsty, my bag is full of very runny chocolate cake mixture (I prefer to refer to it as this) and my back has begun to ache again. Perhaps it's time I started following the rules.

After the kids go, Paolo gets stuck into cleaning the kitchen and hoovering the living room (I help a little) the house is peaceful and quiet. I think about the other women I've left behind in the ward. The lady with lots of money but who is main carer for her husband following his stroke. She has had three separate cancers in less than 2 years, and all the skin has burnt of her hands and feet by chemotherapy. The lovely 92 year old, very polite and middle class. She couldn't understand why the nurses went to such lengths to prevent her getting a clot. "I'm 92" she said "a clot going to my brain and killing me in my sleep feels like a lucky way to go". Another lady who after her bag burst in the bed at home, had to clean herself and change the bedding by herself because her husband refused to help. He said he was diabetic and she wouldn't be able to cope with all he had to put up with. I am the luckiest girl in the world.

When I wake up on Wednesday I've had a good sleep and feel well. I empty the still liquidy chocolate cake mixture into the toilet, I'm quite disappointed that it hasn't thickened up overnight. The nurse told me to take 1 Loperomide pill, 4 times a day before meals and if that doesn't work after two days increase it to 2 pills. I'm very tempted to increase the dose immediately but I don't. I decide that perhaps the nurse with all her education and experience might know better than me. I think maybe I'm learning the meaning of that french word, What was it? Oh yes patience. I don't know what it is with me that I can't accept the things people say until I have tried them. My interpretation of the rules have got me into so much hot water in the past, I will never learn. On the other hand, I can be so naive! When I was younger, my brothers (all younger than me) used to vie with each other, who could tell me the most improbable stories and I would just believe them. I think they probably still find it amusing to do this to me still.

I get up and make a cup of tea and some porridge for me and Paolo. As the porridge simmers I look at all the flowers and cards and once again count my blessings. I have run out of vases for the flowers and the chocolate has been eaten (possibly contributing to the runny poo), but the cards are a permanent source of contentment. In little quiet moments I take them down and read them. Some bring a lump to my throat and a tear to my eye. Some make me smile and others make me laugh out loud. But each of them in turn reminds me of all the people in my life who love and care for me. Money can't buy that.

I take the porridge back to bed and relax. The dioralyte at last is having a good effect, my back is not aching and my mouth and lips not quite so dry.

At 8.30 am, I get up for the second time, wash and dress and go downstairs to keep an eye on the babies while Paolo takes Millie

65

and Keith to school. But he has already put the coats on the little ones. He says he is taking them to "On Safari". I go back to bed with a book. This feels so decadent.

At 11.30 Paolo comes home and begins to make dinner. I sit and sing "Row row, row your boat" with Odelia and Brea, both excited that I am once more sitting on the floor with them. They fight to be the one on my knee. We sing Insy Winsy Spider and 12345 once I caught a fish alive. I try to read Wibbly Pig but Brea wants to turn the pages over and Odelia wants to read a different book, its lovely to hear the emerging language coming from these 1 year olds.

As Paolo lifts the girls into high chairs for lunch, Emma arrives to cut my hair and Mary to Shelac my nails. They bring more "Get Well" cards and more chocolate and ask me how I am. I catch up on all the local gossip while I've been out of circulation. When they leave I eat my dinner (pasta with ham and cheese,) while Paolo changes the girls nappies and puts them down for a nap. Once again I am amazed at how competent he has become while I've been away.

Lynn, an old friend arrives and I brew tea and we exchange stories of children and grandchildren for the rest of the afternoon. I wouldn't wish cancer on anyone, but it occurs to me that it has given me permission to slow down - I could get used to this.

Lynn goes, Brea and Odelia are collected, Paolo sets off on the school run and I make fish fingers, chips and beans for tea. An ordinary day in an ordinary life, I count my blessings.

After the school children go home, Jackie and Steve our very close friends arrive unannounced. Steve and Paolo watch a football match on TV while Jackie and I drink coffee, eat cake and try to interrupt each other's conversation. We both talk too much and either of us would just talk continuously if the other one didn't butt in. We met 39 years ago in Blackpool, she with her eldest daughter Adele, out for a day on the beach, me with a toddler and a 3 month old baby, running away from my husband. Unfortunately, Helen (the baby) got diarrhoea, and used up all the Terry nappies I had with me. I went back home to him and didn't find the strength of character to leave him until 20 years later. How time flies when you are having fun. Before they leave I ask Jackie if she wants a Baileys Coffee and decide a splash in mine won't do any harm?? In the middle of the night when my mouth once again feels like sand paper I question my sanity once more.

Thursday 24th October I have another sleepless night, still not managed to get the contents of the stoma bag to the correct consistency and so I am still a bit thirsty and shaking. When the district nurse came on Monday, she told me to keep the dressing over the drainage hole as dry as possible. Consequently, I have been having strip wash instead of a shower in the morning. Also taking advice from Jean, I have not changed my stoma bag each morning. After my rotten night I decide that I will have a shower today. The nurse is coming to change the dressing anyway. In the shower I am horrified to see I have "nappy rash" all around the stoma, I'm not doing that again.

After taking the older kids to school, Paolo takes the little girls in the double buggy to the bank. He tells me to go back to bed. I feel this is good advice except that the more I rest during the day, the less I can sleep at night. I decide to compromise and sit in the reclining chair. As I am relaxing, a friend drops by the flowers and a card. She hasn't seen this house since we moved in, but she visited it often 45 years ago when it was a children's home and her friend lived here. She is interested to see the changes we have made and I forget about my tiredness as I show her round and re-live my hospital experience.

18 - Good News

Later the district nurse comes to change the dressing and then I decide I will sleep better tonight if I keep active so I clean away the breakfast dishes and wipe down the surfaces in the kitchen. The rest of the day tickles along in a normal way until 2.50 p.m.

Helen and Robert had just dropped in for a quick visit and Alice, a parent had just arrived to pick up Odelia, Paolo is just strolling at toddler pace back home from Ashton's Field.

The phone rings and I impatiently pick it up a snap "Hello" expecting it to be yet another PPI salesman, except it's not.

"Hello Veronica, this is Mr Hobbiss".

I turn to ice, this is the surgeon, this can mean only one thing, bad news. Have they cut away the wrong bit, or have they left an instrument inside me, no wonder I am in pain. Have they found more cancer? I cross my fingers and squeeze shut my eyes. The voice continues slowly and deliberately

"I am pleased to tell you that tests on the tumour removed from your rectum was in the early stages. It had not pushed through the bowel wall and the lymph nodes extracted have been found free of cancer. I will not be advising you to have chemotherapy. I look forward to seeing you in my clinic".

I can hardly breath, all I can say is thank thank you. I try to pass on the fantastic news to Helen and Robert and Alice, the words come out jumbled up but I think they get the gist. Helen and I cling to each other crying hysterically with relief, then I hug Robert and Alice. By the time Paolo comes strolling in we are once more composed and I ask him nonchalantly if he wants to hear some good news. Another round of hugs and kisses and tears. I want to shout it from the rooftop, instead as everyone leaves me to pick up school children I post it on Facebook, then email my friends and family group. It is less than 4 weeks since I was asking how to create an email group. By 5 pm I have 41 "likes" and dozens of answers either on facebook or email. I used to sneer at people "posting" on facebook every 5 minutes but I have to admit it is a fantastic way of getting information to a lot of people very quickly even quicker than shouting from the rooftops.

The news travels fast and I am told that the next day as Paolo is doing the weekly supermarket shop, Lauren spots him and runs and throws herself into his arms. There are few words, they are not needed, they comfort and are comforted and then Lauren runs back to her post on the self-service checkouts. She tells Matteo later that his dad's hugs are the best. Yes they are.

Answers to emails
Helen Harrison tagged you in a status: feeling blessed.
Helen wrote: *"Over the past 2 months my family has been in turmoil as we have watched helpless as my mum, the most beautiful, extraordinary, caring person battle cancer. And today I was there when mum got the call to say that the op had got rid of the cancer, it hasn't spread and mum won't need chemo!! Knew you would beat it mum, on to the next , so privileged to be part of your story. Love you xxxx"*
: **"Ace news Veronica so happy for you xxx"**
Lesley wrote: *"Good job well done Mr Hobbis!! Best news this year. You kicked its ass!!!! Love you. Xx"*
Music to your ears I bet..I'm so pleased Veron..go ahead and celebrate you and Paolo deserve it..lots of love..xx

Darren wrote: "oh bloody hell I'm going to have to get a refund on these wigs then. thanks a lot veronica. XXXXX big kissesXXXX"
"glad glad sooo glad love you sis see you soon"
Rachael wrote: "A new day and a great weight lifted because Veronica Scotton (AKA Super Woman) has done what we all knew she would and beaten it!! But this time has also shown something else that I already knew and that is what wonderful, special and strong family and friends I have. Thanks to you all and a big well done to Paolo Scotton for being so brave and strong. Love you all xxx"
Kevin Tucker wrote: "Great news. We never doubted you would come out on top. It's lovely news for a lovely family. Your own daughter has said it all in her message. :-) Go on out and celebrate and have a drink on me, I will send you a tea bag, while you're out just ask them to put some hot water on it for you."
Top of the world ma!!!
Petra - fan-bloody-tastic
Best news, really pleased
Wow that's fantastic news, so now you can concentrate on recovery from the op. What a relief
Oh Veronica, that's wonderful news, you must all be so relieved. Take very special care of yourself. all our love and hugs. Margaret
Thanks to the Almighty God. He deserves the glory, honour and adoration. He is a faithful God. We as a family are happy for you.

Love the Kanyangas

We have pizza for tea, which I have always thought of as a cop-out, popping frozen food in the oven and warming it up. But apparently for my topsy-turvy diet it is good for thickening up the chocolate mixture. Also less washing up, win-win situation.

Gail calls round to see me, instead of our usual Thursday evening Guinness and curry night. I am not a particularly scintillating hostess tonight and fall asleep.

Friday 25th October. My friend Joyce calls to see me and brings in the post. There is the proof of the phone call.

Dear Mrs Scotton
I have now had the opportunity to see the lab report of the bowel we sent for analysis. This shows that your bowel cancer was indeed an early cancer that had not invaded fully through the wall of the bowel and did not involve the glands around the bowel. No further treatment is required.
I look forward to seeing you in the follow up clinic. Yours sincerely
J H Hobbiss MD FRCS
Consultant Colorectal and General Surgeon

While I am enjoying the tea and gossip with Joyce, I get a twinge, a sharp pain just below the point where the drainage pipe has been. It carries on during the day particularly when I am moving from sitting down to standing up. A normal person would think "I've recently had a major operation, it is quite understandable that I might be in pain" and then maybe pop a paracetamol or Ibuprofen. Not me! First I try walking round the garden to see if it eases it, it doesn't. Then I think having a little lie down might help, it doesn't. Then I consider taking pain relief, after all I have been provided with enough painkillers to commit suicide, perhaps the hospital has a suspicion that I might be in need of a little pain relief. No, first I consider taking the paracetamol, then I begin to worry that if I took it and whatever was causing the pain got worse, I wouldn't feel it getting worse until the paracetamol wore off, by then it might be too late. (Too late for what you might ask). First I try to phone Daren, up to now the most immediate support I could wish for, it goes to answer machine. Then I try the stoma nurses, whose answer machine asks me to leave a message. I phone my GP and am informed by the receptionist that the duty doctor is visiting the sick,, (really??? do

70

they still do that?). I phone the district nurse several times but the line is engaged and then panicking, I phone the surgeon himself. His secretary answers the phone and tells me he is in theatre but she will ask him when he is finished. Finally I phone stoma nurses again and Ben answers. He tells me it is perfectly normal to feel a little pain after surgery (well I never!), its probably caused by a little scar tissue. He says to take a couple of paracetamol and see how it goes. So I do. The thing is, I am 62, used to a few aches and pains, I've probably had worse pains in my gut after a good curry and exceedingly worse pains after a bad one. What's the matter with me, the real me is a reasonably healthy, always on the go, middle aged woman, who is capable of running around after several children for 12 hours a day. My alter-ego unfortunately is a neurotic hypochondriac that worries about the world running out of antibiotic just as I pick up a super bug.

One of our minded kids is Alfie who had his 4th birthday last week. We always have party food and a cake whenever the kids have a birthday during which I re-enforce the idea that whenever you have a birthday you learn to like another food. You would be surprised how many children are persuaded to try and often like several different foods that up to now have not passed their lips. We have the tea today, better late than never. The kids eat masses of sugar loaded fatty food, sing happy birthday several times getting louder each time and then go home with their parents so hyper I know they won't be asleep before midnight. The joys of parenthood.

Note to self, be careful how you answer children's questions when there is more than one age group within ear-shot. The older kids asked me why I was wearing the white socks. I had explained about blood clots after surgery. Rachael later tells me that Isaac has told her if I take the socks off I will have a heart attack.

As the kids are celebrating Alfie's 4th birthday, another friend Trisha calls and brings me a chili plant. I suppose Trisha must be my oldest friend since she was born 3 days before me in the same ward. Apparently our grandparents had known each other. I didn't get to know her until we were 13 when my family moved to Little Hulton and Trisha was in my class in my new school. It occurs to me that I have several different friends who I have known in different spheres of my life with whom I have never argued, is that normal, am I just a pushover. I don't think so, I am quite forthright in my opinions, I think it is just that my generation has learned from an early age to "agree to disagree" before an argument gets personal.

In the evening I look at the list of permitted food and realise that I can eat noodles. We have a take-away chow mien. Now I am really beginning to feel normal and later if I get tummy ache, I can put it down to unhygienic kitchens, or drink a dioralyte and go to sleep unworried. The Chow Mein is bloody lovely, I feel a right slob, leaning back on my reclining chair, watching TV with a take-away on my lap, but I don't care. I go to bed at about 11 pm, and take two paracetamols. I lie there listening to my stomach making noises like a dying kitten stuck behind the gas fire, and then the next minute its 5 am, I've slept for over 5 hours. I automatically go to the loo. The stoma is empty - is this normal, I'm not too sure what normal is. I decide not to over-think things and go back to bed. After checking my phone for emails and Facebook messages, I relax back on the pillows. Paolo tells me to take the loperamide and he will make some porridge, I glance at the clock, it's 9.am - WOW.

I phone Jackie my friend to congratulate her on becoming a granny once more. Then Colin, my cousin from the Isle of Man phones to say he has been in Spain for two weeks and only just got my good news. My relationship with Colin is strange. He is my oldest first cousin and 7 years older than me so I had little contact with him as a child. He emigrated to South Africa when I was a teenager and then to the Isle of Man, I haven't seen his children since they were babies and I have never met his grandchildren. I have possibly only seen him less than 20 times in my life and yet whenever he phones, sometimes with years in between, I recognise his voice immediately and we chat as if we are in daily contact.

Before I go to sleep, I offer a prayer.

'Dear God, whoever or whatever you are, if you have been listening to all these lovely people saying prayers on my behalf, or all these equally lovely atheists sending loving vibes, and if you have influenced the outcome, Thank you from me and my family.'.

I was educated by nuns for the first 13 years of my life. I was taught that God was loving and caring. I was also taught that if I missed Mass on Sunday through my own fault and had not confessed the sin in confession before I died, then I would be banished to hell for all eternity. For years I had nightmares, not about going to hell, God no, I was too good for that and nothing would make me miss Mass. But the thought of eternity. My brain could not absorb the idea of going on forever, nor could it believe in coming to a complete end. When my dad died, I cried and cried until I couldn't cry any longer then fell asleep exhausted. The next day I woke up with peace in my heart and the knowledge that I would not have these nightmares again. And I never have, I believe that was my dad's gift to me and I will always be grateful. It took me a long time for me to come to the conclusion that religions should exist for the comfort of people and not to bully them into anything. Now I go to church sometimes but don't worry about hell fires when I choose not to. A much more civilised arrangement. I thank God for the sun and the rain and don't blame him (or her) for corrupt politicians. I go to church when I have a problem that is worrying me, something about the chanting prayers, the hymn singing and the hugging and kissing as I leave helps me to work through my problems. Sometimes I go swimming early in the morning, this has a similar effect.

Saturday 26th October Fairly quiet day, put some washing in, Nathan and his boys came to see us. Paolo has been shopping and we have hot chicken and bread. Then we decided to go to look for a cheap fridge freezer for our new garage (we need extra storage space at Christmas). I was already cold before we set out so wrapped myself up in boots and layers and gloves. I was still cold and couldn't believe it as we passed dozens of teenagers with bare midriffs and tee shirts. Really feeling my age. I walked about 200 yards to the shop and was worried I might not be able to walk back. As we got home, Paolo lit the wood burner fire and I snuggled down under a blanket to watch TV. I soon felt much better and decided to have a look on ebay. There was a fridge freezer with a starting bid for 99p. I though I had put a bid in for 4.99p but after watching Xfactor, I checked ebay and found I had bought the fridge for 99p just need to collect it from Failsworth. It sounds too good to be true, we'll see what it is like when we collect it.

Ever the optimist, I go to bed on Saturday night with the conviction that my sleep patterns are back to normal. We have had a lovely meal, cooked as usual by my personal chef, of pasta with bacon and tomatoes (all on the permitted list). I'm sufficiently tired having had the trip to Walkden and done various little tasks in the house. I'm relaxed and warm. Two hours after going to bed, I am still awake, my bladder feels like it is on fire. I keep going to the toilet only to pass thimble full's of wee. The stoma contents at last seem to resemble the consistency of toothpaste, but now my waterworks are keeping me awake. I try drinking milk, which helped me in the hospital, but this has no effect, I clear away the tea things and stack the dishwasher, might as well make myself useful. I put the washing machine on and then go back to bed and read a Candis Magazine cover to cover. Eventually I decide that I am really tired and lie down only to have nightmares about losing children.

Sunday 27th October After moaning about lack of sleep and dutiful husband bringing me breakfast in bed. I remember about the 99p fridge. Was I dreaming? I switch on the computer then go and have my 10th wee of the morning. Yep I did actually have a winning bid. I send a message to the seller asking for his address. Then decide to have a game of sudoko. Before the op, I could do these sudoko. Before the operation, I could always complete the intricate level sudoko - each time trying to improve my speed. Since coming out of hospital, I haven't been able to complete one. Success, I complete the game faster than 1% of the 2,366 people playing the game without auto-pencil or hints. Woop woop.

After having a shower and changing my bag I decide to walk to the shop to see if they have any cranberry juice and to buy a "Congratulations on the birth of your daughter" card. It's nearly November but I don't wear a coat, or flight socks, living dangerously. I stride out without pain, with the wind in my hair, so different from my trip to Walkden yesterday. I smile and chat to the shopkeeper, and step out to walk the five minute journey home.

74

Suddenly I begin to feel a bit shaky and I can hear my heart beating. I stop and take deep breaths and give myself a little pep talk, is this what its like to have a panic attack?, or are my muscles just complaining a little?. I stride out again and get home feeling a great sense of achievement.

The ebay seller doesn't get back to me, I guess he is a bit sick about selling the Fridge Freezers for less than a £1

I send a text to Daren to ask him is it OK to drink cranberry juice. He phones back to ask me in more detail about the urine problem. He says cranberry juice is good, but also to drink a lot of water and other clear juices - I can't win. He tells me he will bring me a sample jar for me to wee into so that it can be tested for cystitis etc. But of course I decide I can cure this myself. I realise that I usually go to bed dressed only in a nightie or big tee shirt. Since coming out of hospital I have been wearing knickers to keep the stoma bag snug and thick fleecy pyjamas. I revert back to the knickerless tee shirt to let some air to my nether regions and drink cranberry juice and water and milk and tea.

We have gammon with steamed winter vegetables for dinner, delicious and nice and safe for my ileostomy. Then we have apple strudel and custard. Just as I am spooning the last morsel into my mouth, my sister says "Hasn't that got sultanas in it?" Arrgh - go away Gail.

We move to the living room where we sit side by side like pigeons on a roof. Paolo, Gail, Me and Josie on our big corner unit watching the Changing Seasons of Britain. The background music and the relaxing tones of Richard Attenborough is so soothing, I only stop myself going to sleep out of politeness.

Later I take myself upstairs to the computer to add my latest thoughts to my diary. I start to read it and am surprised how much I have forgotten about already. I sit there too long and when I stand up a wave of pain pulses through my stomach and bottom. I take deep breathes and slowly straighten myself up

Monday 28th October At about 4.30 am I get up and decide to have codeine and I go out like a light. Paolo brings me a cup of tea at 10. am to replace the still full cup he had brought me earlier. I

75

can hardly open my eyes and ask "Can I please stay in bed another half an hour. He tells me to stay as long as I want. It's half term and I can hear all the kids downstairs. Paolo just copes, once more I count my lucky stars that we met all those years ago.

I get up and shower and change my bag. I pat myself on the back (metaphorically of course) that I have not had any problems with this end of the the operation. I spoke too soon. The stoma nurses have demonstrated how to empty the bag by opening the end and pushing the poo out of the opening. Then I am supposed to take a piece of toilet tissue to wipe the end and seal it back up. This to me sounds like taking off a dirty nappy, tipping the contents down the loo and then putting the soiled nappy back on. I have a better plan. After I have forced the contents of the bag into the toilet, then fill the stoma bag with water, while the other end is still attached to me around the stoma, and let it run out and then repeat until the water coming out is clear. I am aware that this may not be convenient when out and about or when using public loos. but when I am at home, it is the method I use. Today as I fill the bag with water the sticky surround becomes unstuck and the warm sewage runs down my leg, all over my clothes and the bathroom floor - shit!

We have a lovely soup for dinner and Lasagna for tea. The district nurse comes to check my dressing. The Fire Officers come to do a risk assessment on the house - very boring , I thought they would at least let the kids see the inside of the fire engine. Daren brings the paraphernalia for testing urine. The parents come to collect the kids. Paolo goes to buy some chicken feed, giving me orders not to tire myself out or do the hoovering. I don't vacuum, but I do tidy the play room that requires hundreds of bending down/standing up movements, but I feel OK and get a certain amount of job satisfaction seeing everything back in its place. I flop down on the chair then feel something wet on my belly. For the second times in a day the stoma bag has come unstuck. . My scar down the middle of my tummy, the two laparoscopy scars that look like cigarette burns and the dressing over the drainage hole are covered in foul smelling faeces. I wrench involuntarily and for the 3rd time in a day have a shower.

When Daren was here, I told him about my flap about the pain. He sits me down and very seriously, like talking to a child tells me "Veronica - you have had a very complex operation. If you could see how much of your flesh was cut away, and how much the rest of your body had to be manoeuvred to get to the tumour, you would expect to be in pain". (I find out later that to facilitate the surgeon, the patient, me, is practically hung upside down on the operating table so that other body parts are moved by gravity out of the way of the bowel to be operated on) "That being said, he continued, don't be embarrassed about asking questions, that's what I am here for. Take your pain relief, and rest when you are tired. You are doing well" He tells me how to take a urine sample, complex mix of little cardboard container and syringes and I nod to say I understand. I will have a play with it later to learn how to do it.

Helen phones me to see if I have any plans for Thursday, Halloween. I say I haven't got the strength to plan things more than a few hours in front. We have more of the older kids on Wednesday perhaps I will do some baking with them with the halloween theme. Or maybe I will give it a miss this year, most of the kids have some kind of celebration at home with their parents, they wont miss out.

19 - One Step Forward - Two Back

Tuesday 29th October, I wake up at 5 am and follow the instructions for taking a urine sample. The syringe doesn't pull back very far so I think I haven't got enough. But then I look at the side and see yellow. Oh great it has got more than I thought! Unfortunately later with my reading glasses on, I realise the yellow is just a label and there is the minutest wee sample in the syringe.

I get up once more at 10 a.m., eat my breakfast and suggest a walk to Blackleach Country Park. I should be OK walking at toddler pace. We walk through St Mary's Park, it is a lovely Autumn day. The weak sun on our faces and wind in our hair. We find golden leaves and wind-fall apples. The kids don't complain about the walk or even the sudden shower of rain.

As we return home, Daren is waiting outside our house to collect the sample. I explain about the mistake, he tells me that there isn't enough there to send to be analysed but he will dip test it. Half an hour later as I am talking to the Stoma Nurse, Daren rings to say there is a chemical in the sample that indicates that I may have a bug. He is on his way back with another sample jar. I tell Zoe, the stoma nurse about my little mishaps yesterday and she makes a few suggestions. After lunch the two toddlers have a nap and Paolo takes the older three to a Halloween activity at the Pavilion and then to the park. Adam tells me that he will keep an eye on the sleeping girls and wake me when they awake from their nap. I get my head down and feet up and sleep peacefully. I seem to feel more refreshed after these little naps than I do after a night in bed.

We have chicken risotto for tea and all the children have been collected by 5.30 pm After everyone has gone home I begin to feel very achy and tired and sickly and cold How can that be after such a lovely sleep only a few hours ago? I snuggle down in my bed and make a few phone calls and leave Paolo to clean up downstairs. Later I go back down and Paolo is asleep in the chair in front of the TV. He looks really tired and I feel guilty for abandoning him. He has been my tower of strength both emotionally and physically. But then I realise that if I don't rest when I am tired, it will take me longer to get back up to strength. I will make it up to him when I am better.

Later while watching the Mentalist, Matteo comes home followed soon after by Lauren his girlfriend. It is good to have my baby home, though he won't thank me for calling him that.

Wednesday 30th October 2013 I wake up at 4.45 bursting for a wee. I wonder if this is too early for the first wee of the day (you may be getting to understand how my strange brain works) I eventually decide at 5.30 that I can't wait any longer and fill the little pot (obviously not clever enough to be trusted with the syringe) and empty the stoma bag. The contents have once more gone too liquid, I will have to make a big effort to remember to take the loperamide. I go back to bed and realise that I am lying on my right side without pain yeah!! another little step towards recovery. I still cannot lie on the left hand side. There are several tender areas and also I get a sensation of pulling when I lie on that side.

I think I may be getting the drugs sussed. Apart from the loperomide that I forget to take before meals, I take ibuprofen to relieve the pain in the morning and hopefully reduce the swelling and two codeine before bed as they relieve the pain and help me to sleep. This is a far more sensible approach than my original plan of putting up with the discomfort until it became unbearable.

Paolo poo poos me when I say that he has been my rock and that I will get up first while he has a lie in. He tells me that I did it for him and now it is pay back time. He insists I stay in bed and he brings me porridge and tea. I give in graciously.

I get up at 9.am and decide not to have a shower. The stoma nurse had put a barrier ring inside the stoma bag so I decide to have a wash and leave showering until the evening. As I clear the breakfast dishes from the table and stack the dishwasher, I feel wetness at the top of my legs. I leave the tidying and shoot upstairs. The stoma bag is leaking once more, well at least its not my fault this time, the stoma nurse had fitted it. I jump into the shower and wash the ileostomy with the shower head. The skin surrounding it is red raw and bleeding. I tap it dry and consider not putting on the sterile powder, but it looks so sore that I shake it on. I dab away the excess with clean tissues, and I wonder why it is not causing me a lot of discomfort. I delay putting on the bag until I am sure that the area is completely dry and none of the powder is left on the part of my belly where the stoma bag sticks. I put clean clothes on and go downstairs to start the day again. I peel potatoes and we have pudding and chips for dinner. The kids go out into the garden and despite the fact I have asked the older ones to tip away any rainwater and dry the toys, the little ones come back in half an hour later soaked. I hang the clothes on the radiator and find substitute clothes. Rachael comes to pick up her car, Jackie calls in for a brew and the man who's fridge freezer I've bought rings to say "Can we come and collect it". I assure Paolo I will be fine. Jackie goes on her way, Rachael lifts the girls into their prams for a nap and then rounds up Isaac to take him to the museum. I promise her I will put my feet up until Paolo gets back. As I wave goodbye, I say to the kids "Have one of you got dog poo on your shoes, there's an awful smell. Too late, I realise it is me once more. Silently the poo had pushed out of the bag, down the legs of my trousers and up under my tee shirt. I fly upstairs and strip off in the bathroom, I wash as quickly as possible aware that there are several children downstairs and they are very quiet - not a good sign. Before I can get dressed again, I hear someone banging on the door. This is obviously someone who has been knocking patiently first. I get downstairs just as Shanay opens the door to Daren. He has come to collect the sample. I give it to him and tell him about the flap. He tells me he was getting worried, he thought the kids had kidnapped me then he tells me to phone the stoma nurses.

Paolo comes back just after this and I go to lie down on the bed. I am beginning to get despondent about the leaks. How can I ever get on with my life if I cannot trust myself to fit the bag properly.

Later I phone Helen to tell her I am not planning to do anything for Halloween. Then tell her I don't feel so good. I feel bloated (possibly too much pudding and chips) and sickly. She gives me a pep-talk. "Mum you haven't taken any time of work, which is amazing but you have to take things one day at a time. You have overcome the cancer do you really think you will let a stoma bag beat you." I tell her that I think Paolo is getting tired and I want to do more. She tells me I am mad and reminds me of all the weeks Paolo spent in hospital and how I coped with children, teenagers and work. How I drove in the dark and rain to see him every evening And how when he was at home I coached him to eat and bullied him out of his depression. She makes me laugh and I think of all the times I have lectured her when she didn't know what decision to make and how often she proved me wrong. If it hadn't been for her working at Daniellis while still at school and college, I wouldn't have met Paolo, but at the time, I didn't think it was a good idea (can't remember what my objections were). We as a family are good at listening to advice, but also not afraid to ignore it and go with our own instincts.

I am beginning to wonder if I have a faulty batch of stoma bags, surely I can't be getting it wrong after getting it right for the last three weeks. Paolo tells me to phone the nurses but I decide to wait until the morning. Then he reminds me to take the Loperomide and makes some pasta soup. Lovely comfort food, I log on to the computer to check out facebook and read emails. I have a game of sudoku, I can't complete it, my brain is obviously still not up to par. I decide that once I can complete a couple of suduko games I will be fit to drive the car. It gives me an objective, I feel like I am in control again. I watch TV for half an hourt then decide to go and lie in bed, I haven't had any accidents while in bed up to now. I tell Paolo I am going to have an early night and he informs me that it is10.40 pm, not so early. Where has the day gone?

20 - Tummy Bugs

Thursday 31st October- Halloween I wake up bright eyed and bushy tailed. The bag has not leaked and I have slept all night, I go to the loo and decide to go down and make Paolo a cup of tea. Then I realise it is only 3.am.

Over the last few days, I have become aware of another discomfort,, I feel like I have slipped and landed on my bottom, my coccyx is really tender to sit on and when moving from the standing to sitting position and vice versa.

AT 8.30 I go down and the girls (4 girls today) help me load the washing machine. Paolo says he is going to take them to "On Safari" so I encourage them to find their coats and shoes. When they are fastened safely in the car I look around for jobs that do not require heavy lifting. Then a little voice in my head reminds me of being in the hospital with all the tubes and wires and thinking "If only I could get rid of all this, I could rest properly. On that note, I take myself back to bed and unbelievably go back to sleep.

When I wake, I phone Zoe the stoma nurse. I tell her about all the mishaps and ask her if it's just a batch of bags without enough stickiness or could it be the powder. She tells me she will put a different kind of bag in the post and to try to go easy on the powder. She tells me not to worry about it. There are thousands of people wearing stoma bags, we just need to find the right one for me. Later Alison the district nurse comes to change the dressing on the drainage tube wound and says it is almost better, she will come again next Tuesday probably for the last time.

Tip: In the morning walk around for a bit before your shower to give the bag time to fill up. Get in the shower with the bag on while you wash your hair and the rest of your body. Finally for the last minute take off the bag and wash around the stoma with the shower. This is much easier and more effective than trying to do it with tissue paper and if a bit of poo leaks out it will wash down the drain without any problem.

I make myself a sandwich thinking the chicken in the fridge is from yesterday. But it is left over from Saturday it tastes OK so I don't worry. Later Paolo makes pancakes, the kids enjoy them but I think they are too salty. I'm beginning to wonder if Paolo is putting too much salt into food or if my tastes are changing. Later he makes pasta with tongue and I can't eat that either. I take myself off to bed, I'll leave Paolo to deal with all the "trick or treaters". I doze a little and then suddenly realise I am going to be sick, I just reach the toilet in time - the chicken! I phone the oracle, Daren and he tells me it is not a good idea to eat dodgy chicken when you have just had surgery, but the biggest danger is that I will damage my wound while I am retching. He tells me the worst is probably over and to learn my lesson.

I phone Gail to ask her not to come around as I am being sick, she tells me that she is also nauseous. She came home from work with a migraine, but it had not got any better and she had been being sick all afternoon. She also tells me that she is very thirsty and has been drinking water all afternoon but her wee is dark orange, I begin to worry about her.

I have a shower and take my time changing the stoma bag, making sure that the surrounding area is dry and completely free from powder. I watch a bit of rubbish TV with Paolo then go to bed.

Friday 1st November I wake up full of energy and ask Paolo if he will run me to Tesco to get my sister a Birthday Card. Paolo sits in the car with the kids while I nip into Tesco, I feel very daring and am looking around for someone to recognise me, such a poser!

I buy a card and a plant for Gail and some flowers for my mum's grave. At the cemetery I tidy the grave and Paolo has a little weep. There is nowhere for him to take flowers to for his dad. We carry on to the farm to buy some chicken feed and for the kids to have a run around, all the farmyard is ankle deep in smelly mud and I pray that non of the kids trips over. I drop off the card and plant at Gail's and make her promise to see a doctor if she is no better tomorrow. A trip to McDonalds and then home, I am exhausted and take myself off to bed for an hour.

In the afternoon a friend Kelly comes to see me with her little boy Ollie who we looked after until September, it's lovely to see them both. Ollie has made a get well card and Kelly brought me a lovely bunch of flowers, just in time to replace the first bunch I got while still in the hospital.. In the evening, I have my first independent evening out when I go round to my friend Joyce's house and meet two other friends Wendy and Dot. They tell me off for "doing too much" but mostly we drink coffee and discuss how we old childminders know much better than Ofsted how best to prepare children for school. My stoma bag has not leaked. End of a perfect day.

Before I go to bed Paolo tells me he has got the "runs". I tell him to sleep in the spare bed, thats all I need. It's one thing having to rush to the toilet, it's another thing altogether if the poo starts pouring out of my tummy.

Saturday 2nd November The worst has happened, despite separate beds Paolo has very generously shared his diarrhoea with me. The bag is filling up a frightening speed with very liquid poo. But neither of us feels particularly ill so we get up and on with the day. Later I phone Daren to see if he has received the microbiology results and he tells me my white blood cell count is 623 instead of 0 - 40. He brings the lab report to me and tells me to phone the out of hours GP. This turns out to be slightly more confusing than I would have imagined but in the end we have an appointment at Salford Royal A&E dept at 7.30 pm.

I decide that I really must start toeing the line and Google dietary advice for Ileostomy. I end off more confused than ever. There are foods that cause gas, foods that cause diarrhoea foods that may block your intestines, foods that don't break down sufficiently within the small bowel. Who would ever know all these complications? I thought I had got it sussed in the hospital just being able to change the bag without help.

My brother phones to say that I seem to be recovered since he has noted that I have been out, so can they come next week and stay over. I answer, "Of course you can, I look forward to seeing you." Out of the window there are flashes and bangs of fireworks of people who cannot wait for 3 more days to celebrate bonfire night. I think of my mum, she really enjoyed bonfire night, but I am glad she is not here to witness my cancer, I know she would be suffering more than me on my behalf.

Paolo drives me to the hospital, just as it comes in sight, I remember that the lab report is still on the dining room table. About turn, Paolo is so patient, I know if it was me driving I would be grumbling by now. We arrive at the hospital at 7.33, my appointment should have been 7.30. Paolo drops me at the door then goes to park the car. I needn't have rushed I don't see anyone until over half an hour later. The nurse tells me the pain in my coccyx may be caused by the bladder infection, she provides me with antibiotics to see if it improves. If it doesn't, I mustn't ignore it but go to the doctor.

As I wait in Tesco's pharmacy to collect the prescription, I begin to feel really ill, I am shaking and aching and nauseous, I find Paolo who is shopping for Sunday lunch and he gives me the car keys to sit in the car. I phone my sister to see if she is any better and I begin to tell her about my week. Eventually we are both laughing, Gail tells me to stop as I am making her migraine worse. By the time Paolo gets back to the car I am feeling much better - laughter really is the best medicine.

I go home, take the antibiotic, change into my pyjamas and go to bed. I sleep all night without pain relief.

Sunday 3rd November I wake up refreshed although still dehydrated, I sip water then Paolo brings my breakfast. It slowly dawns on me that apart from the pain in my coccyx, which is getting worse, most of my pains have gone, I can bend down, walk, or climb stairs with very little discomfort. Not bad for 62.

Later in the morning Helen, Lily, Rachael and Isaac come to see us after church. The kids immediately go outside to play, the girls round on me because I had posted the news about the white blood cells and A&E on facebook and they hadn't seen it until it was too late to phone me, they had both been worried about me all night. I laugh and say "Just keeping you on your toes"

We have our usual Sunday but without Gail, she is still not 100% and decides the settee and a blanket are more inviting to her. We have beef stew, Paolo is trying to cook things that are recommended on my diet sheet. Josie tells me she has two hospital visits this week. One for her eyes and another for a blood test to check for anaemia. She refuses me when I say I will go with her or I will get Paolo to run her there. Mrs Independence, now I know where I get it from.

Monday 4th November I get up early and replace the stoma bag which once more has not leaked, I eat breakfast then take the antibiotic Trimethoprim. By 9.30 I am feeling nauseous and I have strong stomach pains. I decide that I must have gone overboard with the Loperomide and have made the contents of my stomach too solid. I think I just have to lie down and rub my tummy and drink plenty and the blockage will move. In the afternoon while lying in bed and talking on the phone, I get the sharpest pain since child-birth and fling the phone across the room with shock. I think I was right, after the short sharp pain, I feel much better and the feeling of sickness has gone. At 9.30 pm, again half an hour after taking the antibiotic, I begin to feel sick. This is my cue to take myself off to bed with a book. I will deal with this one day at a time, it is only for one week.

It occurs to me I have been quite impressed during this cancer journey with all the information I have been given. But I am beginning to wonder whether it would have been better to have been told "You have a bit of a water infection, just take these antibiotics for 7 days"

Because I have seen the lab report: WBCs 623. RBCS(Non-haemolysed) 2, Epithelial cells Nil,. And the information that three antibiotic have been tried against the bacteria. Trimethoprim - sensitive. Nitrofurantoin - sensitive. Amoxicillin - resistant. My mind is working overtime and the neurotic woman who worries about super bugs and lack of antibiotics is raising her ugly head.

Tuesday 5th November The Stoma Nurse Zoe visits once more with different styles of stoma bag. She is unbelievably calm and sympathetic and promises that we will find, by trial and error, the most suitable bag for me.

The effects of the Trimethoprim antibiotic tablets leave me sickly and in some discomfort, and my coccyx is getting ever more painful, but I no longer have any of the original pains from the operation. I can walk confidently, climb stairs and roll over in bed without a thought, I no longer need pain relief to help me sleep. By the time I come to the end of the tablets I feel I should be able to continue my normal life. Two more weeks and I should be able to pick up the children, push the buggy and drive the car. I will make the most of the next two weeks to get plenty of rest and stick to the rules, I don't want anymore setbacks. As I start cooking the tea one of the kids asks what is sticking out under my jumper, (obviously a child who was not present for the last discussion). I tell them the basic details of the operation and show them the stoma bag. They say "Is there poo in there" I tell them there is "Can I see it?" yuck No ewww. Another of the children says "What's that?", pointing at the scar running down from my belly button. I tell her that is where the surgeon cut my belly to get the cancer out. She says that it looks painful and I reply that I didn't feel a thing as I was asleep. "I think I would wake up if someone cut a big hole in me!" she said.

Tip for reader: if you are woken in the night by a bad smell, don't presume it is your husband farting. Feel around your stoma, if it is nice and dry, then you can punch him in the back.

21 - Bonfire Night 2013

We have hotdog sausages for tea and toffee apples for dessert. I didn't make any effort for halloween and now this paltry offering for bonfire night. I dig out a few fireworks left over from last New Years Eve and persuade Paolo to let them off in the back garden before the children go home. This is a bit cruel on my part. Paolo hates fireworks and has never set one off in his life. The kids all settle down on the garden swing waiting with anticipation, he cannot back out now. He finds a flat surface for the firework (plastic bread tray????) strikes the match and lights the fuse with a completely outstretched arm and then does a Peter Kay run (slightly slower than a fast walk) to safety. The kids were in hysterics, not at the fireworks which were mediocre at best, but at Paolo. To give him his due, I think Paolo was playing to the audience after the first firework and exaggerated his fear. Anyway a new experience for him and another demon faced. As soon as I am recovered, I promise myself that we will have a big party to make up for all these little celebrations that are slipping by.

Wednesday 6th November - Good and bad news. The good news is that I have just been told that I can drive the car after four weeks not six as I understood (that's now - hooray). The sickness and sore mouth I have been suffering from are side effects of the antibiotics for the water infection so only three more days and then I should be fit once more.

The bad news is that the aches and pains I have been getting in my calves and thighs are a dangerous sign after major surgery. (Helen had told me this the day before and made me promise to see the doctor) I decided to phone Daren instead and he had stressed the need to phone the doctor ASAP.

Also today I went back to my Child Psychology class, I decided on the spur of the moment and phoned a friend who attends the class to give me a lift there. I don't know if it was the most intelligent move, an hour into the class I was feeling hungry and shaky but I managed to keep going and it was nice exercising my brain and chatting about other things apart from cancer. Thanks Julie for looking after me and buying me tea and crumpets.

Thursday 7th November Phone the doctor for an appointment, mentally preparing myself for a fight with the receptionist. After a lot of music and a woman's taped voice telling me my call was important to them, I finally get to speak to a real human. I say "this is Veronica Scotton, can I make an appointment with Dr Hyams please" she answers immediately "Yes of course, can you make 11.20 am"!! She has learnt a lesson.

I plan to drive myself to the doctors and then think I will go to the hairdressers to see if she can fit me in before my appointment. I get my cut and blow then come home to find that Paolo has not taken the children out as he was going to do. He said, I thought I might take them to McDonalds so I might as well drop you off on the way and then come back for you. Paolo Scotton, I can see right through you! I give in graciously but tell him to wait in McD's and I will walk over. Little compromise on both parts.

I tell the doctor my fears of a blood clot in my leg and he assures me that I won't get a blood clot because I am too active. I reply that my mum was always very active and used to walk miles and she died of an aneurism. I asked him what to look for just in case I did get one and he said hard, hot painful leg. I want to cry as I suddenly remember as if it were yesterday my mum telling me her leg was really hurting and burning and me saying "Go to the doctor then", not really with any sympathy because I knew she wouldn't, but my attitude had been If you won't go to the doctors what do you want me to do. I didn't know anything about blood clots or maybe I would have insisted she went, but I didn't and a few days later the clot reached her brain. The paramedics said she wouldn't have felt a thing, so a good death then, but it didn't seem like it at the time and I miss her every day. The doctor tells me that the aches and pain in my leg is probably caused by having the injection in my spine. He says that it has probably irritated a nerve but that it will sort itself out.

In the afternoon, a friend calls with flowers and asks if we fancy an evening in Wetherspoons on Monday and I say yes. She is flying out to Oz the week after as her sister is very sick with an undiagnosed illness. I thank her and commiserate about her sister, then we brew tea and gossip for half an hour until Paolo comes in with the children from school, when she decides it is time for her to go.

Thinking about my mum I remember my daughter telling me to go to the doctors so I phone her and tell her I took her advice and the doctors verdict. She says "See sometimes daughters do know best" I agree laughing but tell her that it isn't very often. She says she is going to mark it in her diary as the first time that I have taken her advice.

While talking to doctor Hyams I tell him that I am writing a book. I also tell him the story about the 99p fridge and my subsequent panic when the stomas bag had leaked. He said, are you going to put that in the book and I answer that I already have. He says that will be really good because some people, even though they know what to expect during and after the surgery, still become very stressed and depressed when things go wrong. He says that if someone could inject some humour into a situation it would be a good help. I am inspired once more.

In the evening two more friends drop by Jackie and Steve and then my sister Gail. I make coffee and we sit and talk, but I am not a very good hostess as I don't even think about providing crisp or nuts or offering anything stronger than tea. Jackie would have conjured up something within minutes of us dropping in on her, I have to be prepared and be given notice.

Friday 8th November I don't want to get up today. The nausea caused by the Trimethropin antibiotic has accumulated and I feel like putting my fingers down my throat to see if being sick will relieve it. Trouble is then I would probably bring back the antibiotic and its not going to cure the bladder infection if its not in my body.

I think having a shower would help but I just had a cut and blow yesterday and want to keep the style for at least one more day.

Also I should be catching up on childminding paperwork especially the trackers that have to be submitted by Monday. I procrastinate a little longer and give myself until 9.30 am to lie in bed and wallow in self pity.

Eventually I drag myself out of bed and have a shower wearing a shower cap doh! The house is empty and quiet. I clean the stoma with the shower and take my time to make sure the surrounding area is completely dry. I shake on the antiseptic white powder to the tiny patches of "nappy rash" that have developed around the stoma and then dust if off. When I am sure that everything is dry and powder free, I carefully fit the stoma bag and press it firmly in place. Something isn't right; I look at myself in the mirror and see the bag is upside down!!! Flippin eck (or words to that effect.) I peel it off and turn it the right way. It would be more sensible fit a new one but it seems such a waste. I'll just have to keep checking it for leaks.

I settle myself down to do the paperwork, but the batteries in the mouse mat have run out. I fit the recharged ones and start again. I phone the car insurance who have sent me an email saying that my card has not been accepted and sort that out. Then I phone a lady I met in the hospital and chat to her for over an hour. Then I am hungry. The trackers will have to wait a bit longer.

I wake up in the night with this tickly/achy feeling in my leg. I have had this feeling before the operation but as with everything after an op things adopt a more sinister meaning. I toss and turn, put my leg out from under the covers then back in. I do ankle exercises then rub the calf with my other foot. Finally at 7.00 am I get up and make myself some warm milk and take a paracetamol and Paolo wakes up and offers to message my leg. I am unbelievably ticklish and usually refuse any kind of massage but since I have the flight socks on I let him, it is lovely and relaxing and I must fall asleep, I hardly remember a thing until 9.30.

My brother Kevin calls in the afternoon and stays for a couple of hours talking about his recent golf holiday. I am sure he is getting younger. He is two years younger than me, he is wearing quite a trendy leather jacket, his hair is cut in a nice style and it looks like he has been working out at the gym. I hope this means he has some woman who is taking an interest in him. He has a lovely funny personality, but his shyness holds him back with the ladies. I have tried to "fix him up" a couple of times but with no success.

22 - Remembrance Sunday

Remembrance Sunday As usual we have breakfast in bed and Paolo phones his mum. She is a bit annoyed today. Because, since Gildo (Paolo"s dad) disappeared, the Swiss government, like most governments will not accept that Tecla (Paolo's mum) is a widow. She cannot sell, let out, or raise money on their house. She cannot sell the allotment or the property in Italy (which is costing a fortune to maintain). Last year she was told that if she went to the Town Hall and signed some forms, then this year on the fifth anniversary of his disappearance, they would officially accept that he has died and she was his widow. (His doctors have said right from the beginning that without his heart medication he would be dead within days). They have now informed her that she needs a letter from a solicitor to send to the judge to set things in motion. The charge for the solicitor compiling the letter is 1,000 Swiss Francs (about £750). There have been various expenses regarding his disappearance over the last 5 years. Primarily the £4,000 (or equivalent in Swiss Francs) that she paid for "intelligent information" ie checking his mobile phone signals and more expert dog handlers. At this rate she will have to sell the house in order to be able to afford to sell the house.

We usually go to whichever war memorial our children or more lately grandchildren are attending with Scouts etc, but this morning we decided to stay in the warm and go to our church. It was very moving. I did think though as we sang "Faith of Our Fathers" a rousing song from the Whit Walks of my childhood that this would be an appropriate hymn for Suicide Fighters. In case you are not Catholic, here are a few lines:

"How Sweet would be our children's fate, If they like them could die for thee"

I can remember singing my heart out as a child in church or walking through Manchester waving to all the crowds that came to support the faith. I am sure that the words never upset me or inspired me to become a martyr. I just learned them by rote like the six times tables or the alphabet.

After church I drove the car (for the first time in 5 weeks) to Tesco dry cleaners. I had pulled a coat out of the wardrobe that had been hung there since coming back from the cleaners months earlier. The coat was not clean. It still smelled of stale perfume (the reason I had had it cleaned) and had white smudges all over it, the assistant agreed to send it back for another clean. I got a small trolley and walked round Tesco and then into the new B&M. I resisted temptation to buy even more solar lights. It was a lovely morning and I stopped to talk to several people who complimented me on my fast recovery and my healthy looks (Surprising what a bit of make-up can do).

On the way home I stopped to talk to a neighbour, who surprisingly enough can talk even more than me and without stopping for breath. By the time I got back home I was frozen and got in bed fully clothed with a big mug of tea to defrost.

Paolo made a lovely Sunday dinner. Gammon with lots of vegetables including black peas mixed with chillies and garlic. Followed by hot plums. I did not refer to my list of unrecommended foods and helped myself to two glasses of red wine. The contents of my bag later showed that the wine had liquified the rest of the food but who cares!

Monday 11th November Did the school run today with one of the kids, trying not to lift the kids in and out of the car too much. I should really have got up earlier and walked but have forgotten to take into consideration the extra time it takes in the shower and changing the stoma bag. Oh well it was nice getting into the swing again and getting all the lovely comments about how well I looked and hoped I wasn't doing too much too soon. It's nice that people care.

Went to the childminding group at Sure Start with three little one year old girls and once again met people who have been thinking about me. The kids got really messy with porridge oats and lentils, glad it wasn't on my carpet, and also got soaking wet despite the aprons Never mind, 'they wont rust. When I came home and made soup for the kids dinner I began to feel really tired, and I couldn't change my bag and watch the kids at the same time. Paolo had gone to plant some bulbs for Rachael but said he would be back for one o'clock. On the dot of one o'clock, I began to get angry! How dare he leave me with these kids, I phoned him up and he said he was on his way back. When he got back I say "You're out of order" and suddenly he really lost it and told me I should have phoned him, how he couldn't do anything right. I just walked upstairs, changed my bag and went to bed. It was completely out of character for Paolo to shout, but I guess the stress of the last few weeks had got to him. I gave him the silent treatment for a few hours, I think he deserved it. In the evening we met some friends in Wetherspoons, I had southern fried chicken and chips and a pint of Guiness and Black. I had taken two Loperamide before I went to counteract the liquid but was still very runny when I got home but it was worth it.

Tuesday 12th November I've agreed to help out one of our families. Joseph the dad has to go to Kenya for a week, so Alice his wife needs childcare from 6.15 am. I've agreed that she may drop off their two little girls early in the morning and I shall look after the baby Odelia and take the other, Shekinah to St Edmunds school. Am I mad? Don't I have my work cut out enough for me?

In the morning Paolo takes the kids for a walk in their wellies, looking for muddy puddles while I do some paper work. The Stoma Nurse came and said I was doing really well with the stoma bags and keeping the stoma clean and healthy. She compliments me for getting back into the swing and doesn't tell me to take it easy. I mention that my coccyx is still very tender and she tells me to phone the doctor, but then says, "Its probably just really bruised, if you could see the positions they put you in during the operation, you would understand the discomfort afterwards". Doesn't bear thinking about.!

Wednesday 13th November, Alice brings Odelia and Shekinah as arranged at 6.15 am. I keep the lights dimmed and quickly say goodbye to Alice. I take off the girls shoes and coats and quietly usher them up stairs and into the spare bed. The girls lie down quietly and I cover them with the duvet and lie on the edge of the bed saying as little as possible. Very soon I hear Odelia's breath change as she falls asleep. I can't tell if Shekinah is asleep, but decide to slip quietly out of bed and creep into my own bedroom.

Unfortunately, things didn't go to plan, as I put one leg out towards the floor, the weight counterbalanced my whole body and before I knew what was happening I had fallen on to the floor, bashing into the wardrobe door on the way down. Very undignified for an old age pensioner. I lay on the floor, waiting for the inevitable screams of the girls, but none come, unbelievably, they hadn't woken up. I crawl backwards onto the landing and then stand up and went back to bed. Paolo, sleepily asked what had caused the noise and I told him not to worry, I had just fallen out of bed! I was glad that no cameras were present, it would have given a lot of people a laugh on "Who's Been Framed" or "Candid Camera". Later I give the girls their breakfast and take Shekinah to school. It is the same school that my own children used to attend and I see many familiar faces, teachers and parents who are pleased to see me up and about.

Friday 15th November. End of the first week of being fully back to work. Really looking forward to the week-end, I'm tired and my back is aching, (perhaps the result of the fall from the bed, or maybe caused from picking children up to put into the car).

Listening to my youngest grandchildren Lily and Isaac, both 5 year olds. Lily: "My mummy thinks she is fat, but I have told her she isn't really". Isaac: "My mummy doesn't think her tummy is fat, but it is." She is a size 10. This is the latest of Isaac's gems. Yesterday Rachael (his mum) left him getting dressed for school while she went to have a shower. As she came downstairs she thought to herself, I haven't even made his packed lunch. When she entered the living room, Isaac was lying naked on the carpet watching TV. Taking a deep breath she says to him, "This isn't working Isaac, we are going to be late again. Maybe we should turn off the TV until you are ready for school" without looking away from the television, Isaac answers "or perhaps you could make my packed lunch the night before.!"

Sunday 17th November Spur of the moment decision, we decide to go to Sheffield. Two of our sons are living there. Patrick and his partner Michelle have just bought a new cottage, so we go to congratulate them. The last time we saw Pat was when he visited me in hospital, so much nicer circumstances.

95

We were pleasantly surprised to see Matteo's clean and tidy accommodation, not what I'd imagined a student home would be. Before he had made the decision to drop out of university, he had been misinformed by the loan department that he wouldn't need to repay the loan immediately - but then received a bill for the full amount when he left. He got a job in Tesco selling phones and stayed in the shared house so that his friends would not need to find another tenant. He hadn't known that he would then be liable for the whole council tax bill for the house. He left Sheffield uni, where he had hoped to qualify as a pilot, and enrolled in the school of life. He learned more about money management during that time than some people do in their whole lives.

We spent a relaxing afternoon together having a pub lunch. Huge portions of delicious hot food.

Wednesday 20th November. Went to the dentist to have a little chip on my front tooth polished away and to discuss getting a denture for some missing back teeth. (Need them to chew now more than ever). Missed the Child Psychology Class, I will have to double check when making appointments. Realised that we missed a wine tasting afternoon that Nathan bought us for LAST Christmas but the only available date was 13th November i.e. while I was still in hospital. I phoned the company and told them my sob story and they promised to send me 6 bottles of wine in compensation - sorted.

Sat eating gnocchi in tomato sauce for lunch, encouraging the kids to eat and chatting to Paolo and it dawned on me that I am feeling really well.

Before I started my treatment I really believed that I could sail through it, and I did try but it was definitely more difficult than I expected - ever the optimist. When I came home it seemed to be one step forward, two steps back with urine infections and leaking stoma bags and tiredness and worrying pains. Gradually it became more of two steps forward, one step back with constant hunger, fluid poo and itchy skin. But then suddenly today I realised that I am not in pain, my mouth is not sore and my wee doesn't burn when I need the loo. I have not needed to have a nap and I am not shaking with hunger within an hour of eating. My mouth isn't dry, nor is my skin and hair. I can even, almost, stand up and sit down without pain in my coccyx! Is this it? am I healed? I told Paolo who answered "Oh good, can I go for a rest now?" - I don"t think so Paolo. I think it may be psychological, I have just passed the magical 6 week mark (the hospital said that I couldn't drive, pick up anything heavy or vacuum for 6 weeks). I've already done the driving and picking up, I may as well hoover. Surprisingly it is not comfortable to vacuum the carpet, I can feel my stomach muscles complaining. I decide to leave it to someone else for a few more days. It hasn't dampened my mood though, I pat myself on the back, metaphorically of course, I'm doing well!

Thursday 21st November - Pride comes before a fall. This morning I forget to fasten up the end of the stoma bag. I take the kids for a walk and then to a friends house, I take loads of photos as they play in the garden all wrapped up in hats and scarves. As I walk home I feel something wet trickling down my leg. Thank goodness I had refused the cup of coffee. There is a tell-tale brown stain on the front of my trousers, disgusting. That will teach me to take more care in the morning! After the clean up we have a chippy take-away for dinner (nothing puts me off eating) and then I feel tired. So much for my full recovery. Never mind only a little blip, I'll put my feet up for half an hour and tomorrow will be better.

Friday 22nd November, wake up feeling full of energy. Only got one little girl today until the school kids come home, so I decide to ex-change my Tesco vouchers for toys. Odelia and I walk around the toy section and press all the "Try Me" buttons and sing nursery songs as we go. We buy over £200 worth of toys and then go into B&M and buy Christmas lights, I usually never think about Christmas until December but we are having fun. After lunch we walk round to my friend's house to give Odelia a bit of company and then come back home in time for her nap. After school Paolo and I take all the kids into Weatherspoon's to celebrate Maddie's 10th birthday, marginally easier than celebrating at home.

Saturday 23rd November Continuing on the Christmas theme, Paolo and I go to the Christmas Markets in Manchester. It's heaving, we have a Gluwien but decide not to queue up for anything else, it's madness. No cash now for being extravagant, last year we came home loaded with Italian cakes and sausages and little presents for all the kids. We decide to leave the crush of the markets and to go for a meal, but everywhere seems full. In the end we eat in Browns, never been there before. The food is good and hot and the service is excellent. We are back home and I am tucked up in bed by 10.30 pm. Really showing my age.

Monday 25th November I decide that I am fit enough to push the buggy to playgroup. I am tired by the time I get back but that is only natural after using muscles that haven't been used for 6 weeks. The phone does not ring all day but we don't realise that it is not working until the kids try to put the television on after school. The Virgin Media is not working, no phone, television or broadband. My sister phones on my mobile to see if I want to go to The Bull for an hour, perfect timing. After drinking nearly a pint and a half and eating a plate of chips, my bladder is full and I nip to the loo. When I get back I drink the last mouthful of Guinness and we set off home. As the cold air hits us I tell Gail "I'm bursting for a wee again already!" She says that I can't possibly be as I have only just been. I think about it for a minute and then I realise that when I got to the loo, I just emptied my stoma bag and forgot to empty my bladder. If I had a brain, I'd be dangerous.

Tuesday 26th November, after spending hours on my mobile to Virgin, we are informed that an engineer will call on Thursday and that we will be reimbursed for the two days, I tell them, "I hope you mean three".

In the post, a letter arrives from Bolton NHS:

Dear Mrs Scotton,
I am writing to inform you that your appointment to attend the Royal Bolton Hospital has been arranged.
Your appointment is with Mr J Hobbiss Clinic and will be On: Friday 17th January 2014 at 9.30 am in General Outpatients Department on the Ground Floor G Block

On reading the letter my first reaction is fear, I don't know why, the appointment is to arrange a date for the stoma reversal i.e. the next step towards complete recovery, and is not such a major operation as the tumour removal. But I suppose we don't always have full control over fears. The next thought is disappointment. I thought the operation would have taken place earlier in the year, I was hoping to be back to full capacity with the childminding by then. The next thing I think is "I wonder what the J stands for in Mr J Hobbiss" I will ask him next time I meet him. I also make a mental note to phone the hospital to find out if they have arranged an appointment for a scan as Mr Hobbiss told me that I need to have a scan before he sees me the next time.

Thursday 28th November 2013. I go to the Open access clinic at Salford Royal to be measured for a Fulcionel Easy Belt, for anyone who can remember, it is like a wide waspy belt. The idea of the support garment is to help prevent hernias in people like me who have had a chunk cut out of them. I am hoping that it will also help to stop the stoma bag sticking out under my clothes. I thought that I would be able to bring one away with me, but the nurse says that she will order one and it will be delivered directly from the Surgical Supplies Company who deliver the stoma bags etc. While I am at the clinic the Virgin Media technician comes to inspect the cable that is causing the fault with the internet, TV and phone but he cannot fix the fault.

On Saturday I once again run up my mobile bill and eventually get through to a very bored sounding member of the Virgin Media staff who informs me that an Engineer will try to fix the problem on 14th December - Three weeks without internet or facebook. I threaten to take my business elsewhere and am put on hold with another department, who of course do not answer. To make matters worse I have for the first time in the life of my mobile phone managed to use up all my data by turning on the maps app while we were at the Christmas Markets and forgetting to turn it off, it has been running in the background of my phone for a week.

I spend 8 hours of Sunday sitting in a sports centre watching hundreds of little girls and a handful of boys, with fake tans, thick make-up and thousands of pounds worth of amazing costumes, dance to very loud music. It was worth it in the last half hour to watch my grandson collect a trophy for street dance. But I think I shall enjoy personal demonstrations in the comfort of my living room in the future.

23 - Getting Back Into The Swim

Friday 6th December I get my act together and go to the swimming pool with Rachael, Isaac and Lily. It is amazing to see that Lily has turned into a little water baby, doggy-paddling across the pool and swimming under water as an encore. Isaac is gaining confidence and enjoys playing and splashing and jumping in the pool. It's a nice surprise to see Lesley my friend and her daughter and grandson and also, another family who have a child in the same class as Isaac. After the swim I go into the disabled changing room which I had never noticed before. It has its own shower and toilet so I could change my bag in privacy. Just as I am about to put on a fresh stoma bag I hear Rachael come into the changing room with the kids and I say "let them come in here for a shower". They think this is brilliant as the disabled shower head is lower and they do not have to keep getting a tall person to press the button to keep the shower running. Unfortunately my short term memory lets me down and I forget that I have already taken off the protective cover on the stoma bag. As I am fiddling about with it, my stoma begins to trickle out. I try without success to clean it up and get another bag without the kids seeing. No chance. The questions come thick and fast from two five year olds, where?, how? why? I try to tell them in words that they (and I) can understand. Lily is a bit worried that the doctor hurt me. I tell her that he gave me some magic medicine that made me stay asleep until after he had taken all the bad stuff out of my tummy. Maybe in the future, this impromptu biology lesson will inspire these two grandchildren to become surgeons and save other lives like mine. I have been planning to start going early morning swimming but I have not had the confidence that my stoma bag would not leak. Well now I have no excuses the bag stayed intact during the swim and shower.

Sunday 8th December. Christmas is galloping towards us. I've had this idea to have a family photo taken but I am finding it impossible to find a day that is suitable for 7 children plus partners, eight grandchildren, 2 great-grandsons and the photographer. Not only that but coincidentally I find that I have spoiled a surprise as Helen was trying to arrange for all the siblings to get together for a family photograph as a Christmas present for me and Paolo.

Monday 9th NDecember, My delivery from Brunlea Surgical Supplies with the usual 30 Stoma Bags, Easy Peel Spray for loosening the glue from my stomach, some dry wipes, protective powder to help the skin around the stoma healthy and the Fulcionel Easy Belt. I put them all away in the bathroom ready for use.

Tuesday 10th December, I get up as usual and shower and dress. I look in the bathroom cabinet for the Easy Belt, its not there, I search of and on all day, even looking in the wheely bin in case it has been thrown out with the rubbish. In the end I give up but in the evening I start at one end of the house and look everywhere that I could possibly have put it without success. I ask Paolo if he has moved it but he says that he doesn't even know what it is I am looking for.

I have also been saying for the last year that I was going to recover the dining chairs. I have never undertaken this task before but how hard can it be? On Sunday I finally get started by buying the material and staples for the staple gun. The old covers are almost impossible to come off. After ten years of having stuff spilt on them and being cleaned by various methods (none of them completely satisfactorily) the old staples have rusted in place and the glue is set like concrete. Paolo eventually removes one cover and I use it as a template on the new (child-proof) material. I stretch the material over the old padding and staple it in place and I am quite pleased with the result. I phone a friend to give me some advice on how to improve the corners which are not quite as rounded as they should be. On Monday she comes to give me her advice but I am out with the children. She sets about removing the staples that I have put in and redoing the corners for me. I was not at all gracious with her and told her I would have put that one at the back of the table. In the end I am glad of her advice and over the next couple of days replace the covers on all ten chairs in red leatherette and use a matching piece of material to protect the table. Paolo is really complementary and says that I should start a new career as a furniture renovator. Who says you can't teach an old dog new tricks, I feel real job satisfaction each time I look at them.

Wednesday 11ᵗʰ December. No excuses today, I get up at 6.00 a.m and go swimming. I expected to ease myself in by only swimming 10 lengths but I manage my usual 30. The added bonus is the newly discovered disabled changing room. Private shower and toilet and more room to move to get dressed. The downside is that I miss out on the usual gossip in the communal showers but I can live without that.

Our last day at college. We each take some party food and celebrate the end of the course and Christmas. As Diane (the tutor) hands out the certificates, we clap each others achievement and I think I am really going to miss each one of these class mates.

In the afternoon, the postman delivers a parcel. It is the Belt that I have been searching for. I was sure that it had been delivered with the other stuff, I remember putting it away in the bathroom! Later when I recall the puzzle to my sister, she thinks it is hilarious. "Most people" she says "Forget things - you have to be different and remember things that have not happened" I suppose it is funny when you look at it like that

Matteo and Lauren tell me that her granddad, who was diagnosed with bowel cancer has had his operation to remove it, has not got a stoma bag and is up and about and eating solid food within three days. Well done Ron.

Thursday 12ᵗʰ December. 8.45 am, I get a call from the Thistle Hotel where Adam works to say that he has arrived in work with a bump on his forehead and with obvious signs of having hypoglycaemia. They gave him a drink of coke which sometimes works, but hasn't today and then sent for the paramedics. The paramedics work on him for 30 minutes with no effect and so take him to Manchester Royal Infirmary. Helen has borrowed my car but Rachael offers to drive me there. When we arrive, Adam is in considerable distress. He is freezing cold and is having pains in his chest, and when they give him something to drink, he begins to vomit. He doesn't have any recollection of anything since he left work at 9.00 pm the evening before. The cheerful hospital staff ask questions about family history of heart disease, they give him antibiotics, morphine, aspirin and anti-sickness medication. They take X-rays and E.C.G's, They move him from The High

Dependency Unit to Resuscitation to AMU wards and then later in the evening to Ward 5. They finally decide that his heart is OK and that he must have fallen on his journey to work and injured his chest. We stay with him until 3.00 pm and then Paolo and I go back in the evening. He seems much more comfortable and is confident that they will discharge him the next day. We really have a lot to thank the NHS for this year.

Just after lunch on Thursday, Adam phones to say that he can come home. Paolo decides to take the two children for a ride in the car to pick him up. They usually have a nap about this time, so they might as well nap in the car while I do some paperwork. I have a niggling tummy ache which I am doing my best to ignore, filling in answers on solicitors forms concentrates my mind enough to distract me from the pain. For tea we have sausage and mash and flageolet beans followed by strawberries and custard. I shouldn't eat beans or strawberries but I have been ignoring this advise for the most part without any ill effects, in hindsight I should have thought about it since the pains were getting more acute. Most of the children have gone by 6.30 pm. Helen arrives to pick up Jamie and Lily and goes up to chat to Adam. I make a brew, so it is gone 7 oclock before she leaves. I remember that I wanted to buy something from Aldi and jump in the car before they shut at 8. As I shop in Aldi, the stomach pains are becoming worse, not unlike labour pains and I start to sweat and feel sick. I will myself to take deep breaths while I queue to pay for my purchases then rush out into the fresh air. I am wearing the elastic belt supplied by the stoma nurses to help prevent hernias and decide that it must be too tight, so I pull that off and undo my jeans while I drive home. By the time I reach home I can hardly walk I am in that much pain. I run a bath and try to relax myself into it. Paolo makes me a warm drink and wants to phone a doctor but I assure him that it is probably just a bit of a blockage. I empty the stoma bag and it is completely liquid, like milky tea, no bits of strawberry or beans. I lie in bed rubbing my tummy, then decide to have an ibuprofen and promise Paolo that I will phone the doctor if I am no better by 10 pm. The next thing I am very sick, all the strawberries, hardly digested. Then I start to feel the stoma bag slowly filling and I can feel the shape of little beans. Lesson learned, I will be more discerning about what I eat and concentrate on chewing more. As the pain relief kicks in I decide to go to bed and get some sleep, it's been a long day.

24 - Christmas

Saturday 14th December, I continue Christmas Shopping. The acute pain has been reduced to a nagging ache, ignorable. Virgin Media finally sort out the broadband, phone and TV hurray! I've felt isolated from my friends without facebook, who would believe that I could become so addicted. In the evening we go to Jackie and Steve's house for a lovely Christmas celebration meal. They have some bad news, Steve has been made redundant. He is 62, too old, in his mind to get another job, he says he is going to become a house husband and send Jackie out to work. There are another 5 couples at the party and as the wine flows, more and more ideas on what Steve can do are suggested, several of them not printable. The evening is a great success and Paolo gets slightly drunk and is hung over when he phones his mum for the regular Sunday morning chat.

Its a great talking point, cancer! People who would normally just "nod hello" come up to me and give me hugs. They tell me how well I look. I normally don't take much care of my appearance, a shower and clean clothes each day is suffice, occasionally I look in the mirror in the evening and am slightly shocked at the state of my hair, or the paint hand print on my shoulder, but most of the time I am unaware and unselfconscious about how I look. My first thirteen years were spent in Salford and I can't remember there being a mirror, except a small one near the kitchen sink that my dad used to have a shave. My mum would never pay you a compliment on your appearance (didn't want anyone getting ideas above their station). My first husband, in all our 20 years of marriage, never paid me a complement. Paolo on the other hand is continually paying me compliments, but really he has so little dress sense that I would not trust his judgements and as he says I look beautiful whether I am dressed up or naked (especially naked) When we were working on this house, I single handedly filled a skip with brick, wood, old carpets etc. I had old clothes on and I was filthy and my hair was matted. When I had finished and went back to our other house for a shower, Paolo gave me a kiss and didn't even notice my disarray. Therefore, for opposite reasons, I have given up dressing to please. Recently I have been making a bit of an effort, sometimes having a half-hearted attempt to straighten my frizzy hair or even putting on lipstick, I think subconsciously I am trying to live up to the compliments that I am being paid. Also I am hearing many more stories about people who have had cancer, those that have recovered, those that sadly died and those still fighting. A lady at church who I have hardly spoken to before, came up to me and asked me how I was, normally my answer is "Fine, How are you" but this time I just said, "I'm great thanks" she told me I looked well and I thanked her. She seemed to be waiting for me to say something to her so I just said "How are you getting on" and she told me that she had just been in hospital for a hysterectomy because she had had a very large tumour in her womb. She had only been out of hospital for three days and was back at church coaching the kids in the Nativity. I also know that she has brought her granddaughter up after her daughter died tragically young. I felt humbled and ashamed once more about my "me me me" attitude.

My granddaughter Lily had been chosen to play the part of Mary and the first week of rehearsals she had said her lines perfectly and her mum had cried with pride.

A week later Lily decided that she wanted to be an angel instead and wouldn't be swayed. The apple certainly doesn't fall far from the tree. Helen, her mum, had been just the same as a child. Once their minds are made up, there is no persuading either of them. Fortunately for Lily, her mum is not a pushy mum and she accepted the decision for Lily to be an angel and let another little girl take centre stage and another mum cry with pride for their little "Mary". Lily for her part sang her heart out, not always with the correct words to the carols, but with a beaming smile on her face. And then I cried!

While shopping for Christmas presents, I decide to buy a cheap Bingo Game. We used to have one but the balls have been lost over the years. It was a great success with the four and five year olds who played with much more enthusiasm and a great deal more noise than adults. It got a bit confusing though with Ashton (aged four) reading out the numbers on the balls. Three and Seven.... 77, on its own... 53, nine and nine... 39 (this one should have been six and six... 66). Also the cheap version I had bought did not have a tray to keep the balls in after they had been called so they kept falling on to the floor and the hyperactive kids couldn't keep the score cards still, so the counters slid across onto the next number or onto the table. The kids that were playing were just as "good" at numbers as Ashton so it was anyone's guess who would cover all their numbers up first, and with no way of checking which numbers had been called the game lasted a surprisingly long time.

Friday 20th January 2013 It's the last day with us until after Christmas for some of the kids. We have a party, complete with disco ball, pass the parcel, lots of sugar laden and fatty food - some healthy, and of course Father Christmas. The kids bake cakes all morning and wrap up sweets in layers of paper for pass the parcel. We have a Santa outfit that had been packed away with the Christmas decorations, but as the stuff came out of the loft, the Santa outfit found it's way into the dressing up box and the kids had enjoyed some seasonal role playing. On Friday morning (last minute as usual) I phone my brother Carl to see if he can play the part and take him the costume. He makes me laugh as he tries on the costume and asks me what he has to do. I say "for goodness sake Carl, What do you think you have to do? Say HO HO HO and give out the presents" Carl exceeds my expectations. He arrives with his booming voice and "magic" finger which he touches each child's nose. If it beeps, they have been good. The older kids, while not being taken in at all are just as entertained as the little ones. I think Carl could have a new career.. He hands out the presents and we sing *"Rudolf the Red Nosed Reindeer" and "When Santa Got Stuck Up the Chimney"*, then Santa has to rush off back to the North Pole and Carl has to go back to looking after his son Brad. After the food fest, pass the parcel, musical bumps and dancing competition the kids are too full of "E numbers and start to argue and fight. We put on their coats and boots and send them into the back garden while we make inroads with the cleaning up. Of course after ten minutes, they are back in and getting toys out. Fourteen kids with ages ranging from 18 months to 11 years can make a remarkable mess and we are more than usually relieved when the last one leaves at 6.30. Before he leaves,

Isaac confides in me that *"That was not the real Santa, just a man dressed up"* I ask why he thinks that and he says: *" He had the outfit out of the dressing up box"* Kids nowadays are so observant.

After the children have gone home, we have less than an hour to clean up the mess and set the table again for my friends. We have been trying to organise a get-together for our childminder friends for weeks and this has been the only opportunity. The evening is a success (well I enjoyed it) and I don't even think about my stoma bag until I go up to bed in the early hours. It is bulging like a balloon and when I empty it down the loo the contents are completely liquid. What did I imagine with all those Woo Woos!

On Saturday I wake up surprisingly with a clear head. Paolo goes down to make a brew and then I hear Adam coming home. As I get up to check my emails and make this entry to the book, I can hear tinny music. I follow the sound to Adam's room and find him lying on his back fully dressed and the music is coming from his phone in his pocket. I call his name and he answers me without opening his eyes. I say "where have you been Ad?" and he mumbles "Just the Usual" God knows what that means. I say "Can you sit up" and he says "Yes" but he has not moved. "Sit up for me" He makes a half-hearted attempt but he is either drunk or Hypo. I get him a glass of milk and a banana and he sits up on the bed (with difficulty as his ribs are still painful). After he has had them, I leave him in peace to sleep. I never underestimate how difficult it is for him living with diabetes but it is also very difficult walking the fine line between concerned and over-protective.

By the time I have showered and dressed, Paolo has done most of the cleaning and tidying from the mess of last night. I empty the dishwasher and then fill it again. The phone is ringing constantly. Pat and Joe and my brother and his family are visiting today so I nip to Asda. By the time I return all our visitors have arrived and Paolo starts cooking. I have bought a different shape of pasta than usual and he translates the Italian name. They are called Hanging Priest? Whatever they are called they taste delicious with tomato and basil sauce and salad and wine. Just as we begin to eat, my aunties Josie and Lily arrive bearing gifts for under the tree. Josie tells me that her daughter, Linda is driving from London today, staying the night and then taking Josie to the Isle of Sky, to spend the holidays with Natasha, her granddaughter. She also reminds me that I have invited Linda and her husband Chris for a meal. Arrrgh! I had forgotten and of course we are going to Bridgewater Hall in Manchester to watch the Halle Youth Orchestra performance, including our grandson Arron playing first Oboe. I send Linda a text apologising for my forgetfulness and make a resolution to record things on my phone, so that I can organise my life more efficiently.

The Bridgewater Hall has fabulous acoustics and we all really enjoy the performance, even Isaac, Lily and Jamie sit through the whole performance without many complaints. As we arrive I see a couple from church who are celebrating their 40th wedding anniversary and then in the break another couple that I know from the children's centre. My sister comments that we can't go anywhere without meeting someone I know. At the end of the performance, the audience applaud over and over again and I am the proudest nanna in the world. Arron has given me the best present ever.

Sunday 22nd December I get up early and nip round to see Linda and Chris, before they leave with Josie to drive to the Isle of Sky. I wish them a happy Christmas and a safe journey and apologise for the broken promise of a dinner at our house. When I get home I brew tea and I toast crumpets and lavish them with butter, then climb back into bed next to Paolo. Luxury, tea and crumpets in bed. I must be feeling energetic because I don't stay in bed long but get up and finish off wrapping presents before going to church. I catch up with some old friends at church and then also in the coffee morning. Feeling decidedly "Christmassie" I return home to pick Paolo and we drive to the Trafford Centre. Although the car park is displaying the "FULL" signs, we very luckily get a space almost immediately as another car leaves. We decide to go into Wokooshi to sample Japanese and Korean cuisine - delicious. Once more we spot friends who come and join us and we catch up on the last few years that we haven't spoken (time flies). Once more we saunter around the shops and spot two of our minded children shopping with their mum, I think my sister is right. We don't buy much but enjoy the Christmas frenzy before going home, unbelievably not getting stuck in a traffic jam - unheard of at this time of the year, coming out of the Trafford Centre. Later watching Strictly on catch-up while eating my tea, I decide that life is good. I hope today is a good omen for 2014.

Monday 23rd December I'm awake at 6 am. Might as well go swimming (yes I am mad!). As I drive down Bolton Road listening to Alan Beswick I feel a strange sensation and hear a noise I haven't heard for a couple of months - a fart. How can that be, nothing has passed my bottom since the 7th October. I had been warned that it could happen and I have never done biology but I am glad I am on my own. When I reach the pool, I nonchalantly feel my trousers but its OK it was only wind. When I get back home, Paolo is sitting in the living room in the dimness listening to Johann Strauss. Neither of us can dance but we waltz around the living room, me in my stocking feet and wet hair, all 4 foot 11 inches and Paolo in his shoes at least a foot taller. More Morecombe and Wise than Fred Astaire. We are having fun until Paolo stands on my foot and I kick him in the shins.

We don't have many kids today so Paolo decides to take them to "On Safari" while I turn up some curtains. The post arrives! Along with a Christmas Card and a bill is a letter from the hospital:

Dear Mrs Scotton
An appointment has been made for you to attend Radiology Dept. F Block Fluoroscopy for the following:
For: Water soluble contrast enema
On: Thursday, 02 January, 2014 at 10:00 am in the morning
At: The Royal Bolton Hospital, Radiology Dept, F Block Fluoroscopy
Radiology F Block is located on the ground floor of the Hospital close to the Main Entrance.
Report to Reception and bring this letter with you when you attend for this examination.
Please allow ample time for parking (fee payable).
All Patients who do not attend for their appointments will not automatically receive another appointment. Their request will be returned to the referring doctor to determine the need for the examination.
If you are unable to attend for this appointment please inform us by telephone the above number as soon as possible between 8.3 am - 4.30 pm, Monday to Friday.

My stomach does a somersault. Even though I have to empty the stoma bag several times a day and I talk to people about my cancer, the operation seems like a distant dream. I am glad that things are moving on and this is the next step to having the bag removed but I am not jumping for joy at the thought of another operation.

Tuesday 24th December Last working day until 2014, I need the break. We have been invited to Helen's house for Christmas day and then we (or should I say Paolo with a little help from me) are hosting Boxing Day. We are also doing New Years eve but I have a silly superstition about this. In 1985 I was looking forward to the New Year and had invited a lot of people but then my dad died, so I cancelled the party. I still find it difficult to invite people to New Years Eve party until after Christmas Day. This usually means that everyone has already made other plans and we sit there like Billy No Mates.

Everything is ready(ish), presents bought and wrapped - I hope I have remembered everyone. New tablecloth on the dining table, scented, candles on the mantlepiece and and a fridge full of food. I am off to church for the Christmas Eve Mass complete with Nativity Play. Lily will be acting the part of the angel and singing carols, making up the words as she goes - that's my girl. The Mass starts at 7.30 but it is very popular, so Rachael picks me up and we get there for 7.10 and Helen & family are already there. The atmosphere is lovely with people mingling and wishing merry Christmas and catching up on news. Mary, aka 5 year old Emelie, resplendent in a blue robe and bare feat is balancing on the baptismal font. The shepherds are sitting on reserved seats picking their noses and making rude noises. The angels with an array of white dresses and halos are taking it in turns to hold the baby Jesus (a doll) and also the littlest angel a 2 year old African who is not taking kindly to being picked up. When we get there I am surprised to see that Jamie is playing guitar with the church band. That's all three of Helen and Robert's children showing off their talents. Isaac informs me that he is going to have three lots of presents. Father Christmas is going to leave presents for him at his mummy's house, at his daddy's house and then on Boxing day he is coming to our house for more presents. Lucky boy. After Mass, Father Stephen congratulates the children on their superb acting skills and all the congregation applaud. One little angel gets really carried away, bowing and blowing kisses to her adoring public.

CHRISTMAS DAY - YIPEE

Wake up with the lovely feeling that Christmas brings. I sit up and with my new technological skills, text everyone a Merry Christmas. Matteo brings us a cup of tea and sits on the bed chatting, much more civilised than being woken at silly o'clock by hyperactive children (or am I showing my age). I switch on my phone and an advert for TVs on Amazon pops up. I say to Paolo, "That TV is good value", he says "Get it then" in one click I have bought a TV, this amazon is dangerous. My brother Perry is staying with us for Christmas and we have a chilled morning opening presents and catching up on each other's news. We have lots of wine and chocolate from the children we look after. Matteo has bought me a book and a CD, "Cloud Atlas" - decisions, decisions do I read the book first or watch the film? Pat and Michelle have bought me a big box of Sanctuary Spa pamper products so I soak myself in the bath and emerge soaked, de-foliated, soft skinned and smelling sweet. What a lovely start to the day, no slaving over a hot stove or rushing out to find a shop because I've forgotten to buy stuffing (I have had years like that). We have a good game of "Which label has fallen off which parcel" then I decide to go to see Nathan and his family as they are not eating at Helen's today.

Nathan and his family give us an Italian Christmas Wicker Hamper full of Italian food. Cheese, wine, panattoni, biscotti and baci chocolates - delicious, I'm looking forward to sampling that. They have a huge brio train-set in the middle of the living room that they have bought for their grandsons. I wonder how long that lasts before someone gets fed up of falling over it or hoovering around it! They have a Staffordshire Bull Terrier who wants to jump up to greet everyone as they arrive, Ok when you are in your pyjamas or jeans, not a good idea when you are dressed in your Christmas finery. I go to pick up Rachael, she has made hand-made sweets and biscuits for every one and wrapped them very professionally in cellophane. She has also made a cheesecake and profiteroles for after Christmas dinner today and given us a Willow figure entitled "celebration". I love Christmas. At Helen's the table is full of little snacks, a lovely way to serve starters as we all drift in, open presents, pour drinks, and exchange Happy Christmases. Eventually the roast potatoes are cooked to perfection and the table is cleared and set again with Beef and Turkey, pigs in blankets, parsnips, carrots, cabbage, sprouts etc etc. Having Paolo in the family has set the bar very high when it comes to food preparation, but all the kids have risen to the challenge and are all excellent cooks. After dinner gifts are exchanged, I am given some Daisy perfume, shower gel and body lotion, it smells lovely. I sit and demonstrate to Lily how to knit and Rachael and Helen mock my braiding skills. I used to plait their hair but never mastered braiding from the top of their heads, but today, at the age of 62, I learn how to do it. Why did I find it so difficult all those years age? After a couple of hours I find room to eat Christmas pudding with brandy sauce and even though I thought I couldn't eat any more, manage to squeeze in a small piece of cheesecake. We watch Mrs Brown and Michael Macintyre on the TV and listen to seasonal music. It has been one of the most relaxing Christmas days that I can remember. Nine adults and two children in one house and not one cross word. A miracle at Christmas.

Boxing Day. I start the day by showering in the new fragrances from Helen and Robert then nip to Matalan to buy another dinner service and am disappointed that it hasn't been reduced in the sale. I am also surprised that Aldi is closed (how spoilt we have become, expecting shops to stay open 24/7). I buy some milk and a few bits to put into the Christmas stockings and go back home to help Paolo who is happily cooking dinner for 25 people. Just as I get back, Joseph, who has spent Christmas Day in Ireland with his girlfriend, phones to say that the trains are not running, can someone pick him up from Manchester? I hate driving in Manchester but am sure that I can find the way to Piccadilly. Matteo says he will drive and I go with him to navigate. We chat all the way and as we get into Manchester I just keep saying "straight on" until we are lost. Matteo says "why did you say you knew the way, I could have just put the address into my phone". By the time we get back everyone has started to arrive, so I don't get around to helping Paolo, nor have I straightened my hair.

We have another lovely day. The food as expected is delicious but we run out of dinner plates. How can that be, we always have enough plates and I have just bought eight more. After several people have insisted that they don't mind eating from side plates and just filled up the plates more frequently, I find the new plates in the cupboard (not the cupboard where the plates are usually kept). We have seven children, eight grandchildren and two grandsons and this is one of the few occasions when they all get together, I have such a sense of fulfilment as I watch them laughing and joking and catching up with each others lives. Two of my brothers, my sister and a nephew and niece are also here and I hope that my mum & dad are looking down from heaven with pride at how their children have turned out. Although I often suspect that my youngest son Matteo is my dad reincarnated and that Isaac, my grandson is my mum, so in that case, they will not be looking down but be here among us with no memory of their previous lives.

Our children sign me up for Whatsapp and create a family group. I have tried Whatsapp before when one of the childminders showed me how to send photos, but I didn't know that I could chat on it. For the uninitiated I text a message on whatsapp and all the people in the group get the message. I look forward to my phone "dinging" to say someone has sent a message. Also somehow a very boozy rendition of a few of us singing on the karoake has been posted. It is almost impossible to even identify what song we are singing. Once more gifts are exchanged, toys are played with (not just the children), wine is poured and drunk and the karaoke machine goes on. I have 6 brothers all with reasonable singing voices but unfairly I cannot hold a note and cannot remember the words to songs. Undeterred, I take my turn to sing very badly as is becoming a tradition at Christmas in the Scotton household. I play party pooper at midnight and wish everyone once more a happy Christmas and a safe journey home several of them are actually staying at our house. Another perfect day (although tomorrow brings a few hours of cleaning up).

Friday 27th December, I make an early start by getting up at 6.00 and filling the dishwasher then making a cup of tea and taking it back to bed. I get up again an hour later when Rachael and Isaac get up and I make porridge for us. After they go home loaded with presents and still wearing pyjamas, I make bacon butties for Paolo, Perry (my brother), Joseph and Adam then attack the mess, they all help. Robert brings Lily and Jamie as Helen has gone to work and he has just finished a night shift. Rachael phones to tell me that Isaac has just made her laugh with his first proper joke: As they arrived home he had pointed at the new globe of the world that had been one of his Christmas gifts he pointed at it and said: "What on earth is that? - do you get it mummy EARTH". Good joke for a five year old. I join Lily in painting a toy tea set that Santa has brought her, then watch Dr Dolittle with her and Jamie. We go out to look for a new car without any success then I cook pasta for tea before taking the kids back home. Matteo has stayed at Lauren's parents house and has been shopping at the Trafford Centre. He calls home to have a brew and collect his washing before driving back to Sheffield. I remind him to drive safely and say I will see him on New Years Eve.

On Saturday we get up early and go to the Kia car show room. Paolo and I have decided that we will replace our Zafira with a small, more economical car instead of buying each other presents. We don't really succeed in saving money as we decide to buy a Kia Ceed which is neither small nor cheap but we are worth it! As we are talking to the salesman, Jackie our friend phones me to ask if we are getting a taxi this afternoon. Apparently we have been invited to another friends house and once more have forgotten about it. We go home and get changed. I decide to do without a drink and drive us there, picking up Jackie and Steve on the way. When we get to the house of Linda and Roy we see Pat and Terry arrive at the same time. Terry is 75 and has dementia. You would take him as ten years younger and a bit absent minded. During the evening they are discussing a holiday abroad that they have booked for the middle of January. Pat is worrying about holiday insurance because they have been asked to pay an extra £200 because they are over 70 and because of Terry's illness. Terry pipes up "Oh bloody hell has my alsimons come back again, I'll have to go back to the clinic and get it sorted". If only it was so simple!

Linda and Roy have been trying to sell their house for the last 2 years and I remark that I can't understand why it has not been snapped up. They have lavished money and care on it and anyone could walk in and live there without having to start decorating. They say that it is because the area has become predominantly occupied with Muslim Asian families who come to view but then worry that it is not big enough to fit a prayer room. When we get home, I go to bed and begin to read a book. Amanda Holdens life story "No holding back"- another Christmas present. Paolo makes a brew and then goes to watch telly. My brother Perry comes in. He has been to the pub with my sister, Gail and my nephew Mark and is pleasantly drunk. He sits on my bedroom floor and waxes lyrical about my lovely house, telling me that I am a star and a teacher and many more compliments. We talk about our childhoods, our siblings and children, his job with autistic children and my childminding. He decides that he will not go back to Abingdon tomorrow, but stay until after the New Year celebrations.

Note to self - sort out the sleeping arrangements before 4 a.m. on 1st January.

Sunday 29th December I had planned to go to church but the lazy mood of the season has attacked me and I don't get my act together soon enough. We decide to return to the car salesroom to make the salesman's day by buying the Ceed. Halfway there, I remark that Jackie had told me that her daughter had just bought a new Zafira for less that we were planning to pay for the Ceed, and as the we are not going to save much in running costs we might as well look into buying a new one. We do an about turn and head for the Vauxhall dealers.

At the dealers we look at a Zafira, then at a Skoda before finally deciding to buy an Astra. It doesn't have the Sat Nav or reversing camera of the Ceed, but it is cheaper, is only £30 a year to tax and has lower petrol consumption. Paolo signs the credit forms and we head for home. Only then do we realise that we have spent hours there it is 3 pm and my auntie will be arriving for her dinner at 4. I phone her to say not to come until 5 o'clock and then go to Tesco to buy food.

Minutes after we get home my sister arrives. She is distraught as she has just had a phone call from my brother saying that he is going to jump in the river. Ian lives in Stafford in a one bedroomed bedsit and has problems with depressions when he drinks. Although he doesn't want to live closer to us, at times like Christmas he imagines that the rest of the family are all getting together and having fun and leaving him alone. He complains to Gail that he has had no-one to talk to but when she phones the crisis team they say they have spoken to him several times that day and that he has an appointment for the next day but they say that they cannot do anything for him when he is drunk. When she phones Ian back he tells her that he has been arrested and they wont let him jump in the river! A voice in the background shouts that he has not been arrested but is being admitted to St Georges Mental Hospital. I try to phone him but get no answer. A few minutes later Wayne from the Vauxhall Garage phones to ask if I have taken the car key home with me - Yes there it is in my pocket. Wayne has obviously been in trouble and says he will call on his way home.

Monday 30th December I phone Gail who tells me that Ian has been discharged and sent home in a taxi but that he had an appointment with Atos about his disability payments. I find a number and try to explain why he has not kept his appointment but they will not deal with me without his permission. They tell me to wait until he is feeling better and get him to ring himself. I ask "But what if he doesn't get better?"

I phone Ian and we have a chat, he is obviously over the worst. The police and hospital have sobered him up. He still says he hears voices in his head and he does suffer from delusions. I tell him about my phone call to Atos or Capita (not quite sure which centre I was eventually dealing with) and he tells me that they were supposed to be visiting him but that they hadn't arrived. I asked if they had said they would visit him and he said "No they just sent me an appointment, I told them I couldn't get there - the ball's in their court now!" I have a lot of sympathy for him, he is obviously suffering with arthritis and heart problems as well as mental issues, but he is also very good at manipulating people and very self centred. I phone my sister and she says that Atos had at one point arranged transport for him but then cancelled it so basically the ball was in their court, but that would not help Ian with his disability benefits. I have loved and looked out for Ian since he was a little boy, he is three years younger than me. He has served three tours of duty in Northern Ireland as well as several other conflicts around the world. He has hardly been out of work since coming out of the army and yet now that he is quite seriously disabled with arthritis, heart problems and mental health issues he is having to grovel for his benefits. Hopefully now that crisis in care have been alerted, he might get some help.

I look at the clock, it is 11:19 and I am still in pyjamas and have done nothing but talk on the phone, my ear is burning, I'm sure that talking on the mobile phone for two hours cannot be good for you. I have a shower and change my stoma bag. I am nearly at the end of my supply of bags and the ones I am wearing at the moment are the first ones the nurses brought before we found the best ones for me. They are a bit bigger and when they are full, pull down uncomfortably. I am still being forgetful about taking the imodium so the bag fills up quickly. Only a few more weeks now I hope before the illeostomy is reversed and I don't have to worry about carrying spare bags etc in case of emergencies.

We go shopping for more beer for our party on New Year's eve. Adam has bought the biggest fireworks I have ever seen at a private party. I think I will be watching from indoors. The telly arrives, it is bigger than I imagined it would be, but perfect for the bedroom where the kids watch videos when there are disputes over TV programs.

At 4 o'clock we go to pick up our new car. At the showrooms we are waved casually in the direction of two chairs and a desk. At 4.15 pm a salesman brings us some paperwork to sign and then disappears through a door. Twenty minutes later I am blazing and demand to see the manager. He comes out and I demand to know what is taking so long. He says they are waiting for the credit company to agree the loan. I say "First, Why haven't you sorted this out earlier and second, why wasn't this explained to us and

118

why we were not at least provided with a drink". The manager apologises and sends a salesman to put £30 diesel in the tank. I calm down and think to myself that I am probably a bit on edge because of the conversations I have been having with Ian all day. I do some deep breathing and relax, this has been a lovely Christmas I wont spoil it now.

As we drive home I post a photo of the car on our new group on Whatsapp, I could get used to this technology. At home Paolo makes spaghetti carbonara and I open a bottle of wine. Perry has written a children's book and Jess, his daughter is helping him to compile it. We sit and enjoy the meal and discuss the book and and chat about how facebook and the internet helped me to cope with my tumour and the argument at the showroom is forgotten. I am enjoying having Perry around, but I realise that it is stopping me doing all the jobs I would normally do when I am not working. I usually write out new contracts to my "parents" at this time, and bring accounts up to date. Never mind, I will do it next week-end, when Christmas is a happy memory. We watch a James Bond film on TV then I take myself off to bed with "Amanda Holden" (The book).

New Years Eve. I take a ride out to Tesco in our new car. First I can't start it - you have to make sure the steering wheel lock is off. Then I turn the engine on but the car doesn't move, (you have to put your foot on the brake and then take it off). Eventually I get going, out of the drive and along the street and it is great. I go to Tesco to buy washing up liquid, bread and paper plates. I come home with everything I set out for plus two pillows, two door mats, several pounds worth of party food and some more alcohol (just in case we haven't enough). I get home and dig out extra bedding, blow up two inflatable beds and do a quick tidy. Then I set the table and realise that it is 3.pm and I haven't eaten since my breakfast. We have crumpets and tea (don't want to spoil my appetite before the party. Ian phones me several times. He tells me that he has set fire to his hair and that it smells. This is Ian being ridiculous and I don't rise to it. I say "Tell me about it, I had a curly perm in the 80's and an eye level grill, I set fire to my hair regularly". I ask him why he is setting fire to his hair and he answers that it is getting long. So I ask why he doesn't cut it and he answers that the police have taken away his knives and scissors, so I tell him to tie it back in a pony tail. This conversation is not going the way he has planned, he intends to shock and worry me, but I have been here before. I know it is attention seeking. I consider telling him to get a taxi to the train station and come to Manchester and I will pick him up and pay his fare. But then I decide against it. Ian has spoiled many of my parties by inappropriate behaviour and also, in his present state of mind the last thing he needs is a glut of alcohol.

I straighten my hair and put on the shortest dress that I have worn in a long time, I feel good. My sister Gail arrives first and I go and pick up Rachael and Isaac. Soon Pat and Michelle, Joe and Ciara arrive carrying crisps and drink and belated Christmas presents. I fill a drink fountain with a fruit cocktail for the kids and we begin to chill. I have a drink of hot mulled wine and sip it slowly, primarily because it is hot and also because this is the only alcohol I am going to have. Once more I have chosen not to drink. Helen and Robert with their two youngest children arrive (17 year old Arron has chosen to party with friends, maybe letting in the New Year with your Nanna and Pappy is not cool. Carl (of Father Christmas fame) arrives with his family. Brad in his wheelchair shows off his reversing skills. Another brother and partner followed by four more friends are the last to arrive. The party is fabulous, all my friends and family celebrating the end of 2013 and welcoming in 2014. Jamie and Isaac provide entertainment by street dancing and Lily joined in with a "Thriller" dance. At midnight we all go out into the garden and Adam lets off the fireworks that he has provided. We were expecting pretty colourful sparks and a few rockets! What we got was explosions. Very loud explosions. And lots of them. After one of the rockets failed to shoot up into the air, but bounced along the lawn, nearly knocking Lily over and almost taking Matteo's head off, we move back into the safety of the house and drink champagne and sing Auld Langs Ein. At about 1.00 a.m., Lily and Isaac are persuaded to go to bed to watch a video and Patrick demonstrates a party game that consists of tying a banana to a string suspended from your waist and swinging your hips so that the banana taps a tangerine onto a piece of paper. The idea being that you get your tangerine onto the paper before your opponent. Players and audience alike enjoy the slightly risqué game. More tame games follow and then karaoke. Perry stands up and performs a few of his poems, that reduce me to tears and then at about 3.am a few people begin to leave. After running a few people home I slip into my pyjamas, my tights are pulling on my stoma bag and it is getting uncomfortable. I eventually go to bed at 4.30 and the younger members of the family who are staying overnight continue to chat and party for another hour. Happy New Year

Wednesday 1ˢᵗ January Rachael is first up (only one with a child) and begins to clear up the proof of the celebrations, followed soon after by Paolo and Me. We drink tea, eat cereal and then Rachael gets dressed and Paolo takes her and Isaac home and fills her recycle bin with bottles and tins (our's is full). We continue to clean up, helped by the rest of the family as they rise bleary eyed from their beds. I check my emails and text messages and chat on the phone with a few people and then realise that it is nearly 3.p.m. Time to go to Rachael's house. Rachael has made taco's and fajittas and apple strudel. It is so relaxing, the children play and the adults eat lazily all afternoon and then we drift off home to watch TV and go to bed early. Whatever 2014 holds, it has had a good start.

25 –A New Year 2014

Thursday 2nd January, 10.00 a.m. my appointment for the next step of my treatment, a Contrast Enema. The appointment letter reminds me that I need to pay a fee for the car park and I have parked there so often over the years that I need no reminder. I forget. I always have coins in my coat pocket, but today I wear a newly washed one with empty pockets. I always have money for parking in the car, but today I am driving the new car and the last owner selfishly took all the change out of it. I invariably have money in my handbag, but today I take a different bag that will fit my book in case my appointment is late and an emergency stoma bag plus all the regalia.

I don't have time to return home so I grovel at the reception and tell her I am coming for treatment and should only be 20 minutes. I arrive a bit early but don't wait long. I have to take off all my clothes and put them in a basket and put on a hospital night gown, the one with the fasteners at the back. I am ushered into another room and invited to climb onto the bed. I climb on with my usual grace, flashing my bottom at anyone who is interested to look. I begin to lie down when the nurse says "Oh you should have sat up first" so I sit up and then she tells me to lie down??? I lie on my side while she inserts a tube into my rectum with the promise that it will not hurt. It hurts like hell - what is she doing? She tells me to help by clamping my bottom around the tube so that the fluid doesn't leak out, then she tells me to relax. It is impossible to follow both instructions at the same time. She has told me that the procedure wont be too unpleasant because the scar is low down and so she wont need to put too much coloured fluid into me. But as she instructs me to change positions so that she can scan me from different angles she repeatedly says "I'll just put a bit more air in, or a bit more fluid" It doesn't take long and then I am shown into a spacious toilet and the nurse says that I can go as soon as I am dressed and the report will be sent to the surgeon. I sit on the toilet to empty my bowel while I get dressed. When I think there is no more to leak out, I quickly leave the hospital to see if my car has been clamped. It hasn't but as I begin to drive home I get a pain like trapped wind. I feel like I am going to soil myself and my new car. I once more clamp my bottom cheeks together. The hospital is only 10 minutes away from home (especially when you drive as fast as I do), as soon as I reach home I abandon the car and run into the house, calling to Paolo to park it for me. I sit on the toilet moaning as liquid squirts into the toilet, it feels lumpy, like having a runny poo (I know! - too much information). Paolo makes me a warm drink and I sit there feeling sorry for myself. After a while, I think it will be safe to get off the toilet, but as soon as I stand up, I feel the need to "go" again. This carries on for a few hours, I'm really lucky that the doctor didn't need to put much liquid into me!!

I gradually begin to feel better and help Lily and Jamie to bake cakes. My friend drops in for a chat and brings me a bottle of wine and two plants from her garden.

She works in a hospital and tells me that she has not had a day off all over Christmas, she looks really tired and I make a drink and try to help her relax. She was born in the next bed to me in Hope Hospital. Our grandmothers lived near each other on Coronation Street, Salford and we went to school together after we moved with the Salford overspill to Little Hulton when I was 13. Her family were already living in Little Hulton when she was born. We went youth hosteling together and I had my first holiday abroad with her. But our paths have taken different routes. Her husband died tragically about 12 years ago and she has had to work hard to keep the wolves from the door for her two children. She is very domesticated and can turn her hand to anything practical (she made all of our holiday clothes for our holiday in Minorca when we were 17). She does the gardening, sews curtains and makes batches of food to keep in the freezer for emergencies. She puts me to shame. But whereas my children are always showing their appreciation, her children seem to do nothing but complain. I sympathise with her and promise to visit her on her next day off.

After tea, I go to visit my auntie to wish her a Happy New Year. She seems a bit distracted and she is bending over more than usual, she doesn't offer me a drink as she usually does. I make a mental note to keep a closer eye on her. This old age is a bummer.

Before I go to bed I write a few sentences on Facebook, telling everyone about my hospital visit and the following discomfort and get the following comments:

Wendy Marshall Tell Paolo to stroke your bottom better!!!!
Wendy Marshall You also might need to tell me to stop making inappropriate comments on Facebook!!
Veronica Scotton Don't encourage him Wendy I keep telling him I am too old. But he doesn't believe me.
Veronica Scotton I look forward to your inappropriate comments Wendy Marshall
Gail Wieczorek TMI sis way TMI !!!!!
Gail Wieczorek Sharing is one thing but there is a limit - love you tho xx
Veronica Scotton TMI Gail???
Gail Wieczorek Too much information !!!
Veronica Scotton It's a whole new language lol, WTF, PMS
Gail Wieczorek Don't know what you mean, you've been using a whole new language all your life !!!
Gail Wieczorek It'll soon be tomorrow so I've going to bed - night night xx
Veronica Scotton It is tomorrow now Good Night, God Bless xxx
Lesley Hopwood-Ryan Rofl..... But then find it hard to get up again!! Love you vron. Xxx
Veronica Scotton I've seen you rolling on the floor and getting back up. You are a lot fitter than you suggest. Love you too
Linda Kenny So glad your feeling better love always xx

Friday 3rd January. I phone my brother Darren to wish him a happy birthday. I usually forget. It comes too soon after Christmas so I usually give him a birthday card and present if I see him at Christmas but then I forget on the actual day. I have a list of phone calls to make and a few errands to run. I need to drop off Ofsted medical forms with the doctor so that he can verify that I am fit for work. Take a jumper back to Tesco that I had bought but brought back with the security tag attached. Then pick up a McDonalds chicken nugget Happy Meals for Jamie, Lily and Isaac.

As Paolo is cooking our dinner, Daren, the nurse from Bolton returns my call from yesterday. I tell him that I am OK now but ask him why I was in so much discomfort and why I needed to spend so much time on the toilet. He explained that when the doctor poured the enema into me and then asked me to get into different positions on the bed to facilitate different view of the bowel, the liquid would travel back up the bowel. Sitting on the toilet in the hospital while getting dressed would have allowed about 6 inches of the bowel to be emptied. The fluid going back up the bowel would effectively given me a clean out, a colonic irrigation with compliments of the NHS and thats why I had to keep returning to the toilet. The discomfort was probably caused by wind as the doctor had pumped air into the bowel to allow a clearer view on the camera, all clever stuff!

Paolo and I have Pasta and Salmon and then I take the kids to see Walking With Dinosaurs taking boxes of chocolate received over Christmas and left-over cordial. It's ages since I have taken children to the cinema, Paolo usually takes them while I entertain the younger children. The film is brilliant but afterwards I follow Lily into the mens toilets - embarrassing (she had followed Jamie and Isaac). I take them into Poundland and let them pick two toys each (last of the big spenders).

When we get home the kids want to "make sparks" with the fire-pit in the back garden. I light the fire and the kids throw wood on, then poke it with sticks to make sparks. Not recommended by Ofsted but I believe in letting kids take the lead in choice of activities and I stayed close to remind them that fire is hot. They came in for tea with sooty hands and faces and clothes smelling of smoke and big smiles on their faces. After tea Rachael picked them all up to take them swimming, these kids have such full lives.

Paolo and I decide to go out for a meal to Danielli's Restaurant. We know the owner and his two daughters are working there. They are shocked to hear about my cancer - obviously the grape vine hasn't reached everywhere, the restaurant was quiet for a Friday so it was nice to have time to chat to the staff and take our time. Afterwards we dropped in on some friends and helped them finish off the Christmas wine. At least I did, Paolo was driving this time.

Saturday 4th January. A bulging bag wakes me up early (all that wine). I empty the bag then go down stairs to make a brew. While there I empty the washing machine and fill the dryer. Then fill the washer with more washing. Let the machines do the housework while I go back to bed and read my book. Matteo comes into the bedroom to say goodbye as he is off back to Sheffield. I am sad for him having to work at a job he dislikes and then having hardly any wages left to spend after paying bills. But proud of him, he could easily have given up and moaned. I wished he had stayed at University, perhaps on a different course but I respect his decisions and am confident that he will make a success of his life. Paolo gets up then to move his car which is parked in front of Matteo's. He brings me another cup of tea on a tray with some "Fruit and Fibre".

As we lie there, me reading and Paolo playing candy crush (we lead such exciting lives) my stoma starts making little noises. I say to Paolo, "If I close my eyes, I can almost imagine that I am in a forest, listening to all the little animals" Paolo, bless him, doesn't bat an eyelid, he is used to me. But the bag continues to whistle and pop and shiver as the fruit and fibre and milky tea leaves my body and fills my bag. I think I will almost miss this after my next operation. I get up and dressed and think I will send Lesley a text about going out for sushi. As I think about it, I receive one from her saying she is just taking her dad to Morrisons and then she will pick me up. Half an hour later she sends me another one saying that her dad has decided he would like to go to Asda, it seems they have a bigger choice of toilet rolls and salad, he is also examining the sausages even though he doesn't want to buy any. I tell her to chill, the sushi can wait, her mum died of cancer last year, her dad has cancer. I tell her to spend as much time with him as he wants, I wish I had spent more time talking to my mum and dad.

Eventually we reach the Trafford Centre and spend almost as long looking for a parking space as it took us to get there. But the sushi was worth the wait (except the rice balls). We have a stroll around, not looking for anything in particular and then stop for a coffee. I've known Lesley for 30 years and we used to see each other almost every day (I looked after her foster children), but now we rarely get time to chat so we make the most of this opportunity.

When she drops me off at home, Paolo tells me that I have just missed Nathan with Bobby and Bailey, he has taken most of the Christmas decorations down so I spend time climbing the loft ladder to pass him stuff to be stored until next year. I give thanks that I am still fit enough to do this. Then I phone Nathan and have a chat with him.

I phone my cousin Jackie who lives in Boston as she has left a message on the answer machine. We talk for over an hour, I'm not looking forward to my phone bill, but it is only once a year.

Sunday 5th January I decide to wash the covers off the car seats and the bedding off the spare bed (what is it about January that induces me to do this?). Paolo goes shopping and I clean the house (I usually do this on Saturday but I was eating sushi instead). As I finish hoovering, I notice that I have got a message on the answering machine, it's Jackie my friend who lives near, not my cousin in Boston, saying that she has had a fall and broken her arm. This is the one whose husband has just been made redundant. I think this is going to be their bad luck year.

Paolo cooks Lamb and my auntie Josie comes for dinner and then Gail arrives just as we finish eating, she is full of a cold. I put the TV on but we mostly talk over it while we drink tea and eat chocolates. I should be doing new contract for the children I look after but I keep procrastinating. I will definitely do them tomorrow.

Monday 6th January. One of my parents tells me she is going to work four days instead of five. Beginning earlier and finishing later. I tell her she will have to pay us extra for the extra hours but she says she can't afford it. I say "OK, leave it as it!!" What kind of business woman am I? I'm such a pushover. The problem is that I have never paid for child-care. Some of the parents who bring their kids to us get help via tax credits and some don't pay anything at all as they get 3 or 2 year old funding. I have sympathy with the ones that are working but earning just over the band for benefits. I'll never be a millionaire, but then I would not get as much job satisfaction if I did it just for the money. A couple come to see us about childminding. I tell them that we are not taking any other children on until I have completely finished the treatment. But they talk us round saying that they have plenty of contingency plans to cover hospital appointments etc. They just want their baby to come to us because we have such a good reputation. (See what I mean about job satisfaction - or have they been told we are mugs as far as fees are concerned)

At 11.30 I have a dentist appointment for a fitting for a partial denture, (bottom back). I wonder what they would say if I mentioned that I couldn't afford it?

My friend phones to say that she has just seen an advert for a cruise. Leaving Southampton and visiting Russia, Finland, Stockholm, Copenhagen, Denmark and Berlin. I have been putting off booking a holiday until after I have had the stoma bag removed, but the holiday sounds just what the doctor ordered. We have to co-ordinate holidays with all the families that we service, but if we book early enough they can usually work around us. Our friends have been trying to get us to go for the last three years but with the expense of buying the house and the necessity to go in school holidays we haven't gone. Because of the reduction in the number of children that we are looking after at the moment, we really will be struggling (especially now we have a car loan). My practical self is saying wait until next year, wait until the stoma has been removed successfully, save up until we have enough in the bank to pay for it fully. The emotional side, is saying, live your life to the full, don't put off till tomorrow what you can enjoy today. I have been reminded over the last few months that I won't live forever (I think up until now I was kidding myself that a magic elixir of life would be found before I kicked the bucket).

I think about my sister who has saved all her life so that she could enjoy seeing the world with her husband when they retired. She lost a huge percentage of her savings when the banks crashed and then her husband had a stroke and had to give up work. They could still afford to have a few nice holidays, but he would not appreciate them. I think about Paolo's mum who has missed seeing us this year (we planned to go last August). I need to make sure that all of our "parents" including our two daughters can get these two weeks off work.

After taking everything into consideration, I begin to get excited, I really would like to go. My eldest son is forty and since his birth until a couple of years ago we hardly took a holiday without children accompanying us. A cruise is a really selfish holiday and I feel the need to be a bit selfish. Two weeks of visiting places I have never been, two weeks of eating delicious food and wine without considering the cost. . Two weeks of doing nothing, or everything, two weeks of good company of four of our best friends. A fortnight's break from changing a nappy, wiping a snotty nose or writing an observation - heaven! I love my job, but I have decided its time to prioritise my free time.

I phone Helen and she tells me that she has booked one of those weeks off and to "go for it", she will sort something out for the other week. I get a similar answer from Rachael.

I will phone the hospital and ask for an educated guess about the date of my operation and recovery time. I will do the maths with our incomings and outgoings and look where we can save money (we have one more child coming to us three days a week from next week) We can look for cheap flights for Paolo to visit his mum for a long week-end, or make her a firm promise for next year. By tomorrow I will have thought of 1001 other reasons not to go, but I will deal with each one separately and not be put off. I think May 24th will see us sailing from Southampton.

As I am writing, I can hear a lot of hammering coming from downstairs and consider investigating. After a while I hear the dishwasher being filled (whoops I forgot that the cleaning up had not been done when I came upstairs to use the computer). I can tell from the noise that Paolo is probably a bit aggrieved with me leaving everything to him, but I know that in a while he will brew a drink and bring it up and tomorrow I will go the extra mile to give him some space to do whatever he wants to do.

No he didn't bring me a brew up. When I heard him making himself a cup of tea, I knew I was in trouble. I went down into the kitchen and made a drink and some salmon and Boursin cheese on toast. I took them into the living room and started chatting about who I had been talking to on the phone, the responses to my text messages and emails. I told him that I had been writing my book and what I had written. By the time he had eat his toast and drunk his tea, he had forgotten to sulk. But I know it was a close call, I don't take his calmness for granted and thank God everyday for his gentle character. I will make sure that I do at least my share of housework tomorrow.

Tuesday 7th January, the day is quite mild for January so I take the kids into the back garden in their wellies. I tip all the collected rainwater away which leaves plenty of puddles to splash in but hopefully no cold water to soak their clothes. Bailey soon discovers that if he jumps on the mat under the swing, the mud oozes up through the holes in it. Before long there is a muddy puddle big enough to please Peppa Pig's dad. They find water that I have missed and the ash in the fire pit. What's the matter with the bikes and scooters and doll's prams. Why don't they play in the play house or wooden den so lovingly built by Paolo. I leave them to it, who am I to tell them how to play, I fill a bin bag with the remains of the fireworks and broken toys and snapped pegs. All this bending down and walking in the fresh air is surely better than a session at the gym. The kids by this time have found some worms and are feeding them by hand to the chickens and I remember playing with my friends and brothers and sister in Salford. We would have dinner parties. The plates being slates from the roofs of "bombed" houses, the food being mud and worms. We never knew we were poor, but watching these kids play today proves that even though they have each been given hundreds of pounds worth of toys for Christmas, they still prefer to play the same games that prehistoric children could have played. I wonder if their mothers told them "get out into the fresh air while I sweep this cave, and watch out for the sabertooth tigers"

I don't get any answers from the hospital about the estimated date of my operation, but I do get a reply from the photographer about the photo session. We are on for the 22nd February. It is Lauren's and Joseph's birthdays around this time so birthday celebration meals are on the menu. I'm excited!

Matteo phones to say that his flat has a leaking roof and the landlord wont take responsibility for it. I might get my baby home sooner that I was hoping for. Fingers crossed.

Thursday 9th January After the kids have gone and the house is tidy, I go to see my auntie Josie. She comes for dinner on Sunday and I usually call one night in the week to give her a bit of company. As I am leaving my sister phones and says "Are we on for tonight?" I'd forgotten that Thursday is our Wetherspoons night! Christmas and Gail's friend Catherine being home from Tanzania have interrupted our weekly routine. I can do both, cup of tea with Josie, then Guinness and chips (or curry) with Gail. As I walk round to Josie's house, I pass my friend Joyce's, she spots me and tells me to wait. She brings out a bottle of Gin to give to Gail. How come my friend knows that my sister likes gin and I don't? At the pub Gail tells me that she had been to visit our brother Ian in Stafford and said that he seemed to be a bit happier, and that the crisis care team were trying to get a social worker assigned to him and to get him somewhere more suitable to live. The evening was pleasant and Paolo picked us up later so that we didn't need to walk.

Rachael phones me to tell me the latest Isaac-ism. Isaac nags like all other 5 year olds, "Mummy can I have some sweets" "No Isaac", "Mummy please can I have some sweets", "No Isaac", Mummy please may I have some sweets", "NO". Rachael had read an article on Facebook that the way to stop this is to say. "Do you remember asking me that question before? - Do you remember the answer I gave". She tries it on Isaac and he replies "Yes I do remember asking, but I don't remember your answer!" Smart Alec. At bedtime Rachael says to Isaac "bedtime Isaac, what do you want to drink?" He answers "Mummy, do you remember asking me that question last night?, Do you remember my answer?" God help us when he is 15.

After the majority of my "parents" saying that they will sort out their kids for the two weeks in May, our friends seem to be chickening out. Too expensive, not enough time to save! Never mind, we can still take the time off and drive into Scotland and maybe even visit my cousin on the Isle of Skye. We will still be visiting somewhere we have never been, we can stop and eat wherever and whenever we choose, and it will be cheaper. Win, win situation.

Monday 13th January I get an email from my brother's ex-wife

Hi Vron,
just a quick message. I still need to get myself a portable computer device to enable communications. Meanwhile I am in the library again.
Hope you and all of the family are continuing well.
Gary has a cardiac tests appointment this or next Friday to check

I try to phone him but his phone is going straight to answer phone. I don't worry too much, I'm sure he will let us know if he needs anything.

I am up early and so decide to go for a swim, I am always hot and sweaty in the mornings so it doesn't take so much motivation to get out of bed with the promise of a nice cool pool. When I first started going early-morning swimming it was with the idea of losing weight but I have never lost any. But my ankles had started to swell and I had a fungal infection on one of my toe nails that refused to clear up despite spending £s on creams and medication. After a few weeks, my ankles had slimmed and my nails were healthy and even though I did not lose weight, I started to sleep more soundly and have more energy during the day. Some days I turn over and spend another hour in bed but I am trying to get back into a routine of going swimming a couple of times a week.

When I get home, the young mum with her baby who is starting with us today is waiting, the baby is fine but her mum is obviously very nervous. I tell her to go to work and I will send her photos all day to reassure her. At lunchtime I get a phone call from her to ask how the baby is and I tell her she is fine and ask her had she not seen the photos. What a time for my phone to play up! I also get another call from another mum with similar enquiries who says she was panicking because she has been trying to get in touch with me all day. I try my phone by ringing it from the house phone and it seems OK, then I take another couple of photos and fire them off to the young women who text me back to say that they have received them. Have I not been doing it right, is dementia creeping up on me - only time will tell.

On Tuesday, I persuade Paolo, with a little help from Robert to bring an old chest of drawers out of the loft. My intention is to clean it up and repaint it to put in the spare bedroom. It smells musty. I clean it with soapy water then sand it down, not the best idea, the room is soon full of grime accumulated over several years of being in a loft. Still the results are promising so Paolo carries it outside and uses the electrical sander on it. As he is doing it, Nathan brings his grandsons to see us. He suggests that we wax the drawers instead of painting them. I say OK we'll give it a go, if the results are not good we can always paint over it. Only after applying the wax do I learn that you can't paint over wax. Never mind, they no longer smell musty and will serve the purpose of supporting a small TV at a suitable height.

Wednesday 15th January I make a new group on Whatsap and am soon sending photos to all the parents of the children and getting some lovely comments back. Why did I not think of this before? We also get some favourable comments at "home time". The parents of the new baby tell us that she slept all night after her first day with us and they cannot believe it when she ignores them completely when they come to pick her up after they finish work. She is loving being the centre of attention with the other children and not at all in a hurry to go home. This is the maddest, most stressful time of a childminding day. several parents arrive within minutes of each other, they each want to know how their child/children have been and also tell us about their day. The kids don't want to get ready to go home until they have finished playing or watching a TV program, and use delaying tactics such as asking for a drink or saying they need the toilet, they know that if they give their parents a chance, they will start talking and it will buy them a few more minutes. Shoes, reading folders, coats, lunch boxes go missing, despite the fact that we have dedicated coat hooks with each child's name and photo above them and they each have a drawer in which to keep personal belongings. The problem is that as the kids pour out of my car and into the house, the smell of food draws them into the dining room and coats and belongings are deposited in the porch and shoes are kicked off at the bottom of the stairs. After tea, as the older children disburse to various activities, the toddlers pick things up (such as folders and boxes) and carry them around until they find something else of interest, when they will drop the first item. Which is why odd shoes are often found in the garden and lunch boxes in the utility room. We have had several attempts to organise them, but then what does it matter if we have a madhouse for an hour each evening?

After most of the children have gone home, I log on to Amazon to see if I can buy a lead to connect my iPad to the TV. I have downloaded Disney HD onto the iPad and I think it would be good to be able to connect them so that the movies can be seen on the TV screen. The part I need is only a few inches long with a lightening connecter at one end and a USB at the other. It is £40. Forget it, the kids can watch the movies on the iPad.

Thursday 16th January has a disappointing start when I receive a call from the dentist to say I have missed an appointment. I didn't forget the appointment; I just forgot it was Thursday already. I finally get to speak to Gary (the brother with the heart problems who lives in Leeds) He tells me that the hospital are going to give him shock treatment to "reboot" his heart, but before that he will be given warfarin to thin his blood slightly. Obviously the warped sense of humour runs in our genes as he post on Facebook that he is going into hospital to be poisoned and electrocuted. He tells me that even though this is the second time he has had this treatment, he is more worried about it than he was the first time. I empathise with him. When I first opted for the treatment for the bowel cancer, it was a "no brainer" the choice was Radiotherapy and major surgery on one hand or painful death on the other. My next operation is different, although it is not quite so major and not so invasive, it is still surgery on my body. But it is not a matter of life or death. I could live (not exactly happily ever after) with the stoma bag. Should I put my body through another operation just for a bit of convenience. Also I have had more time to think about it. "What if I die in surgery, what if something goes wrong and I am left disabled?" A friend today told me about her mother going into hospital for this operation, but when she came back the stoma bag was still attached but her appendix had been removed. It had happened several years ago and she couldn't remember why they had removed the appendix but I can't understand how this could happen. While I was in the hospital, a day never passed without someone asking me to confirm my name, date of birth, address etc and also making sure that I understood what was going to happen to me or what the risks were. The niggling worries creep up on me several times a day and distract me. Probably the reason I seem to be more forgetful at the moment.

Rachael tells me the next episode of the "Do you remember me asking you that question...". Last night after putting Isaac to bed, she was just about to get into the bath when he asked her for a drink of milk. She told him that he had already had his supper, but if he was still awake after she had bathed, she would get him one. A few minutes later Isaac once more shouted to her. "Mummy, Toby (a doll), wants to ask you something" she says "What does he want to ask", "He wants to ask you if him and me can have a drink of milk, right now". You have to give him A for effort.

Friday 17th January tea time. We have beef burgers chips and beans. Isaac says "I will just eat the chips Nanna". I say you can eat the beans too, and also have a taste of the burger" He tells me that he doesn't like the burger so I say that I know that, but if he keeps having a little taste, after 15 tries he will like them. He says "But I don't want to like them" The problem is that Isaac is a trendsetter. Whatever he does or says, the other children copy. If Isaac doesn't like burgers, neither will most of the others. The only person who almost made him change his mind was Lily. On Monday we had roast beef, she told him that if he didn't eat the meat, he couldn't be the wolf in the game. Isaac struggled with this for a few minutes, until he thought of an answer. "I am only pretending to be a wolf, I will eat pretend meat" After tea we have Apple Crumble and custard. Fortunately Isaac likes this and asked for seconds, so the other children followed suit.

A good outcome. When Rachael arrives to pick him up, he jumps up and runs to get his shoes on. He says Yes, yes, yes, I'm going to my daddies" Rachael comments, "I'm glad you like going to daddies, but I wish you could be a bit more enthusiastic when you are coming home with me. "Yes!" he says "But daddy buys me treats!"

As I am typing this book, I notice I have missed a letter out, I drag the mouse across to the word and type in the letter "i". The Whole Book Disappears. I do everything in my knowledge to bring it back. I am not panicking at this point, the icon for the book is still on the front of the screen and it is still showing 116 pages, unfortunately all the pages are blank. In the end, with the help of Matteo (who had just gone to bed in Sheffield) and Face -Time on the mobiles, I manage to go into iCloud and retrieve the book up to the last saving point. I had lost everything that I had written today, but the rest of the book was back. Phew!

I decide that I will forward my book - up to now - to my sister and friend so that if I lose it again, they can send it back to me. By return email I received a reply from Wendy:

You have a new car????!!!!!
I think you'll find that it is in fact.......Daddy Pig and not Peppa Pigs Dad. I'm an expert you know!!!
You got rid of your toe fungal infection in the swimming pool??!!! Dear god !! I hope no one was swallowing any water!! You minger!!!'

I would like to point out that my fungal infection was not a weepy, crumbly thing. Just a thick nail that was difficult to trim. After a few weeks of early morning swims, you could see that the "new nail" was growing healthy and smooth, not thick and corrugated. It did take while for the whole nail to become healthy.

Saturday 18th January. It is lovely waking up with the alarm at 7 a.m. - then rolling over and relaxing, the whole day available to do anything I want. Today I am going to see if they can fit me in at the hairdressers, take a jumper back to Next and meet some friends at a recommended curry house to celebrate their son's 6th birthday. If there is time in between, I will do some washing and cleaning, but if not I will do it tomorrow after church. I loved being a mum when my kids were younger, but I do appreciate my week-ends now they are not full of rugby matches and swimming lessons. I am sure I am much calmer with the kids we mind, now that I get to chill in the evenings and week-ends.

The restaurant in Levenshulme is called Nawabs. It is the ultimate Indian fast food. You just find a table, then fill your plates as often as you like. There are lots of waiters to bring you drinks (no alcohol) and to clear used plates. Apart from all the usual Indian curry dishes there is lasagna, pizza, sweet and sour chicken and very sweet deserts.

The friends who have brought us here Debbie and Murtaz and their four children (the eldest is 7 years old), discovered it when they were invited to a wedding here. You can understand why it would be suitable for a wedding party, it is huge, with plenty of parking space outside. There are lots of families dining here and the waiters fuss over the children who mostly sit at the tables when they are not serving themselves with food.

On the way to Nawabs, I receive a phone call from my friend Linda, to enquire if I am OK. I say "Yes of course, why do you ask?" She tells me that she has not seen me on Facebook all week and wondered whether I had been ill! Am I really that predictable? She also has some bad news. Her sister, who lives in Australia has been taken into hospital again. Since returning from Thailand last year with a virus, she has been rushed into hospital a few times with collapsed lungs. She is on steroids. Linda only returned from visiting her last month, but says that she will not be going on the cruise as she will need to return to Oz if her sister deteriorates.

Sunday 19th January - 5 days to go until my appointment with Mr Hobbis to find out if my bowel is water-tight enough to get rid of the stoma.

The alarm wakes me up at 7 am. Just as well, the stoma bag is ready to burst, I have never felt it this hard before (no innuendo intended here). I get up and go to the bathroom, then go downstairs to make tea and breakfast. I put the washer on while I am down and then take the tray back to bed. I have 3 hours to relax before I need to get up if I am going to church. Paolo's mum rings at 8 a.m. and I try to pick up the conversation - as I can only hear Paolo's side of the conversation and I don't understand much French, I only have a bit of success. Afterwards he tells me that his mum and brother are upset because Sonia (Paolo's niece) has just got her new passport and has changed her surname to her mum's maiden name. I don't understand why they are upset, if she got married she would change her name! She is also worried because Pietro's (Paolo's brother) boss has been rushed into hospital for a hernia operation and she is sure that the restaurant will not be able to run without him. She is also stressed because Pietro's wife, Maria has had an accident at work and needs treatment for a hand injury. I wish my French was better so that I could have a good heart to heart with her. As my daughter always says "choose your attitude". Tecla always looks on the sad side of every situation, I always feel like giving her a shake. It's true that when Gildo (Paolo's dad) disappeared, it was unbelievably heart-breaking and if she had only

137

carried the world on her shoulders since then I could understand. But she has always been like this. She worried about Paolo when we first met because I was an "older woman" with four children. She worried when we decided to get married, because I had already been divorced, (so had he), she worried when we decided to buy this house, and I am truly grateful for the financial help she gave us at the time. Her attitude doesn't help. You have to choose how you are going to cope with a situation. When the results of the screening showed that I had cancer I could choose to go into a depression and ask "why me, what have I done to deserve this" or I could say, how lucky I am that it was diagnosed early, now I have a better chance of beating it. When Paolo had an accident on the motorway and the car was written off, we could have worried about how we could afford a new car to get him to work. But we chose to be grateful that he had not been injured. I want to say to her, "Don't stress the small stuff" Her life has not been all plain sailing, but she was married to the one love of her life for over 60 years. They worked together to drag themselves out of poverty and ended with two houses in Switzerland and Italy and enough money to ensure that she can live comfortably for the rest of her life. She has a garden where she grows all the fruit, vegetables herbs and flowers that she needs. She has two lovely healthy sons who care about her. I want to say to her "Look around at what you have got and be happy, choose to look on the bright side". When I was a child, I remember my dad saying that my mum was not happy unless she was worrying about something. Maybe it is just the same for Tecla.

As we lie there discussing his mum, I suddenly realise that it is 10.15 a.m. I am still in pyjamas and the Mass starts at 10.30. Where did the last three hours go? I jump out of bed and manage to wash dress and get to church in 20 minutes (only 5 minutes late). I'm glad I made the effort, I young boy from the parish sings a solo "Amazing Grace" with a beautiful voice and the congregation cheer him and it puts a smile on my face. My oldest daughter Helen, tells me that Jamie has been in trouble for telling lies. She has been really angry with him and banned him from his XBox for the next week. Jamie is really subdued and seems to shed a tear in church. My heart goes out to him and I want to cuddle him and tell

138

him that I am on his side. But I don't, Helen's children are a credit to her and they have not got like that by being lenient towards them. As Helen says, soon he will be in High School, going to school independently and having a key to let himself in. He needs to be trustworthy.

Afterwards at the coffee morning several people enquire after my health and tell me I am looking well. I feel well today, with my new hair style and lipstick, but I don't want to be reminded about the cancer. I am trying to put it out of my mind for a bit longer. Jamie by this time has cheered up and is chatting to a friend and I get to talk to Helen. We have busy lives and don't spend enough time chatting like this. I am proud of my daughter and remember being just as strict with her as she is with her children. Its hard work being a parent, and trying to find the balance between keeping your children happy, and giving them values to become stable adults is difficult. It strikes me as I chat to my daughter that I got it right, she has grown into a happy, strong and hard- working woman. She is a brilliant mum and my friend. I sometimes think that she is being too hard on her kids, as my mum did with me. What goes around comes around. My mum must have got it right, although it didn't seem like it as I was growing up, but the lessons she taught me have been passed down to my daughter and now to my grandchildren. I am very proud.

26 - Birthdays

Tuesday 21st January, Nathan phones me to ask if he can borrow the car. (Mine is a people carrier, bigger than his) so that he can collect a dryer that he has bought from someone in Bolton. I agree and he picks it up and leaves his car parked outside my house. Paolo trotted off to take the kids from Barnados swimming and I go to see my auntie Josie. On the way back I see a man in uniform, (I took him to be a policemen) and I asked him if there was a problem (as if he would tell me if there was). About 5 or 10 minutes later I hear a scraping, metallic sound outside and see a car transporter loading a car onto it. I had forgotten that Nathan had left his car and so didn't put 2 and 2 together. Shortly afterwards, Nathan came in and said, "My car has gone, have you moved it somewhere". Then I remembered! I told him about the pick-up truck and he said "Oh no its the tax". Of all of our children, Nathan is the worst one at handling money. The tax on his car was due at Christmas, so he thought he would leave it for a few weeks. But he had spent hundreds of pounds on his kids and brothers and sisters on Christmas Presents. God knows how many times I have told him to pay his bills and then decide how much he can afford to spend on gifts. He never learns, but he is one of the most kind hearted men I know, and also know that he will manage to get himself out of this mess as he always does.

Wednesday 22nd January, I have my final fitting at the dentist for a small denture. Some of my bottom back teeth are missing and I have been finding it difficult to chew my food sufficiently as I have been instructed by the stoma nurses. The denture is a good fit and I am soon chewing more efficiently. The only slight problem is a tiny clip that fits round two of my front teeth and helps to keep the denture secure. I keep thinking that I have some food stuck in my teeth. I don't know how these young people with a mouth full of teeth braces get on, I suppose I shall have to be patient.

Wednesday evening, I go to Tesco to buy a birthday cake for Lily who will be six years old tomorrow. I feel a bit guilty that I am buying one instead of baking one myself. But I find a princess cake that is much nicer than I could decorate so I don't feel too bad. I also buy one for Joyce, my friend who will be 60 on Saturday. I have volunteered my house for her to have a party on Friday night as her house if not big enough. I choose a card for "Mummy" to give to Isaac for Rachaelher , birthday is on Sunday, and a few random Christmas gift items that have been reduced. At the till I am shocked to learn that I have spent £106 - and I only came in for a card and two cakes. I think I will leave the shopping to Paolo in future. When I get home Paolo is beaming with pride because Patrick has phoned to say that he is being promoted. Well done Pat.

Thursday 23 January, Lily is 6 years old today. We have party food for tea and sing happy birthday to Lily several times. We also sing Happy Birthday to Brea who will be two on the 29th January because she is crying and we can't work out what she is saying she wants. Anyway singing Happy Birthday to her works - she stops crying! Among all the party food is a Ham and Pineapple pizza, cut into quite small slices. I am surprised to see it has been eaten so quickly until I realise that Jason (22 months) has been helping himself to it, picking of the pineapple then dropping the rest of the pizza on the floor. That's called enterprise!

Friday 24th January - the big day.. Going to find out if the intestines have healed enough for the stoma bag to be removed. But... I can't find the letter of appointment, can't quite remember if it's at 9.00 a.m. or 12.00 p.m.

Find the letter. The appointment time is 9.30 a.m. I drop Keith off at school at 9.00 a.m., drive to the hospital, park the car (I've remembered the fee this time) and by 9.20 a.m. I am at the receptionists desk asking for directions to Block G. There's a lot to be said for living in a "built-up" area.

My bum has hardly touched the seat in the waiting room when my name is called and I am ushered into a little room and weighed. Then I am sent back into the waiting room where I read magazines for half an hour. Eventually I am called into a scruffy little examination room with yellow walls, two chairs, two doors, a sink, a bed and a computer and I sit impatiently waiting for another 20 minutes. What's the point, I would have been happier in the waiting room with the magazines and other people to moan with. A nurse enters the room, takes a paper sheet off the bed and throws it away and pulls a fresh one from a roll, she doesn't say a word. I say "Hello! How are you?" and she nearly jumps out of her skin, the room is about 10 foot square, with barely enough room to swing a cat, how did she not notice me there?

Eventually I hear a familiar voice, it is the Chinese doctor with the lovely bedside manner. It had not occurred to me that I would not be seeing Mr. Hobbis and I smile at the memory of Dr. San Yong (I've made that up, I can't really remember his name). A few minutes later there is a light tap on the door and the doctor enters. It is neither Mr Hobbis nor Dr. San Yong, but a female doctor who is also on Mr. Hobbis 'team. She examines my tummy very gently and I wriggle and jump as I am very ticklish. Then she feels up my bum (Is it really necessary?) and tells me that everything has healed nicely. She comments that I am looking amazing, that she hardly recognises me from the ward. I suppose fully dressed, with lipstick and a comb through my hair, I do look different from when I am wearing a nightie, no knickers and my face in a sick bowl. Or maybe she has just been taught at medical school to compliment all senior citizens as we are suckers for a kind word. She asks me about my diet and tells me it is important not to eat sweetcorn or peanuts, apparently she has had to fish peanuts out of stomas and it is not pleasant. I tell her I have eaten everything and the only problem I have had is with fraggolet beans, which although very painful, managed to pop out by themselves eventually. Finally she says that according to all the examinations and tests I have made a good recovery and she is pleased that I have had no weight loss (what? That's what I was expecting and looking forward to!) She tells me that it is up to me whether to elect for a reversal of the stoma. I tell her I am nervous about this procedure but that I would like to go ahead and she tells me that I will go on a waiting list and should receive a letter in the post within a couple of weeks. She asks me if I have any questions and frustratingly I can't think of any, I meant to write down all the things I had been thinking about on the run up to this appointment, but unsurprisingly I had never got round to it. As I get into the car to drive home I remember I had meant to ask if I would have to have a catheter and oxygen mask and all the other paraphernalia that I had been attached to at the last operation.

When I get home, Paolo is sitting on the floor playing with Odelia and Jason, two little children, they are completely absorbed in the marble run game and barely acknowledge my entry. I make a brew and Facebook everyone with an update on my condition then I go into the kitchen to make lunch and chat with Matteo and Lauren. Lauren says her granddad is having chemotherapy and does not want anyone to see him. I hope he is ok! I make chicken goujons with pasta and garden peas which the kids really enjoy. Afterwards, I give the kids strawberry jelly and yoghurt and they both put their hands in it, spread it over themselves and the table, some of it even goes into their mouths. Two for the price of one, strawberry dessert and sensory experience rolled into one.

After a sing song including "Banging, banging" which is very noisy and popular with both of them, I change Jason's nappy and cover him in grease to ease his dry skin and I encourage and praise Odelia for using the toilet. Then I dress them in their warm coats and put them in the double buggy and walk to the pharmacy to see if they have any dry wipes. By the time I have reached the pharmacy they are both asleep so I walk to "Cut Above" the hairdressers and as the kids sleep peacefully, I have my eyebrows waxed and tinted. I have never in all my life taken so much care of my appearance. Maybe when I was younger, I didn't need to!

On the way back I knock on Joyce's door and ask if she needs any help for tonight. She has just come back from Asda and I can't believe how much food she has bought for this evening. "Joyce, How many are you catering for?" I ask, "I think about 10" she answers. She has a full carrier bag of biscuity nibbles, a gateaux, some hot and spicy chicken wings, barbecue chicken thighs, half a dozen jars of dips, jars of pickles, a tray of sandwiches, a tray of cream cakes, three tear and share garlic breads. Also a selection of wines and spirits. She apparently was planning to get a taxi to bring them the couple of hundred yards to my house. I say, I will go home and bring the car, then I ring my sister and a friend to say to come to my house this evening as there will be an abundance of food and drink available.

I do the school run - three schools with 15 minutes space in

143

between each one, it can be done, while Paolo makes tea. As I go through the gates of the last school, St Pauls primary, Isaac and Ashton run into the gap between a privet hedge and a wall. I know they are going to have a wee, (they don't know that I know). I shouldn't allow it really I suppose, but it is a bit of naughtiness that I turn a blind eye to and I am sure the privets are glad whenever we have a drought.

By the time I get home and the kids are eating their tea and trying to out-do each other with wishful tales, I see that I have 10 messages of encouragement in answer to the Facebook status I posted earlier. Including one from my cousin Claire in Canada, a friend in Tanzania and another one in America. I also have 26 "likes"

I tell the kids that I am going to have a party and I would like them all to keep the place a bit tidy, by putting the toys away after they have finished with them. Surprisingly as the last one leave at 6.30 pm I find I only need to hoover the living room and sweep the dining room floor. I think I will just have a quick wash and change out of my work clothes and I will be ready. It's never that straightforward is it? As I strip off my elastic belt, I see it is full of poo - lovely. Into the shower. My hair that had been lovely and straight this morning had been frizzed up in the rain anyway and it doesn't take that much longer to shower as it does for a good wash. I'm soon kitted out in a new stoma bag and party clothes. My hair will have to dry curly as it is by now 7.30 p.m. time for the party.

Paolo is talking loudly in french to his mum in Switzerland, (he always shouts on the phone) telling her the news of my hospital appointment, and I presume listening to her worries of the day. I shout bonjour, ca va to her then I ring Joyce to tell her I will come to pick her up, I know that the food she sent earlier was only the first wave. As I go through the door, Julie arrives with cards and presents for Joyce and Dot (both their birthdays on the 25th) and more wine. I tell her to make herself comfortable and I will be back in 2 minutes. Ladies arrive in quick succession. Jackie is dropped off by Steve who also takes Paolo back home with him. My sister arrives even though she had warned me she had had a bad day and was too tired and I stick a bit of stuff in the oven that

144

needs to be warmed up and connect my Ipad into the Bose so that we can Spotify the music (doesn't that make me sound clued up?). The night is a complete success with chats about husbands, weddings, divorces, kids. We insult each other (actually I was the only one doing this) as only really good friends can and laugh until we nearly split our sides and I begin to worry about hernias (that would put a delay on my next op). As the first friend tries to leave, she find that she is locked in. Adam had come home from work and automatically locked the front porch door, made himself a drink and gone to bed. How he didn't hear us in the front room baffles me. When Steve and Paolo return and help to eat some of the left over food, the rest of the girls start making tracks. Steve takes one home, my sister takes one and the rest walk and Paolo and I are once more left in peace in our lovely house, BLISS.

Saturday 25th January 2014. I wake up to find Paolo standing at the side of the bed and ask him "What's up" He says he can't remember if he paid the tax bill! Is this normal? I get up and empty my stoma and go down to make a drink and breakfast - I have priorities. An hour later we are both washed and dressed and fed, the bill has been paid and I am reading even more comments and "likes" on Facebook. I find that I am to be Sherlockupyourdaughters" as the character for Rachael's Murder mystery party next Saturday. I should go and buy an outfit.

My auntie Lily calls round for a visit as she has decided that she will not travel to see Josie without calling on me. I decide that I might be a little unfair with my image of her. Maybe I will take her at face value from now on. As we are chatting, the representative from Virgin Media phones to ask why I haven't paid my last bill. I explain to him that we have cancelled the direct debit until we get the reduced bill which takes into account the lack of services for four weeks (he says it was only for 19 days, I haven't made a record of the exact dates and I do know that I exaggerate but I still argued), in the end he reduces the bill by one month and I pay the balance with my credit card.

I think I will go and write a chapter in my book (this book) for half and hour, but the next time I look at the time it is 3.00 pm. We have had no dinner and I haven't been to look for an outfit. Where does the time go to? On Whatsap, I see pictures of Lily and Isaac at Legoland, (Rachael's treat to Lily for her birthday) and then pictures of Lily on her first horse riding lesson - lucky girl.

I haul myself away from the computer and put on my outdoor clothes just as Paolo returns from shopping. I had forgotten to mention to him that I had invited Rachael to come for Sunday dinner and was thinking of asking Helen and Robert to come. Bless him, he doesn't bat an eye lid, just tells me that "In that case we need more lamb". I go out to buy lamb and a Sherlock Holmes outfit and come back with the lamb and the deerstalker hat and pipe, but also a Birthday Cake, a jumper and shirt for Paolo, a jumper for me, a letter rack, a present for Lily (another one), and several other items I didn't know I needed until I saw them. What has happened to the woman who watched her pennies? I think she had a brain transplant along with the ileostomy.

I call to see Lily with the extra present, then to take Isaac the presents we have wrapped up for his mummy and the card I had forgotten to give him to sign. He takes them into his bedroom so that he can surprise Rachael tomorrow. I show Rachael the Sherlock Holmes accessories and she tells me she is going as a Laura Croft type character just wearing a shorts and tee shirt outfit. I am beginning to look forward to the evening. I text Paolo to tell him I am on the way home so that he can start to make the tea. We are supposed to be going to the cinema but the weather is freezing cold and it is raining sleety rain. I think I will suggest we give the pictures a rain check.

Paolo cooks inky spaghetti and prawns with a lovely salad and we eat it on our knees, watching Tom Daley in Splash. I light the wood fire and open a bottle of wine, a much cheaper and more pleasant alternative to an evening out at the cinema, the old "careful with money" Veronica is still there somewhere.

As we watch TV, Matteo and Lauren arrive home with a sound box. He asks me where the Dyson is, then I hear hoovering sounds coming from his bedroom. Is it normal for an 18 and 19 year old to clean the bedroom without being asked? I'm not complaining. Paolo and I settle down with cups of tea and Sudofed for blocked up noses and watch "The Perfect Storm". By the end we are grateful we haven't booked a cruise.

Sometimes Paolo gets on my nerves and I know that I must disappoint him occasionally but on evenings like this I count my blessings and know that we are perfect for each other.

Sunday 26th January 2014 - Rachael's 34th Birthday. I wake up after a blissful sleep not even been up to empty the bag. I first of all think "It is Rachael's birthday, I'll get the phone and send her a text" Then as I get up the stoma bag swings on my belly and I remember that I have had cancer. It's amazing what your brain can block out or forget. I'm getting very casual now about emptying the bag and am not really concentrating on the job in hand when I sit on the loo and start to wee. I nonchalantly flip open the velcro fastening on the bottom of the bag and it bursts open covering the whole of the toilet bowl and running down the outside onto the floor. It's my own fault, I do not take the loperamide pills as regularly as I should (they thicken the poo). I actually don't mind it being runny as it is easier to empty away. I wash the toilet and the splashes on the wall and get into the shower I will remember to take the pills today.

Paolo wakes up and asks if I am going to church. It's freezing cold outside, there are several jobs to do that I can do in my pyjamas, I think I will stay at home. I'm a fair weather church goer. I go down and make breakfast and bring the tray up. I like Sunday mornings like this. When I eventually rise from my bed the second time, I realise that I hadn't done such a thorough job of the bathroom so give it a good clean then put some washing into the washing machine. I read my emails and facebook and play a bit of sudoko on the computer then drive to Rachael's to give her a card and gift for her birthday (she is coming for dinner later, but I need the fresh air after all that smell).

Paolo is cooking lamb again, (we don't usually eat lamb so regularly, he must be feeling flush) so I peel and chop vegetables and set the table. I like this time of a weekend when there are no interruptions. I phone my auntie and tell her that dinner will be at 4.30 pm as Lily is having a birthday party from 2 - 4 and then they are all coming round here for dinner. We end off with eleven people around the table as my brother and his wife and daughter have been at Helen's for the birthday party and decide to tag along I settle the kids down in the living room with sticker books and lego (they are stuffed full of party food) and we have a delicious meal. It's occasions like this that I admit Paolo is correct when he cooks huge portions. We toast Rachael's birthday and I produce another shop bought cake and discuss what costumes we are going to wear next week at Rachael's murder mystery party.

Saturday 15th February After everyone leaves and we have stacked the dishwasher and cleaned up, we watch a bit of telly and then I decide that I am going to have an early night with a cup of tea and a book. I think I will pack my bag for the swimming pool so that I don't forget to take shampoo or towel or stoma bag. I become aware that the stoma bag is full, all that lovely food and wine, but I have taken the loperomide so it should be thicker. I sit right back on the loo and point the opening of the bag into the toilet - not making the same mistake twice. I don't know what happens but the bag once again explodes, this time with worse consequences. Thick black grunge covers the bath mats, the toilet, me and even through the radiator to the wall behind. First I try to mop it up with toilet paper, very ineffective. Then I pick up the mats and throw them into the shower and turn the shower on while I clean everything else. Surprisingly it doesn't take much effort to clean the bathroom, the walls and floor are covered in tiles. When everything is clean I get into the shower and clean myself. The mats are clean, why did I never think of washing them like this before, much more effective and quicker than the washing machine. I bring the maiden up and put it into the shower cubicle and let them drip dry. From start to finish it has taken less than 20 minutes.

I think this little episode should go in the book so I settle myself at the computer. I am just thinking about how to start when the phone rings and it is my cousin Colin from the Isle of Man. He tells me he has been following me on Facebook, but will not answer me on there in case he does something wrong - technophobe! As usual we chat about everything and nothing, mostly me giving him news of his remaining relatives and by the time he puts the phone down it is eleven o'clock. Not such an early night and I haven't even started my latest chapter.

148

I eventually get to bed after 12 but still read for another half an hour. I would expect to go straight to sleep, but no. I look at the clock at 2.00 a.m. and then regularly all night until at 6.00 a.m. I might as well get up and go swimming, even if I go to sleep now it will do me no good. When I go in the bathroom to clean my teeth, I see one disadvantage to washing the mats in the shower, they are still dripping wet! Good job I am not showering at home today. Adam is heading for the door as I get down stairs so I give him a lift to the bus stop in Walkden. When I eventually get into the pool, I notice that I am swimming just as fast as some people and faster than at least one other swimmer. My competitive streak kicks in and I find myself trying to catch up or overtake other swimmers and turn around quickly at each end instead of stopping to see if anyone is up for a chat. But somehow as I reach 30 lengths I look at the clock and I have taken 30 minutes, the same as always. It must have been the other swimmers swimming more slowly today. Never mind, I'm sure the extra effort must have done some good, I might treat myself to a hot buttered crumpet when I get home.

After doing the rounds of three schools (one of them twice because two girls were staying late at after school club) and sitting down to tea, the house becomes a bedlam. We have 9 kids tonight between the ages of 11 months and 9 years. I scoop the baby up because she crawls between legs without a care in the world and I dread one of the kids tripping over her or on to her. The two 9 year old girls go on the computer and three of the boys are playing a very boisterous game of "dogs??". In the middle of this mayhem Oliver comes crawling into the kitchen on his hands and knees but with his forehead brushing the floor in front of him"Oncika! What I am?" I say that I don't know "Are you a dog or a duck" no he says with derision "I'm a turtle, I've lost my shelf" I think he meant shell.

Tuesday 28th January I have a big glass jug with a glass screw on top. It used to belong to Paolo's mum and was one of the things that I happened to mention that I liked. I learned to be careful about this because on returning from Switzerland, we used to find all sorts of items in the cases that I didn't know had been packed. (Paolo's dad thought of himself as a professional packer and always insisted on doing it for us). Today as I poured Odelia some blackcurrant cordial, the top, which had apparently not been screwed down, crashed onto the tiled floor of the kitchen and smashed into a thousand pieces. I was gutted, the jug was over 50 years old (Paolo's mum said she had got it with milk shake when Paolo was a toddler). I hope this isn't a bad omen.

Yesterday the girls, Maddie and Alise (aged 10 and 9) Were telling me about their plans to sell jewelry in school to raise money for St Annes Hospice. I was only half listening when they asked me if I would drop them off at the shop to buy some rings and bracelets. After school I remembered to ask them how their new business was coming on. They had spent £3 and sold the stuff for £16.50. I gave up trying to explain that they needed to take their own £3 out of it before they counted their profits, but even so that was quite a success. They go back to the shop and spend £5 out of the profits and return after school on Thursday with £21. Budding entrepreneurs

Thursday 30th January. In the post is a letter from Bolton NHS. My heart misses a beat as I imagine that it is the date for the next operation.

Dear Mrs Scotton
I am pleased to say that your recent CEA blood test was entirely normal. Yours sincerely
Dictated not signed
J H Hobbiss MD FRCS
Consultant Colorectal and General Surgeon
Well thank you Mr Hobbiss for letting me know that.

Yesterday was Brea's Birthday, she is 2 years old. She doesn't come to our house on Wednesday so we are having a party tea tonight. The problem is that the kid's pick up times are staggered, how do you keep1 & 2 year olds away from the party table until all the school children have returned home. As I get home with the first batch of kids, Paolo is looking a little harassed. The baby has been sick, the older ones are mithering to go outside in the garden. I swap jobs, Paolo goes for the last school children and I take over the mayhem. I let the kids out in the garden, close the dining room door so that the kids can't get to the party food for a few more minutes and change Jason's nappy. I am just washing my hands

150

when the baby starts crying again, I pick her up just in time for her to projectile vomit all over me and my lovely black carpet. The joys of childminding!

After all the kids have gone, except Isaac as he is sleeping the night here, I give him some supper then shoo him upstairs to get ready for bed. I listen to him read and am quite impressed how quickly he has picked it up. I read his library book to him and he tells me whats going to happen on the next page. He asks me if he can watch a Disney Film on my iPad and I have just put in the pass word when I hear my cousin arriving. Linda lives in Muswell Hill in London but is visiting her mum and so nipped round to catch up with the Scotton news. Soon after, my sister Gail arrives and I almost forget that Isaac is in bed and not shouting downstairs for drinks etc as he usually does. It's only after Linda leaves at 10.30 pm that Paolo comes downstairs and tells me that Isaac is still awake and saying he is still hungry. I suppose it will be my own fault if I can't wake him up in the morning.

Friday 31st January, I am going to a pie and peas ladies evening with Lesley. Her sister is the minister at a local church and this is a fund raiser organised by a lovely lady called Eilene who is 82. The theme of the night is poems and prose so I "google" myself a poem. I didn't really have time to think about the evening until I was ready to go and then I thought, "What am I doing? Going to sit in a freezing cold church with a lot of old biddies, when I could be slobbing in front of the telly with a real fire and a bottle of wine"

The church is freezing as the man who normally turns the heating on, guards the working of the system like a national secret - and he has gone away. Lesley and Karen (the minister) find some instructions and turn the heating on, but this is a church and churches don't heat up quickly. And it is full of old biddies - actually some of them younger than me, and two or three men. But I enjoy the evening nonetheless, and surprise myself by getting up and reading my poem. The host for the evening Eilene reads a couple of her own poems and a "bit of writing" as she introduced it. It was hilarious and the church was filled with belly laughs. Then her husband also read a poem that he had written about their honeymoon 60 years ago. He said that although he wasn't an accomplished poet, he realised that this was the way to win Eilene's heart and his rhyme also had everyone laughing as he related the story of Eilene jumping on the bed and falling off the other side. In the interval over pie and peas and a glass of wine, a lady began telling me about her breast cancer and I was able to join in the conversation, comparing operations and treatments. Oh the joys of old age and illness.

Saturday 1st February 2014. Tonight Rachael is hosting her "murder mystery party". My character is SherlockUpyodaughters. I have bought a deerstalker hat and pipe from Boogy Knights and a gaudy waistcoat from St Anne's charity shop. But the hat is too small and keeps jumping off my head, I should have tried it on earlier. Oh well it will be something else to laugh at.

The evening is a laugh a minute, Rachael's friends are a scream. Rachael tells me that before he went to his dad's house, Isaac offered her some advice for her murder mystery party, when he suggested that we could push someone over the bannister at the top of the stairs. He didn't realise that we weren't actually going to murder someone.

When we arrive the table is full of nibbles and drinks and a bloody corpse is lying on the floor. The guests arrive , Arnie de Nironator, Bridget Bones, Buffy Spears Bunny Boiler, Dana Scullerella, Deadwood Cullen, Dr Evil Kernevil, Eli Cronenberg, Jack Blacksparrow, Jem Hunter, Marilyn Gungho and last but not least me as Sherlock Upyodaughters. At the beginning of the game everyone picks a card and keeps it a secret. This is when you find out if you are guilty or innocent. You are given an introductory speech to read and then a list of questions and answers. There are two lists of answers, one for if you are innocent and another list if you are guilty. After the first round Rachael disappears into the kitchen and brings out the first course. A lovely salad of potato, black pudding, apple and onion. Delicious! The game continues with each guest getting into character. Haley (Jack Blacksparrow) raises a laugh when she reads that she is a willy pirate instead of wily. The game becomes sillier as the drinks flow and at intervals Rachel serves us with another course of chicken and pasta with garlic bread and then a bit later homemade profiteroles. Well done Rach. The closing part of the game is when we all choose who we think is guilty and then each of us reads out our alibi or confession. The guilty party is supposed to wait until the last to read out the confession. The second one to read is Haley aka Jack Blacksparrow. Bearing in mind that she has picked me as the guilty party, she gets halfway down her confession and as she says "And I hit him over the head with the golden globe" stops reading open mouthed and says "Oh! it was me!" She had definitely lost the plot.

Soon after this I look at my watch and realise that it is gone midnight and Paolo is waiting for me to ring him to bring me home, he is also giving Helen and Gail a lift to their houses. Gail would have stayed all night as she has just retired and can sleep as long as she wishes on Sunday, but Helen is doing the children's liturgy at church and has not prepared anything. The rest of the young ones plug in the Xbox karaoke and prepare to make more noise for a few more hours. Happy Birthday Rachael, good party.

Two guests were missing from the party, Nichola gave birth to a baby in the early hours of that morning. Her babies always arrive quickly, I think we should be grateful that Sophia Louise didn't decide to arrive 7 hours later or that would have added another dimension completely to the party. And Laura didn't come because she has lost all feeling down one side of her body, she has "googled 'the symptoms while waiting for the results of hospital tests and is very worried and upset. She arrives early to help Rachael "set the scene" but doesn't want to join the party. I pray to God that she is OK, she is one of the most creative women I have had the pleasure to meet and she has three lovely children. She used to be Rachael's dancing partner before University interrupted, and would "whip up" two costumes in a couple of hours before a dance competition. At the time I was oblivious to the cost of bought costumes and I thank her in arrears for the money she must have saved me.

Sunday 2nd February I wake up with a sore throat. It has been coming on for a few days but I have been ignoring it. Good enough excuse for staying in bed a bit longer. I eventually get up but don't do much except stack the dishwasher after dinner and answer emails. After dinner I watch "Lewis" on the TV with Paolo, Gail and my auntie Josie. Josie seems to be asleep, until I ask Gail "Who was in the shower then" and Josie without opening her eyes says "another body"! Obviously just resting her eyes. By the evening my throat is worse, cold sores have broken out on my lips and each time I cough it feels like my stomach is going to burst. An early night is called for I think.

Monday 3rd February, Tahapenes does not come. Her mum says she has been ill all week-end with sickness and diarrhoea. I take Odelia, Jason and Lexia to the Sure Start Childminder's drop-in. Once again the organiser has left water out for the children to play in. The children love water-play but it is just not practical in these circumstances. At home I can cover the floor with towels and strip the kids off. Or cover them with rain coats waterproof trousers and wellies, but here the only protection they have is plastic aprons. The kids get soaking wet, the floor gets soaking wet, a toddler slips several times on the slippy floor. There are no facilities for drying clothes, good job I have come in the car.

Tuesday 4th February, after the school run and an inside picnic complete with picnic mat on the living room floor, We wrap up warm and go out for a walk in the windy weather. The baby falls asleep in the pram and Odelia and Jason splash in puddles. I talk about road safety, window cleaners, bin men, recycling etc etc, building up their vocabulary before they start reading. As I get home, Paolo is levelling sand out where he is going to lay a new path. I go inside, change nappies then start dinner. I think I will do fusillini with tomato soup. But the tin I think is soup turns out to be chopped tomatoes. As I am deciding what to do I become aware that I can't see Odelia. She is washing her hands. She is drenched from top to bottom, the water is actually dripping from the bottom of her dress. The mat is soaked, a full packet of nappies has fallen on the floor and they have soaked up some of the water. Odelia has put the plug in then just held her hands under the tap. It feels like I only took my eyes off her for a minute, How could she have caused this flood in such a short time. I strip her off and sit her on the bottom of the stairs naked, saying "Sit there on the naughty step" (I know, I am not supposed to use the N word). If there is anything that she loves more than water, it is being naked. She sits

154

swinging her legs singing B I N G O, B I N G O, B I N G O, HIS NAME IS BOBBY BINGO. I am obviously not scary enough. I carry the soaking wet clothes, towels and mats outside and hang them on the line, then mop up the remainder of the water. Then I smell the burning coming from the kitchen - shit, shit, shit. I think I have just sworn inside my head, until I hear Jason saying "shit, shit, shit" I don't think I will write this down on his words list. Oh well! it will have to be omelettes.

Wednesday 5th February. Nathan arrives with Bobby and Bailey and tells us they are still having problems with his step-daughters. I feel so angry with them. Nathan was not much older than they are now when he moved in with their mum and became their dad. He has supported them financially and emotionally ever since and now at a time when he should be in a position of a bit more financial security, he has become main carer for his grandsons. He is juggling his time between working, attending court with one or other of the girls and looking after his baby grandsons. On the one hand I am immensely proud of him. On the other hand I want to shout at him to stop running around after these two spoilt girls. Make them stand on their own two feet, make them face up to their responsibilities.

After the younger children go home, we pick up the school children and take them to Bolton for a Chinese buffet. It was so relaxing. Maddie was an old hand, having celebrated her 10th Birthday here in November, so she and Alise helped themselves. The younger ones enjoyed picking bits of food and trying it, (they didn't push the boat out eventually only eating chicken nuggets, chips and rice crackers) but they had tasted several other foods they would probably not have. Then of course there was desert, cakes, ice-cream, jelly, custard, popcorn. The staff were polite and helpful, the kids extremely well behaved (although very messy) and I ate far too much. By the time we got home all the parents were waiting to pick up the children, money well spent.

Its hours later when the pain begins. I've done a bit of housework, Paolo has gone to do his charity work (visiting an old lady with cancer) and I am sitting playing games on the computer. I think about the fraggolet beans and hope that the pain is not

155

going to get so bad again. I can't think of anything that I have eaten that should cause problems. I go to bed at about 11.30 pm and read a book then lie down to sleep, but the pain is gradually growing stronger. Paolo comes to bed and asks if I am OK and I answer that I will be fine, my usual reply, and he goes to sleep. I start to hear little pff pff sounds and I think, at last the food is pushing its way into the bag. But then I realise that it is Paolo, sometimes he snores and sometimes he makes these strange noises. For better or worse. By 2.00 am the pain is getting too much to bare, I go downstairs to the kitchen and make myself a cup of tea (cure all) and a crumpet. My reasoning being that the crumpet will push whatever it is along. I sit in the dark drinking and eating and listening to the rain and thinking how lucky I have been. Seeing this house for sale, winning the auction, having understanding workmen willing to wait for their money. The bowel screening, picking up the cancer and treating it before it caused me any trouble. Having such a lovely family and great friends, compared to so many people in this world, I am truly blessed. I begin to feel chilly and go back to bed and take two codeine. Paolo puts his hand on my belly and massages it gently, but it has no effect, I can't get comfortable and one of us has to get up before 7 am. Once more I get out of bed, I think I will just walk around a bit until the pain relief kicks in. As I swing my legs out of bed, a voice from under the blankets says "it was probably the plum". Of course, I had to push my luck. After eating all that authentic Chinese food, I had spotted the fruit bowel and eaten the plum - Why do I have to be so greedy? this pain serves me right. Five o'clock in the morning finds me sitting at the computer chatting on facebook to the rest of the insomniacs, but the pain has started to subside so I go back to bed and sleep soundly until the alarm wakes me at 7. I go to the loo and empty the bag, it is full but there is no tell-tale undigested food just a load of chocolate brown sludge - I know, too much information.

I am supposed to be meeting some childminder friends at the wacky warehouse but I don't think I could trust myself to drive. Paolo take the eldest children and leaves me with the baby. I go for a walk and she goes to sleep, so I get my head down on the sofa and have a power nap. At lunch time I make some pasta soup in time for Paolo returning with the kids. They are all hungry after all that climbing and running and jumping so they make short work of the soup and even ask for more. After changing nappies and supervising teeth cleaning, I think they will be ready for a sleep. No such luck! They are all still full of beans, so we play ring o roses and other action rhymes. In an attempt at "quiet time" I bring out the lentil box. It is full of green and red lentils and rice with containers of various sizes. This is a favourite pastime for all ages, but today they seem to have become hyperactive and are throwing it up in the air like confetti. I think it is probably just because I am tired that they seem hard work today. We put them all into various prams or sofa and tell them to go to sleep, all but the baby go. Miraculous. I put my feet and have a drink of coffee. I don't think I will have any trouble getting to sleep tonight. Only while I drink the coffee do I remember that we should have had a lady coming to see us about minding a little girl. I know the grandmother of the baby and make a note to call and see her to see if she has changed her mind.

After all the kids leave and the house is tidy once more, I phone my sister to see if she wants to go out. I really hope she doesn't, but I don't want to be the one to cry off again. She has seen my comments on Facebook and asks how I am. I tell her I am tired but didn't want her to think I was a wuss not going out again. She is fine about it so I think I will go to bed before something else interrupts me again.

Friday 7th February. I am awake early thanks to the early night last night. I think I will give swimming a miss and be the first up to give the early arrivers a welcome. Paolo usually does this while I am in the shower or swimming. I go for a shower by 6.30 a.m. plenty of time before the first arriver at 7.15. The trouble is that as I think I have plenty of time, I take my time. By the time I stroll into the bedroom to get dressed, Paolo has already been woken by the 7 a.m. alarm and brought me up a brew. Oh well, the thought was there.

Jason is the first to arrive with his dad who informs me that his wife is ill in bed with flu. He also tells me that Jason has a bit of a fever and gives me written permission to administer Calpol if

157

needed later.

The day trickles along as usual with the school run etc, Nathan phones to ask if we will have Bobby and Bailey for a couple of hours while he goes to a meeting with Shauna's social worker. He brings them at about 10 .m and we stand chatting for a little while then I play with the kids while Paolo prepares a snack. As the kids tuck into tea and toast and kiwi fruit and grapes, Jason suddenly does a back flip off the stool and begins to fit. At first I worry that he has choked on something and trip to see into his mouth, then I think, he can't have choked, I was standing right next to him, I wouldn't have missed that. I tell Paolo to ring 999 and I phone his mum and tell her that Jason is having a fit and to get here quickly. The emergency operator asks me questions about Jason and I ask her what I should do. She tells me to lie him on his side and not to leave him unattended. I take his jumper off him as my reaction to the fit is that he must be too warm. The paramedics arrive promptly and test Jason for oxygen absorption, blood sugar and temperature. They say he has a high temperature and to take all his clothes off immediately. At this point his parents arrive and the paramedics move them all into the ambulance where they have more equipment at hand.

Paolo by this time has taken the other children into the play room and they are oblivious to the crisis. If they hadn't been there we would probably both have gone to pieces at this point or at least hit the brandy bottle, instead we have a cup of tea and sit on the floor with the children and the building bricks. I send a text later to see how Jason is, his mum says that he has been asleep but is just waking up, the hospital doctors want him to stay for another couple of hours to monitor him. He goes home later in the afternoon and his mum thanks us for looking after him and I record the episode in the accident/incident book as if it is a normal day. I think I might have nightmares tonight. The next episode to this story is that after Jason leaves the hospital and goes home, he has another fit and is taken back to the hospital where further investigation reveals that he has tonsillitis.

In the evening Adam arrives home and tells us that he has a stomach bug. He had been out the night before and had a Chinese buffet. (Not the same one that we went to). He had roughly calculated the food he was going to eat and injected his insulin, then decided to have a bit more, as you do at an "eat all you want" buffet and so injected a bit more insulin and then when temptation in the form of Chinese deserts had appeared, a bit more. Later in the evening he started vomiting and worried about how much insulin was in his blood and how much food was now not in his stomach. Not wanting to take any chances of the "falling off the bus incident," he sat in a friend's house sipping lucozade and testing his blood sugars. And I, wonderful mother that I am, had not even noticed he hadn't come home. I tell him not to lock his bedroom door and to let me know immediately if he starts to be sick again and to continue to check his blood sugars until they are OK. There's never a dull moment in this house, I should write a book!!

On Saturday, I go the hairdressers to see if she can style my hair in a curly style as a trial run for our photograph shoot in two weeks. Emma, the hairdresser comments "Oh your going to mind Tilly aren't you" At first I don't recognise the name until she says "Its Brea's cousin" and I remember it as the lady that should have been calling on Thursday. I tell Emma, that she hadn't turned up and she tells me that they had rushed the baby to the hospital on Thursday as she had stopped breathing several times. I was concerned for the baby and sympathetic to the poor mum, but I must admit that my reaction was that I was glad she hadn't held her breath at my house, two ambulances at my door in two days would be enough to make me paranoid.

Patrick comes for a flying visit in the afternoon after visiting his grandmother who has been a cause for concern for over a year. In her late eighties, she is suffering from dementia and her memory seems to be deteriorating rapidly. But when Pat arrives he tells us that she is much better. Apparently she had been taking two sleeping tablets each night for over two years. Her doctor had paid her a home visit unannounced (didn't think doctors cared so much nowadays) and told her she must stop taking them. Practically overnight she has become much more coherent and her grandson was much happier going home than he had been before he had seen her.

We go for a curry night with our friends tonight and Linda, our hostess and cook admits that she had mistaken ounces for grams and has made a curry that would blow your socks off. After she realised her mistake she had made another one, but we all had to taste the mega hot curry. Well it certainly sorted out my sinuses.

Monday 10th February, I get up to go swimming. The car is completely iced over, I nearly change my mind. The pool has been divided into lanes, apparently some fast swimmers have been complaining about having to swim around other people. As I haven't been since last Monday, I have missed all the fun. There are three lanes, slow, medium and fast. On the first day the people who normally swim in the far lane were asked to move to the other side, into the slow lane. They refused because that side is colder (What???). So the marker boards were changed over. Then people ignored the instructions to swim in a clockwise direction within the lanes because they like to swim alongside each other and chat. The problem is that a lot of the people who do the early morning swim are pensioners and this is a social occasion. The pass is very cheap, it keeps them healthy in mind and body and gives them a reason to get up in the morning.

The ones that want to swim fast, do exactly that. Lengths and lengths of front crawl, or sometimes with the use of a float using legs only, or arms only, I have never seen any of them having a problem as each person tries to swim in a straight line up and down and definitely keep away from the "professionals". But they are in the minority, most of the people who go there would be classed as slow swimmers, so this system means that the few fast swimmers would have a lane to themselves and the stalwarts would be crammed into one lane. Anyway by the time I got there today, The three lanes were still in place, but everyone was swimming up and down (not in clockwise directions) in whichever lane had the fewest swimmers. By the time I had had this story related to me, I had lost track of how many lengths I had swum, so I just carried on for 30 minutes then came home.

Rachael came in to pick up Isaac to tell me that the lady over the road had asked her to move her car up a bit, "as that was where she parks" The space is right outside my front gate and opposite

160

her house. The ironic thing is that whenever I, or any of out guests park there she complains that she cannot get out of her drive, but at the moment because she is having work done, she has a skip on her drive. It has never bothered me, but several of my "parents" have commented that she is taking the P***. Anyway, this evening, Rachael, answered that of course she will move her car, but would it be noted that this was a kind act and would it be reciprocated by not being scowled at each evening. The lady over the road said, it has got nothing to do with you if I want to scowl. Rachael tried again, she said, "I am a nice person, I would not purposely park anywhere that caused you inconvenience, so when I smile at you, it would be nice if you didn't pull your face at me" to which the lady said, "Well I don't think you are being nice now". So Rachael said, "Oh well then, I wont move my car, good evening" My children have been brought up to be polite, but there is a limit. Later still, we go in Wetherspoons. Gail, Helen, Rachael and me. The story of the altercation with my neighbour is related and the rest of the world put to rights, we should do this more often.

Tuesday 11th February, Paolo has a hospital appointment in Manchester at 3.00 pm. The appointment cannot be changed for an earlier one so I need to get myself organised so that I can pick up all the children from school, look after the younger ones and make tea. Jason is brought by his dad in the morning because his mum is still off work so I ask if it's OK for me to drop him off at home at 3 o'clock and I will make up the time at a later date. His dad says that will be fine. Odelia usually goes home at 2.55 as her dad picks her up on his way to pick up her sister. I have three babies in car seats and Odelia dressed in her outside clothes ready for 2.55. Her dad doesn't arrive, so I phone him and it goes to the answer machine. I reshuffle the kids and fasten Odelia into the car. I am just driving out of the drive, already late when her dad pulls up. He had decided to get the sister first. I set off once more but when I knock on the door to drop Jason off there is no answer. I am panicking now. I am sure the mum is in. In desperation I ring her mobile and tell her I am outside her door. She strolls to open it and apologises for not hearing me banging very loudly on her door. I can still get to Isaac's school on time, but I have to find somewhere to park and then unfold the trolley, unfasten the other two babies

161

from the car seats and fasten them into the buggy, then run around to the back of the school where Isaac's classroom is located. I am only a couple of minutes later than usual, but because of this, I am now at the back of the queue, filing slowly to pick up each child. I shuffle along, apologising for the buggy, then the teacher calls "Isaac, your Nanna is here". Isaac strolls out, handing me his back-pack of spare clothes, which he insists on bringing home each evening, his lunch box and his reading folder, saying, "Just hold these Nanna, I am going for a wee." Aaagh!!

Eventually, we emerge from Isaac's school, pack everyone back into the car, fold up the trolley and set off for the next school, where I repeat the fastening, folding, lifting and shifting. I am not late for Keith, and I have time to chat for a couple of minutes with Robert, who is picking Lily and Jamie up. Lily wants to come home with me, but I can't fit her into the car and pick up the next lot of kids. I promise her she can come for three "sleeps" the following week, during the school break. The last school I pick up from is usually the first. They finish normally at 3.00 pm, Isaac at 3.15 pm, and Keith (on some days Millie, Oliver, Lily and Jamie) at 3.30 pm. But today, Ashton, Alise and Maddie have after school clubs, so their finishing time is 4.00. I was hoping that Paolo would be home in time for this one. I fasten everyone back into the car and phone Paolo. He answers that he is still at the hospital and there is a backlog of an hour. There's no point in going home, I go to the last school and collect the children ten minutes early and go home to make tea.

Paolo has made some bolognese sauce so I just need to boil some pasta. I put the pan of water on the stove and then change the baby's nappy. I warm her bottle and feed her while the pasta is cooking. The boys sit quietly watching TV and the girls go to the shop. I put the baby down to play but she starts screaming to be picked up again. I can't carry her and make tea so I fasten her into a trolley where she can see me and ignore her cries. Her mum arrives early and asks what she is crying for. A few years ago, I would have been embarrassed in this situation, but now I have more confidence in myself. I tell the mum that, her child has been fed and changed and that she is crying to be picked up, but it would be dangerous for me to do so. The mum accepts the explanation, and stands chatting while I liquidise some spaghetti bolognese for her baby. Lexia aged two wants me to pick her up, but I sit her at the breakfast bar, close enough to watch me cook, but far enough away to be safe. The baby's mum remarks how quiet it is with 7 children in the house (now that her child has stopped screaming), and I tell her not to speak too soon, its not usually so calm.

As we all sit down to eat, the blue sky suddenly darkens and it begins to snow. That snow that comes down fast like rain, and soon everything is covered in a thin layer of white. The boys can't wait to go out in it, so teas are eaten quickly and without complaint. The baby and her mum go home. By the time that Paolo arrives, expecting chaos, the table is cleared and he sits down in peace to eat his tea. What a wonderful wife I am!

Wednesday 12th February, I don't wake up until the alarm at 7.00 a.m. Paolo gets up and goes down to greet the first arrival. I know he will bring me a drink of tea so I think I will just read a chapter of my book (The Storyteller by Jodi Picoult) The next thing I know it is 8.15. I have a quick wash and get dressed, I had promised Millie and Keith that they could go to school on their scooters and so we need to leave by half eight. The walk to school makes up for not going swimming and uses different muscles as I push Jason in the trolley. On the way back I see my "nearly" auntie Elsie through her window and wave to her. She waves back and so I go and have a cup of coffee with her. She is amazing, at 82 (or thereabouts) she still has the energy to help her daughter-in- law with babysitting and is getting excited about visiting her son who is living on the 67th floor in an apartment block in New York. By the time I return home, four more children have arrived including Bobby and Bailey. I do some more exercise by dancing to a children's CD then rest on the floor by playing Sleeping Bunnies. We have crumpets and tea for snack keeping a very wary eye on Jason who seems to be his usual energetic healthy self and then I bring out all the glue and coloured paper and bits of confetti and wool etc for the kids to create their own works of art. The good thing about working as a team with Paolo is that when the kids get bored with one project, (two year olds don't have a very long attention span, however interesting the task) I just wash their hands

163

and move into another room while Paolo cleans up all the mess. This time it backfires on me because he gets involved with sharpening pencils, throwing away dried up felt tips and separating scissors into the correct tray and when dinner time comes around, he has not given a thought to dinner. It doesn't matter, the snack time was a bit late because of my chat to Elsie, the kids can hang on a bit until I make something. I peel a few vegetables and put them in a pan to boil, then slice some ham left over from Sunday dinner. The kids climb onto the stools and eat the ham quicker than I can slice it (maybe they are hungry after all) and talk. I suddenly realise that I am having conversations with these kids who are not yet two, when did they start putting words together like this? I need to start doing their trackers. I manage to save a bit of the ham and put it into the pan with the veg and wizz it up with the food processor and guess what? Its delicious (or bloody lovely as my mam would say) The kids practically lick their bowls clean - you see sometimes I can cook just as well as you Paolo Scotton! I reward the kids for the clean bowls with ice lollies, then we have a sing song while they are all sitting still at the table. The next task is nappy changing and teeth cleaning then quiet time. I spread blankets on the settee and chair and the children lie on them and watch TV. I don't expect the eldest two to go to sleep (they are nearly three and four) but I tell them to lie quietly. In ten minutes a miracle has happened, three out of the five have gone to sleep. I take Alfie and Bailey into the play room and they decide to go outside. They are not outside more than 5 minutes when Bailey has found a huge puddle of mud to fall into and by the time that he has rolled over to get into a position to stand up, the mud is on the back and front of his coat and trousers and shoes. I do have wellies and waterproofs, why did I forget to dress him properly before he went out. The good thing about childminding is that I just put the dirty clothes into a carrier bag and send them home, I don't have to worry about washing them. I sit on the floor with the duplo and try to do some colour recognition with Alfie, his inability to match two colours together is worrying me and I make a note to get some help with this.

School pick-up time comes around quickly and the wind is getting up. After picking up Ashton at one school and Isaac at another we arrive at St Paul's to collect Keith and Millie. Ashton wants to take his coat off. I say "Are you mad? it's freezing!. Then I suggest that he holds onto the bottom of his unfastened coat to make wings. His face lights up in excitement. He grabs hold of the hem of his coat and says "Do you dare me". Bless, he really thinks he will be able to fly. The boys run around the playground perfecting take off techniques, Millie comes out about 10 minutes later with her coat buttoned up and hat gloves and scarf protecting her from the February weather. She is loaded up with lunch box, flute, reading folder. She says "sorry I'm late, I kept forgetting things" I say don't worry Millie, the boys are learning to fly" even at this age, men are from Venus and women from Mars (or visa versa).

The wind picks up and Rachael comes to pick Isaac up and says that next door to her, the trampoline has blown over a 6 foot fence. She advises Paolo to check the weather conditions before he goes to see Norma (the lady he visits each week from CALL). Even though it is only about 4 miles away, he realises that most of the roads are either closed or traffic is crawling along. He phones her up instead and has a chat on the phone, promising to visit her tomorrow.

27 - Good Samaritan

At about 9 o'clock I hear Matteo come in. I go to see him and comment "Are you mad? What do you think you are doing driving from Sheffield in this? You should have waited until the weather and road conditions improve. Then I see that he is visibly shaken up. He had been in a training session all day and so hadn't seen the weather and given a girl a lift home then just set off, heading toward the motorway. This is actually the longest way, but usually the least problematic at rush hour. It wasn't until he had been driving for half an hour that he realised that everything was white and traffic was slow. Suddenly, the Sat Nav on his phone changed his destination time to 11.00 pm and asked if he wanted an alternative route. He just clicked "yes" and was directed on the scariest route of his life. The route took him to the top of the pennines, the road was icy with a sheer drop at each side. The traffic was nose to tail and visibility only a few yards. He began to tremble as if he was going to faint and he worried that he was going to cause an accident. He reached into his pocket to find some sweets to bring his blood sugar up and then the traffic came to a standstill. Someone else had had an accident up in front of him. The only thing to do was to turn around and go back the way he had come. He began to do a three point turn, which turned into a five point turn with the restrictions of the width of the road and the traffic. By this point he was terrified, there was no signal on his phone and he hadn't a clue how to get home. As he was turning round, the man in the car behind him wound his window down and asked him if he was OK. Matteo answered that he wasn't and signalled him to go in front of him. The man waved him to follow him and drove very slowly back the way they had come. Matteo put his trust in this samaritan and followed him through tiny villages that nestled within the Pennines, at each turning the man waved him to follow. After an hour the signal returned to his phone and it was saying he was 30 minutes from home, then 20, then he began to recognise his surroundings and thanks to this very kind man arrived home safely. Thank you stranger whoever you are.

Friday 14th February Valentines Day. After going to bed fairly early with a book, I awake and lie there wondering what has woken me. I can't see the time on the clock so I get up and go to the loo and have a drink of water. It is 4.32 and I am wide awake, I consider going to make myself a drink, but then decide to try to go back to sleep. I doze until nearly 6.00 and get up. I might as well go swimming if I am not going back to sleep. After I am ready I remember that Adam has told me he is on work early today and wonder why he is not up. I tap on his door with trepidation "What if he has gone hypo during the night? I should have checked on him when I woke" He is not hypo, just stealing a few more minutes in bed.

When I get to the pool, it is packed, Who are all these mad people getting up so early? I lose count of the lengths after about 5, so just swim for 40 minutes then get out. It is not until after the school run that I catch a glimpse of myself in the hall mirror. I look like a scarecrow. My hair has always been quite greasy and for the last 40 years needed washing every day. But last week I used a new shampoo and conditioner called Argon Oil. I also put a colour on. I don't know the cause, either the shampoo, the colour, or the accumulated effects of the chlorine in the water, or maybe even the effects of the radio therapy or operation, but my hair is dry and standing up like a halo around my head. Only eight days until the family photo and my hair decides to misbehave. We only have three small children today so Paolo offers to take them out while I try to do something with it. I go to the hairdressers where Emma and Mary very cruelly laugh at the vision when I take my hat off. I ask Emma to give me a trim to see if that makes a difference. She washes my hair gently then thickens it with conditioner and leaves it to soak in for 10 minutes before she trims and dries it. It is marginally better than when I came in, but not fabulous. To cheer myself up I have a run into Swinton to Matalan to see if I can buy myself an outfit for the photo shoot.

At three o'clock I get drenched and so do the kids as I pick them up from school, they strip off their wet clothes (except Isaac, who as usual has to be different and says only his hair is wet) We have tea (I only have a very small portion because Paolo is going to cook for us later) then clear the table and get out the glue and glitter to make Valentines Day cards.

After all the kids leave, Paolo cooks a lovely meal of Vietnamese river cobbler with white wine and pepper sauce, pilau rice with asparagus, fennel and pear salad. And for dessert strawberries in red wine. And to think, before I met him, I thought I was being adventurous eating spaghetti bolognese. He's brought me wine and flowers. I give him a card and a kiss. His reward is my happiness. I used to complain that my ex- husband never bought me anything, and I am going down the same route.

On Saturday my hair is still very dry. After my shower I apply conditioner again, I am not going out, I can tidy and clean with my hair resembling a greasy haystack. I clean the bathroom and shower room and spray air freshener everywhere. The smell of the bathroom after I have emptied a stoma bag is awful and I am getting a bit paranoid that the smell is lingering. Paolo has gone shopping, Adam is working and Matteo has returned to Sheffield. I put Beautiful South on the iPad and enjoy the music while I load the washing machine and dishwasher. As I potter about, I notice how grubby the floor is under the dining table, then when I look more closely the table top and chairs are not particularly clean either. I always wipe down the table and chairs after tea and sweep under the table and I thought I had done a reasonable job. In the cold light of day I see I haven't done a great job. There are traces of glue and glitter still clinging to the table and chairs and the floor needs a good mop. I have a steam mop that I don't use often enough. I fill the reservoir in the mop with water but it just runs out again. I dismantle the whole thing and find that the container inside has been broken. How could that have happened. I could understand it if a bit of the outside had been broken. I get out the old fashioned mop and bucket and by the time Paolo brings the shopping home the house has been cleaned from top to bottom, the dishwasher has been emptied and dishes put away, clothes are hanging from the rack and clothes maiden and the chickens have been fed and are enjoying the run of the garden. It's surprising how much can be done in a morning with no distractions. Paolo has bought a hot cooked chicken and fresh bread so we sit down to enjoy it then I set the table for 10 as we have invited our friends round for dinner tonight. Later Paolo cooks spicy meatballs in pasta and chicken and mushroom risotto and lovely tomato salad.

We have a pleasant evening with our friends, a couple of whom have not seen the house before, so I enjoy showing them round my "mansion" and relating the story of how we bought it and renovated it. They all leave before midnight and I go to bed relaxed and happy telling Paolo that I will get up early in the morning to clean up the mess. Sunday, I wake up with that lovely Sunday morning feeling and lie there without opening my eyes. I think that I will wait until the alarm goes off at 7 a.m. Then I hear a cup being placed on the bedside cabinet and open my eyes to see Paolo. He had been down and brewed a drink. I look at the clock and it is 9.00 a.m. I can't believe that I didn't hear the alarm. I get up eventually and begin to tidy and stack the dishwasher but I am still in my pyjamas when Robert brings Lily and Jamie with their overnight bags and Xbox and Huddle. Robert and Helen are going to Paris for a three day break and Lily and Jamie are staying with us. They both start talking as soon as they are through the door so I am glad of the excuse of going to have a shower and getting dressed to give my ears a rest. We bake cakes in the morning and then make a replica passport for Lily so that she can play going abroad with the dolls and Lily also decorates a kitchen roll with glue and glitter. The dining table once more is sparkling. She tells me that her daddy is going to take pictures of the Eiffel Tower and her mummy is going to bring some Chinese?? food home. In the evening Jamie, Lily and I sit in bed eating crumpets, drinking tea and watching the Tooth Fairy on DVD. There are bonuses to babysitting.

Wednesday 19th February. After two days of school holidays looking after 10 children including 5 under threes, today seems like a stroll in the park with only 5 kids. Two 5 year olds, two 6 and one 10. I make the most of it by taking them to the cinema to watch the Lego Movie then on to Frankie and Benny's. Before we go, I ask Lily and Jamie if they have any homework they are supposed to be doing before their mum and dad come back from Paris. Jamie has some maths that I have to read out the question and then he has five seconds to give me the answer. I am blown away by his skill. The last time I tried to do some number work with him (probably years ago - time flies) he was really struggling. Schools take a lot of knocking but St Pauls Primary, with a lot of

169

support from parents are doing a cracking job. Lily has some number work, then she has to write the story of Jack and the Beanstork in her own words. Ever the drama queen, Lily sighs and puts her head down "I have heard two Stories about Jack and the beanstalk, one with a giant in, and one with a giant and his wife in, I can't decide which one to do" I tell her to do whichever one is the the shortest or I will have to leave her at home while we go to the cinema. She tries again, "But I don't know how it starts!". Isaac for ever the helpful cousin says "Once Upon a Time of course, thats how all fairy tales begin" I help her by writing a selection of key words to prompt her and so that she doesn't have to struggle with spelling then I leave her to it while I try to change my Tesco points into cinema tickets. When I return, I am once more impressed with her writing and story writing skills. Eventually we set out for the cinema, Jamie says "I think I know the way, but I wont tell you or I might get us lost" and I reply "Yes Jamie, I don't need any help getting lost do I?" Even my grandchildren know my poor sense of direction, I'm glad they don't seems to have inherited that from me.

Thursday 20th February, we have five children aged between 1 and 6. We go to the park in Swinton and unbelievably the weather is so mild that the kids take off their coats. They run and play in the fresh air giving me hope that they will have a nap in the afternoon. After lunch, Paolo takes the 5 and 6 year old to see the dinosaurs at Bolton Museum and I think I will get the three youngest down for a nap. Unfortunately they don't cooperate, they are still full of beans, (where do they get their energy? I am definitely getting old!) and I am exhausted by the time the last one leaves at 6.00 pm.

Friday 21st February We have 5 children again, but not all the same children. I ask them if they have any preferences of where to go. Isaac answers that he doesn't want to go anywhere, but he wants to eat gnocchi in the living room. I say, its OK to stay at home but dinner will be eaten in the dining room. The day turns out to be fine. New playdough in bright luminous colours keep them all occupied for half the morning, followed by games with the model animals, hide and seek and hide the dolly are played with the minimal arguments. A bit of quiet time watching TV but once again no naps. With gnocchi and hotdogs for dinner and beans and egg on toast for tea, I think this has been the cheapest day of the holidays. In the afternoon the solicitor rings to say that the sale of the house to Rachael has gone through and our mortgage has been paid and the rest of the money is in the bank woopee!!!

A few years ago, Rachael had tried to buy a house, but because of circumstances completely out of her control, was unable to get a mortgage. We got an interest only mortgage and she has been paying the money into our bank to pay for it. Now she has the mortgage and house in her own name. I am so proud of her. Single parents are often lumped together and get a bad press, but many of them are like Rachael, hard working members of society who are put into a situation that they would never have chosen and get on with it without complaint. My brain is finally getting back to normal (my normal, not normal normal) I have just completed a sudoku puzzle in 11.54 minutes which is apparently faster than 23% of all the other people not using autopencil or hints.

Saturday 22nd February The photoshoot day has arrived. Must be excited, or nervous, I keep needing a wee. I am up and showered and at the hairdressers for 8.30, leaving Paolo with instructions to get a new headlight for the Toyota. (Just realised that is why I have been having trouble seeing when I am driving in the dark). Joe and Ciara arrive by 9.30, Nathan drops by just after to borrow the people carrier and stays for a cup of tea, of course then I need to use the loo again. Rachael has told Matteo she will pick him up by 10. She has not arrived by 10.15 so I ring her, she says she will be another 5 minutes. Matteo says he thinks he will take Lauren in his own car, but I persuade him to wait for Rachael in case she needs someone to navigate. As it happens, it is a good job as when we arrive at Bernards Farm Cottage for the shoot, there are not enough parking spaces for the 4 cars, another one would have had to park miles away. When we get there, Patrick has already arrived and he comes out of the cottage to meet us. I had followed a man into his back garden and knocked on the door and was asked to go round to the front. It is a bit cold so I say to everyone, lets go inside and I go into the door that I think Pat has just come out of. Just as I sit down on the settee in the tiny lounge, leaving the door open for everyone to follow me, a van drives down the narrow lane and asks "Is this number two" There is no number on the door so I shout upstairs (where I think the photographer must be) "Hello Gill, is this number two?" a young girl dressed in a nurses uniform comes down and says, I don't think so I will just ask. I realise that I am in the wrong house, Bernard Cottage and not Bernard Farm Cottage next door. When eventually I scuttle out of the wrong house and into the correct one and tell Gillian of my mistake, she laughs and says she knows the lady next door. She is a lovely lady but she has dementia and will have forgotten about it already. The cottage is quite small so the photos have to be shot in smaller groups and then slotted together and the ground outside is very boggy so not enough opportunity for all the outdoor shots we expected. Isaac is being argumentative and refuses to sit where he is asked to sit, or smile for the camera. Rachael threatens him and cajoles him but for the most part he only joins in on his own terms. Patrick finds it difficult to smile on demand and has to settle for his mean and moody look and Rachael practices smiling in the mirror as she doesn't realise how beautiful she is and worries the photos wont show her "good side". The proof will be in the quality of the photos when they are printed Only disappointment was that Josh and Michelle could not come. Michelle could not get time off from her job in the police and Josh was not well on the day. After the shoot, we follow one another down the road to the Printers Arms Pub/Restaurant which Gill has recommended. The food is lovely and I have brought a birthday cake to celebrate Joe's and Lauren's birthdays. Helen gets a phone call to say that she has got a promotion (she had been for an interview the day before) and we raise a toast to Rachael to celebrate her getting a mortgage. Jamie, Lily and Isaac discover that they like bread dipped in balsamic vinegar and olive oil, and strike up a rapport with the waiter and order their own desserts. Afterwards, only Joe and Ciara come back to the house and watch the England v Ireland Rugby match on TV. Ciara is Irish so there is a clash of support in our living room. Nathan drops in to return the car and we have a bit of a chat about Josh, who is Nathan's son but who lives with his mum. I tell him I am disappointed that he didn't come for the photo, but he is 17 and Nathan says he is going through a "teenage period". I can't get him on his mobile to ask how he is but make up my mind to go and see him tomorrow. When Joe and Ciara leave to watch a friend in a gig at a local pub, it is quiet, a bit of an anticlimax after the busy day. Paolo and I end off falling asleep watching Vera on the TV and then afterwards I lie awake in bed in the early hours. It doesn't matter, it is nice to lie awake sometimes and think about the lovely day we have had. It is Sunday tomorrow so I can sleep in if necessary.

Tuesday 25th February - I have an appointment with the optician at 10. I think my reading glasses are not quite strong enough as I seem to be finding it more difficult to read instructions on the side of medicine bottles. I haven't had an eye test for about 3 years or more, but I don't really think I have a problem. After the usual questions i.e. do I drive, do I use a computer, how far away do I hold a book to read etc and resting my chin on a chin rest of a machine that looks into my eyes, we eventually get to the actual eye sight test. I am quite confident about this, my short-sightedness has just got a bit worse, but I can see into the distance as well as ever. The lovely handsome optician asks me to cover my left eye and read the letters projected on the wall and I trot them off smugly (well a bit of a squint at the bottom line) Then he asks me to cover the right eye and to once again read the letters on the wall. I can't even read the top line, I am blind!! He magnifies the letters until I can read them, then read them again with both eyes. The rest of the test goes past in a blur, I can't believe that my left eye has deteriorated so much. He asks me if I wear my glasses for distance vision and I tell him that I don't need them. He says that my eyes are still within the legal limit for driving but that they will go worse without the glasses especially night vision. I then remember that I have been having problems driving in the dark (I had been blaming the headlights on the car). More symptoms of advancing age, not a happy thought.

28 - Chinese Food

Wednesday 26th February - I walk to school carrying bags, flute and reading folders for Millie and Keith while they ride the scooters. It is a lovely mild day, or so it seems, it might just be that I was very warm due to the weight bearing exercise and brisk walking. Anyway when I get back, I suggest that we take the kids to Moses Gate Country Park. The first thing I notice is that the clouds are black and it isn't as warm as I had thought, but the kids don't seem to mind as they run and swing and slide. The visitors centre, which is a listed building has closed down, which means we cant use the lovely warm toilets and have to find the freezing cold, metal, smelly ones, and all the park rangers have been made redundant due to the tax cuts, what a shame. Time flies while you are having fun, and we soon realise that it is 12 midday and we haven't thought of anything for dinner. Since we are already in Bolton, we might as well eat at the Chinese Buffet that we discovered a couple of weeks ago, and which doesn't charge for under three year olds. We have two, one-years olds, a two year old and a four year old, so we only have to pay for one of the children. I just give the kids a selection of food that I think they will try, then Paolo and I have quite a civilised meal, with starter, main and dessert and I come away absolutely bloated. (Didn't eat a plum this time though). While I am enjoying my rice pudding dessert, I notice that I have missed several calls from Nathan so I ring him back. He has some forms to fill in for the fostering course he is undertaking and needs me to fill in aspects of his childhood and information about his dad and me. As I chat to him, Bailey, having eaten his fill, decides to slide off the chair and sit on the floor under the table, a habit I am trying to get him out of before he gets much older. As I finish my conversation with Nathan, Paolo asks "Where's Bailey?" I reply "He is here under the table", but he isn't, I look around and can't see him, then begin to panic. I run into the toilet and and near to the hot serving dishes but don't find him. I make my way back to Paolo who is supervising the other children and just as I think I am going to start screaming out his name, I spot Bailey, sitting like a little budda under his chair, very quietly enjoying watching me running around looking for him. After the school run, I still feel bloated so I don't eat with the kids, I think I will get myself a butty later while watching TV. Just before the last parent arrives to collect their children, Patrick and Michelle drop by. They had driven to Manchester to visit Pat's grandma and so came to see his dad and me. I go to make them a brew, but Pat says "I will do it, you sit down, you have been working all day", then the door bell rings and I answer it to my sister. I say "you've arrived just in time, Pat's brewing tea." She looks at me and says "You have forgotten again haven't you - we are at the W.I.T.S tonight" (Worsley Intimate Theatre) Arrgh I had told her that I would go to watch an Amateur Dramatic version of Educating Rita and it had completely slipped my mind. While Gail chats to Pat, Michelle and Paolo, I quickly change my clothes into something not covered in sticky finger prints and sweet and sour sauce, comb my hair (doesn't look any different) and put on some lipstick. I shove a spare emergency stoma bag and baby wipes in a bag along with my purse and glasses, apologise to our guests and we are on our way in less than 10 minutes. As usual the performance is hysterical, with Simon and Esme starring as Frank and Rita and the lighting man scaring the life out of me by accidentally shining a light onto his own face as he sat in the dark and doing a good imitation of a ghost in the rafters. It startled me so much, I nearly spilt my lager shandy. We are back home by eleven o'clock, drinking even more tea and falling asleep while watching rubbish TV. Another fun packed day.

Thursday 27th February. I wake up feeling lousy at 5.00 with a full-to-bursting stoma bag. When I empty it, it is like orange water. I take a Loperamide and go back to bed. Twenty minutes later the bag is full of liquid again - another trip to the toilet! Where is it all coming from? I haven't had a drink since last night. Just before 7, Paolo gets up, he says he as been getting up to the toilet all night and he feels rotten. He gets dressed anyway and goes down to greet the early arrivals, Millie, Jason and Tahapenes. I take my time having a shower. My usual routine after showering is to stand with the stoma overhanging the toilet, while I dry the top half of my body, then dry the stoma, put on a clean bag, then dry the rest of my body. I can't feel anything coming out of the stoma as there are no nerve endings there. I towel dry my hair and

175

arms and shoulders then glance down and see that the stoma has been "spitting" foul orange liquid, not into the toilet as it usually does, but against the wall and there are little worm-like squiggles slowly making their way down the tiles. I quickly clean the wall with one hand while holding a dry wipe over the stoma with the other hand, then dab the skin around the stoma dry and fix the new bag. I'm feeling guilty now because Paolo is not feeling well and I am leaving him to cope with the kids single handedly, so I trip down stairs and start pouring out breakfast cereal. Suddenly I feel something wet trickle down my leg. More haste less speed obviously. In my haste I had not dried the skin around the stoma sufficiently and the bag had become unstuck.

Rachael phones to say that Isaac has been sick several times during the night so she is keeping him home. Several of the kids have had sickness and diarrhea and both Paolo and I are not feeling well today so I guess it is all one bug, and probably not the Chinese Buffet to blame. I Whatsapp my friends to say that I will not be meeting them at the Wacky Warehouse today and settle down for a lazy day. Who am I trying to kid with four kids all aged 1 or 2 and several more after school?, I think an early night is the most I can ask for.

I get out a magic painter and the kids enjoy painting without the mess of paints. Then the jig-saws and picture books. The weather outside is cold but dry so we wrap them all up in coats and wellies and take them outside into the garden, then bring them back in again for snack. I look at my watch, it is only 10.00 a.m. I have emptied my bag three more times and despite taking the pills the contents are still like dirty water, Paolo has been running to the toilet. It occurs to me that having the runs is easier with a stoma bag. Its a pity we don't all have velcro on the opening to our bottoms then there would be no danger of soiled trousers if you didn't get to the toilet quickly enough. The rest of the day drags as slowly as the beginning and I am impatient for the last of the parents to pick up their children. At last we have the house to ourselves. Paolo cleans the kitchen and I put away all the toys and hoover the living room, playroom and dining room. Paolo has a soak in the bath while I do a bit of paperwork, then I get in after him (water recycling). I am feeling much better, but he goes to bed

176

because he can't get warm and he is aching. I have a feeling that I will be working alone tomorrow.

Friday 28th February - My prophecy has not come true, Paolo is fine and so am I. We only have two kids today so Paolo says he will go to Rachael's house to put up a curtain rail for her. I am just getting Odelia and Jason ready to go for a walk when Nathan phones to ask if I will look after Bailey and Bobby while he runs some errands. Oh well so much for having only two kids. I take the the kids to the shop to buy a loaf and on the way back call to see my friend Joyce and ask if she wants to bring her minded kids to play in our garden for the morning, at least I will have a different adult to talk to. It's a lovely day, belying the forecast of snow and the children play out all morning in the garden. We have tea and toast for snack. The kids play on the slides and swings, dig up the soil (much to Joyce's concern, she doesn't "do" dirt) and feed the chickens with bread. Later I bring out the bubbles and Joyce woops around the garden, getting much more enjoyment and exercise than the kids who are trying to catch them. I cook some pasta and mix it with some bolognese sauce left over from the day before. As before, Bailey sits under the table and pretends to be a dog, I ignore him, at home they think this is funny and just a phase he is going through and they pass him food to eat, but he will be going to school in September, so I think it is important to get him used to sitting at the table and eating with utensils. After the spaghetti, the other children have a yogurt and Bailey climbs up on his chair, but I say "I'm sorry Bailey but doggies can't eat yoghurts" I hope he has learned his lesson and will be hungry for tea. Paolo can't fix the curtain rail for Rachael because she has bought the wrong one so he takes Matteo to Ikea to buy a wardrobe as Matteo can't fit it into his car. When he returns he takes Teo's old wardrobe to Rachael for her spare bedroom then I realise that it is time for picking the kids up from school and I haven't even thought of what to give them for tea - this is usually Paolo's jurisdiction. Looking into the freezer I find some battered chicken breasts, but not enough to feed 6 children, a pepperoni pizza also not big enough to feed 6 children. I peel some potatoes for chips and put the pizza and chicken in the oven and open a tin of peas and a tin of beans.

Bobby, Bailey and Odelia have gone home so I only have Jason.

177

I nip upstairs to see how Matteo is getting on with assembling the wardrobe, I shouldn't have bothered. "Can you just give me a hand for a minute?" he asks. I should never move away from the kitchen when I am cooking, when I return, I discover the chips are burnt just as the children troop in from school. I give them each a small portion of pizza, half a chicken breast, burnt chips and a choice of peas or beans. Paolo takes one look and goes upstairs to help Matteo. When the kids have gone home and Matteo has gone to meet Lauren, I tell Paolo, "Sorry, there wasn't enough food for us" and he replies with too much relief in his voice, "Oh good!". We clean up the children's mess and order a curry take-away.

While waiting for the delivery of the curry, I read my emails and am excited to read that the photos are ready. I am so disappointed. The long photo of us all just looks like the individual photos she took, joined together, which of course is what it is. Some of the individual family photos are good and one taken of all the grandchildren is lovely, except that Josh is missing. I am never happy with photos of myself, I must think that I am much more attractive than I really am, but my hair looks thin and flat, after all that messing with conditioners and hairdressers. I light the wood burning fire and open a bottle of wine. We sit eating our meal watching the news, Russian tanks in Ukraine. This brings a bit of reality to the situation. I am sulking about photographs and these poor people must be out of their minds with worry of what tomorrow will bring. I give myself a shake and look around at my life, it makes me smile with contentment, there will be other photos, it is Friday, two days of relaxation, then I relax and watch TV.

Saturday 1st March I wake up and wonder what is missing. Oh yes! it's the sound of the hens squawking to be fed. I look out of the window and see that I have left the door to the chicken run open and the ladies are happily digging up my lawn for worms. Good job mister fox didn't come calling last night. I phone Helen to see how Arron got on at Sheffield yesterday (he's deciding which university to go to. She says they had a great day. Arron asked intelligent questions and made friends within minutes of getting there. He is going to do a pharmacy degree but was worried that he would not be able to practice his music, but he needn't have

178

feared as there are enough facilities for him to do both. He is a bit of a dreamer though, I hope he doesn't get lost in his oboe practice and forget to go to lectures.Then again, I hope he doesn't have too many lectures that he forgets to enjoy playing his music. I think he would prefer to play for an orchestra in New York, but knows it is very difficult to make a success in music and so is hedging his bets by doing a pharmacy degree. I allow myself a little regret that Matteo didn't stick it out at uni. or that I didn't insist on him keeping up with his music lessons, he used to play the clarinet beautifully.

It is a lovely day, the sun is shining and on goes my spring cleaning head. I put all the dolls in the washing machine, complete with clothes. It spooks me to watch their little faces as they turn somersaults in the water and I can't bare to watch as they spin. Joyce brings me some tow-rope and we put new rope on the swings and we go to see another childminder, who's husband has made a "messy play bench" but I resist the temptation to buy one. Paolo and I had planned to go to the cinema in the evening, but after a day out in the garden, he looks shattered. I tell him it would be a waste of money if he fell asleep watching the film, so we take a raincheck and watch The Voice while eating bacon and eggs (complements of our hens) and Paolo falls asleep.

Sunday 2nd March I decide to use a tall book shelf that Matteo is getting rid of, and put it in the bedroom that we use as an office. Of course I need to clear out a lot of stuff and organise and file things that have been pushed into drawers or left in piles. By 4 pm the floor of the office and my bedroom is covered in paper, books, photograph albums and files. I wish I had never started.

Monday 3rd March, One of the kids does not arrive. His mum phones to say that he is sick and she is taking him to see the doctor. The sun is shining once more so I put the baby into a buggy and walk the two other girls to playgroup. On the way we talk about shadows and worms, flowers and cars, warm and cold. We look at numbers on doors and bus stops. The girls are getting fresh air and exercise and practicing new words. I love this aspect of my job, but I don't look forward to recording these observations later. After dinner, Paolo shows the girls how to plant seeds and I continue to clean up the back garden, sweeping hen poo from the patio and washing winter grime off garden toys. I hope this is the beginning of summer (I know, it's not even spring yet). I don't yearn for it to get any warmer, just would like to give the snow a miss and would appreciate a bit less rain, I'll keep my fingers crossed. After tea, I send Alise out into the garden to hide chocolate easter coins for the rest of the kids to find. They don't come back in but continue to play outside until their parents arrive. Another bonus of mild weather. Isaac is staying with us for a couple of nights as Rachael has to go to Birmingham. After the other kids leave, I listen to him read his school books then pull out a sheet from his reading folder. It has the alphabet drawn on it with dots and arrows to guide a child learning to write. I ask him to write over them. He says, "I don't need that sheet" and proceeds to show me how he can write his letters. I am astounded, I always sing the ABC with the kids but I didn't realise that he could not only remember it but knew how to write each letter correctly and in order. I put the sheet of paper in his reading folder with a note to tell his teacher what he has done. We bake some cup cakes, then he has a bath and a milk shake and he goes to bed and is asleep within minutes. Rachael should be proud of herself for producing such a clever little boy.

Wednesday 5th March, Our baby boy is 20 years old today. No longer a teenager. Where did the time go? Lauren bakes him a cake with the help of her grandma so after tea with the help of the minded kids we sing Happy Birthday to Matteo. This is the only celebration of his birthday, he didn't want a fuss. He has just refurnished his bedroom (how did I produce this Stepford child) and we bought him a wardrobe and I presume his brothers and sisters have texted or phoned him, but I miss the childhood birthdays.

Friday 7th March We take the kids to IKEA (New experiences, it's in the EYFS) We buy a bookcase and filing cabinet to accommodate all the paper work that is being added to the job of childminding. Also bought a lovely brightly coloured door screen for the playroom and some plastic child sized glasses for the play kitchen. We have meatballs and chips for dinner in the Ikea cafe and I sit in the play area with the kids while Paolo collects the items and stows them in the car. All three of the babies fall asleep on the way home so I look forward to having a cup of tea in peace, but they wake up as soon as the car pulls onto the drive so nappy changing, potty training, pouring juice and wiping noses takes priority. After all the kids have gone home, Paolo begins to assemble the book case while I clean up downstairs, then the work really begins, hauling out the old chests of drawers that were filled with photograph albums, throwing away stuff that has been hoarded and organising filing systems. Of course this involves a lot of looking at old photographs, reminiscing and laughing, discovering books that need to be read again, finding files that had been lost, so the job tumbles over into Saturday morning. Trips to the tip and charity shops doesn't seem to diminish the mess of the bedrooms, where has all this stuff come from?

Saturday evening after having a lovely soak in the bath to get rid of the dust in my hair, we go out on a date. A chicken shashlik in Spice Valley (where Paolo spots a minor celebrity from Cbbees,) and then the cinema (curtesy of Tesco vouchers) to watch "12 Years A Slave". I am full-up as we leave the restaurant and I feel I could easily fall asleep so I buy a drink of coke, something I never drink, and a packet of twix mix. The film is tear-jerking but somehow the combination of wine, curry and coke deadens my usual emotions and I don't cry once throughout the film.

Sunday 9th March. The weather is bright and sunny and I spend almost the whole day sorting out paper and dividing it into rubbish and filing. The re-cycling bin is full, the black bin is full and the office looks as cluttered as it ever did. The highlight of my day is hanging washing on the line after 3 months of drying in the dryer. How sad am I? Rachael and Isaac drop in for dinner as well as Josie and Gail. We have stuffed roast chicken with cabbage, leaks, tomatoes, peppers, potatoes, onions and carrots followed by apple tart. I think I have had all my weekly quota of 5 a day's on one day. We also finish off a lemon cheesecake that Matteo and Lauren made and I wonder why I have not lost weight!

Monday 10th March I am awake at 5.00 a.m. Good opportunity to start the early morning swim. But I haven't packed a swimming bag. I am on the last stoma bag, so it's maybe not a good idea to go swimming then having to try to dry the bag before getting dressed again. I'm not sure where my pass is. I go back to sleep. 6.00 a.m. I am once more awake and have stopped making excuses. I get up and pack the bag with towels, shampoo, goggles etc, not really such a big deal. I find another stoma bag in my handbag along with the swimming pass. Adam is just on his way out to work as I come down stairs so I give him a lift to Walkden, my good deed for the day. The weather even at this time in the morning is bright and sunny (the weather forecast said it was going to be cold and cloudy). Have we had a winter this year? I know we have had a lot of rain, but I can't remember it getting very cold. If this is global warming bring it on. My mood takes a little nosedive when I arrive at the pool. The lane markings are on and it looks like the swimming squad are taking up three of the lanes, which means the rest of us casual swimmers have only three lanes to use. As I get into the water, I remember my goggles which are still in my bag in the locker. Too late, I can't be bothered to go back to the locker, I will swim with my head out of the water. I lose count of the lengths and didn't even make a note of the time when I arrived, so I might have swum 30 lengths or I might not. I make my way to the disabled shower room, but it is occupied. How dare someone use my shower! I take the shampoo to the ordinary showers but of course, I would get arrested if I stripped off my costume here so I can't change the stoma bag. I walk back through the changing room to see if the disabled shower is free yet and realise that it is empty, it has just been locked from the outside. I go and find an assistant who tells me that I can open it with any key. It has just been locked to prevent the kids messing in it.

The rest of the day passes happily. The weather remains warm and sunny, who would believe that officially we are still in winter. We have a "new" little girl starting with us. Mia is 3 years old. She doesn't bother when her mum and gran leave her with us, barely acknowledging them leaving. She is quite bossy with the other kids, but they don't let her get away with it. She eats her snack toast, helps Paolo to plant some flower seeds, plays in the garden then back inside with the play dough. She pulls out one toy box after another and soon the playroom has no floor space at all. I explain to her that she will have to help me to put some things

182

away before she gets anything else out and she complies without complaint. At lunch time, she demolishes my home made vegetable soup and chats away as if she has been coming to our setting all her life. It is amazing how much confidence some children seem to be born with.

When all of the school children have been collected, we have homemade beefburger with proper chips (As the kids have named them - as opposed to oven chips.) and then Paolo lets them plant some more seeds in trays. Life is so much easier when your husband can cook and likes gardening. I'm glad I married him! The last child leaves us at 7.00 p.m. and a solar panel salesman arrives at 7.30. We are both tired, We can't remember how much we actually pay for electricity, I can't find my glasses and the lights in the dining room are quite dim so I can't read the facts and figures he is presenting me with, he probably thinks I am a moron. I apologise to him and ask him to come back again on Saturday morning. I will do my research before then, and prepare some intelligent questions. I don't think we will buy them. We haven't got any money in the bank spare and so it would mean borrowing money with interest if we went ahead, which would defeat the object. Possibly if we were a bit younger it would be a good idea, but by the time we had paid the loan, we would probably be looking for sheltered accommodation, (if we are still around that is)

Tuesday 11th March I get up and have an "all over wash" rather than a shower, because I have definitely run out of stoma bags. I don't fancy trying to dry one after it is soaked. Millie and Keith want to go to school on scooters, but we have Ollie today, he's four and its 8.30 a.m. and I don't think he would walk fast enough to get to school on time, so I tell them they will have to go in the car. At 8.45 another solar panel representative phones and I start a conversation while Paolo gesticulates to tell me to watch the babies as he is taking the kids to school. The next thing is that he is back - the car won't start, the battery is flat. He transfers the kids into his car and shouts Matteo up to move his car so that he can get out of the drive. Matteo comes down all groggy eyed and tousled hair without a word and gets into his car. His engine doesn't start either! After a couple more attempts, the car starts and Paolo is able to get the kids to school with seconds to spare. Good start to the day. Our battery charger has little effect on the battery so we phone up our local mechanic and he lends us his commercial charger. A couple of hours later the battery is charged and the culprit is discovered. Someone had turned on a light in the back of the Toyota, it must have been burning electricity all night.

After a frosty night, the day turns bright and sunny once more and the kids play out in the garden for most of the morning. The rope that I had used to re-string the swings has stretched so that the seats of the swings are now on the floor. The rope was advertised as tow-rope. Can you imagine trying to tow a car with elastic rope? Odelia arrives with a three-wheeled scooter and I am amazed that she can ride it, she isn't two yet, I really must get stuck into some observations. Since my operation, I have been very lackadaisical with all the paperwork involved in childminding. I make a note to make some time this evening.

When Paolo leaves for the swimming session with Barnados, taking with him the last two children (dropping them off at home on his way), I make myself a cappuccino and sit down at the computer to read my emails before I get stuck into the tidying up. My stoma makes a rude noise and then I smell a disgusting aroma. My jeans have been dragging down the top of the stoma bag all day, giving me an uncomfortable tummy. I look down and find that the top of the bag has become unattached from my belly, allowing the stench to float up. Time for a shower and a change, sod the housework.

I usually go to spend some time with Josie, while Paolo is at the pool, but I am not going round in my pyjamas so I ring her up for a chat instead. I tell her about Doreen, my ex-husband's auntie who is the same age as Josie. Doreen has a pace-maker fitted which has been causing her some concern over the last few months. She also has cataracts, making it difficult to see. There have been a lot of delays to her appointment for the eye operation mainly waiting for the consultant in charge of her heart condition, to tell them that she is well enough to undergo a cataract operation. But then another problem crops up. She has been completely deaf in her right ear for years and wears a hearing aid in the left ear. She gets an infection in her right ear and is sent to see an ENT doctor to sort it out. The doctor washes out the right ear, then for some reason, washes out the left one. The result is that he perforates the "good" ear and so she is then completely isolated. She can't hear or see anything. I spoke to Doreen earlier and she had gained a little hearing overnight but still not perfect and is swearing more than I have ever heard, saying that the stupid bloody doctor had ruined her social life as she usually goes ballroom dancing, but now she cant hear the music.

Wednesday 12th March. Another lovely day, I wake up early after getting to bed before midnight. Jason arrives just after 7.00 a.m. and is not happy to see me, he much prefers to be met at the door by Paolo. He waves bye bye to his mum through the window and takes off his hat and coat. Then says "Poo poo" and points to the toilet. I take off his nappy and encourage him to sit on the loo. He doesn't do anything but insists on tearing off the toilet paper to wipe his bum, flushing the toilet and washing his hands. I praise him, it's a good start when they actually want to sit on the toilet. I replace his nappy and go to make his breakfast. Ten minutes later he once again says "poo poo" and the whole routine is repeated, with me once more congratulating him for trying. The third time I am just making a cup of coffee for Paolo and me so I say "Just hang on a minute darling, and I will put you on the toilet" He just stands there and fills his nappy. Arrrgh!

We spend most of the day in the back garden and I manage to do two lots of washing and get it dry on the line. Odelia impresses me once more by making a good attempt at balancing on a two-wheel scooter, Bailey sits at the table and doesn't pretend to be a dog (lesson learned from last week), my sister comes to chat and drink tea and gets roped in to entertain the kids while I clean away the debris after lunch. Paolo brings home some block paving bricks, so she also gets the pleasure of helping to unload them too. At about three o'clock, Gail goes home, Nathan collects his two grandsons, Odelia's daddy collects her and Jason wakes up from his nap. Paolo elects to do the school run and I cook tea. Actually I pull fish fingers and potato wedges out of the freezer and open a tin of peas - a chef I am not.

Thursday 13th March - Cooler today but still dry. Seem to be going through the motions today, not really getting stuck into anything. As soon as I change one dirty nappy, another one needs changing or one of the other children need help on the toilet. I make snacks, take photos, kiss bumps better, sing songs, mop up spills. I can't organise myself into putting any of them down for a nap, with the consequence that by tea time, they are all tired and it is too late for them to sleep now. There are 12 children around the dining room for tea - I'm sure we don't usually have that many! Have I collected someone else children by mistake?

We have some training tonight and I have volunteered to pick up several childminders on the way, but I haven't told any of the parents that we need to be out before 6.30 p.m. In theory all of the children should be collected by 5.30 but I know that several of them will be later than that. At 5 oclock I start to ring around the parents to ask them to pick up their children promptly. Jason mum says she has only just left work and so cannot guarantee it, but says that his dad will be home if I want to drop him off. Rachael collects Isaac and says she will drop off Lily and Jamie with their dad. The only one that I don't phone is Keith's mum. He is at Marshal Arts this evening, he is already changed, so I don't predict any problem. At 6.15 pm she still has not arrived, Keith is late for his karate and I haven't had a wash or changed my clothes. I have told her before now that if she is going to be late on a Thursday to ring us and we can drop him off and then she can just get there in time to pick him up, but she has never taken us up on that offer.

Ultimately we get out on time (washed and changed no less), pick up the other childminders and arrive on time. I needn't have worried, I also shouldn't have bothered, it was just a waste of time. We all came out an hour and a half later and said "Did we learn anything new then" and agreed that we hadn't. I phoned Gail on my way home and told her I would meet her in Wetherspoons, half an hour later than normal.

Friday 14th March One of the latest "brilliant" ideas from Ofsted is that children should be supplied with adequate mark-making materials outside as well as inside the home. We have a huge blackboard and a good supply of chalk, but one of the

186

childminders had managed to acquire some white boards and gave us one, so Paolo fixed it to the wall in the back garden. I buy some marker pens and the kids set to as they always do with something new. After a while they begin to feel the cold and come back into the house so I go out to erase the marks, but they wont rub off. I whatsApp my colleagues to warn them from buying the pens from Asda. One of them replies with "Have you taken off the protective film?" - Film? What film? Needless to say I am the butt of the jokes for the rest of the afternoon.

Saturday 15th March Mornings are the best. I always wake up early, but on the weekend I can choose to snuggle back down under the blankets or go down to make a brew, or sit up to read a book and kick Paolo out to make a brew. The last is the best option. I am reading the autobiography of Peter Kay and laughing out loud at some of his antics and agreeing with his ideas on Catholicism. I too was educated by nuns and the things he writes about the church asking for money ring very true. By 10.30 a.m. I have dragged myself into the shower, dressed and washed one washing machine load. I am just hanging it up to dry when the salesman arrives for his second attempt to sell us solar panels. His name is Hani, he is a nice guy and I want to buy something from him. I ask lots of questions and then promise him I will phone him on Monday with an answer. This of course is not what he wants to hear, he wants us to sign on the dotted line. He explains that the refund that is paid out from the electricity companies goes down on 1st April and that if I sign now I will pay £10 a month less than if I sign on Monday but I am adamant,I have made many rash judgements in my life, I stick to my guns. Hani persists, saying what else is there to think about, but now I am getting exasperated. He finally admits defeat and says that he has to phone his boss. I know from experience that this is just an encore of a selling technique - he will phone the boss, who will offer to sell at a fraction less. I am not interested I have decided to look over the paperwork over the week-end, so I go outside to continue hanging the washing. When I come back in, the salesman has gone and taken all the paperwork with him. His loss, I might have decided to have them if he had given me the chance.

Sunday 16th March - Once again I decide to give Church a miss, I think I will continue to sort out the playroom which I had started on Saturday afternoon. Throwing out broken toys, sorting them into the relevant boxes, printing new labels. I don't know if other men do this, but Paolo, if walking naked can't resist adopting a flamenco pose and shaking his penis at me. I used to laugh, now I just roll my eyes at him. Today I get my own back. As I come out of the shower, Paolo is on the phone to his mum. I adopt the pose and swing my stoma bag. Not a sexy sight, I admit, a 62 year old flabby woman swinging a full stoma bag, but then neither is a floppy willy. Paolo starts laughing, but doesn't tell his mum the reason.

Monday 17th March, It is a cold and bright day the kids play indoors then out, then in then out, I should have a turnstile fitted. I had decided that I would order sand in bulk instead of buying a couple of bags every week. It arrives at 2.30 pm. and is left on the drive. I had not considered how I was going to move it to the back garden. When the kids arrive back from school, they fill buckets with it and carry it to the sand pit, I guess that is the only way to do it, without a wheel barrow. At 5 pm I start putting things away. The double buggy is in the back garden so I try to put it into the garage, but Paolo has locked it. I walk back through the house, open the garage door, drag the buggy in, lock the door once more and go back through the house to the garden. As I get there, Paolo asks "Where's Jason?" I say "He is in the back garden. But he is not there, a frantic search through the house reveals nothing. I know that I saw him in the garden, the front door is closed he couldn't have gone outside. I ask the kids if they have seen him. Alise says "The last time I saw him he was climbing in the buggy". I unlock the garage, there he is, happy as Larry trying to fasten himself in the buggy. I had not noticed him when I had dragged it in.

Tuesday 18th March, Odelia's birthday. She walks around all day singing "Happy Birthday to Didi, Happy Birthday to me". Overnight it seems she has grown from a baby into a beautiful little girl. 18th March was also my mam and dad's wedding day 64 years ago. We take the kids to the Fun House and have dinner there, then come home and have a mini birthday lunch with birthday cake and a few crisps. Usually we have a birthday tea when the school children arrive home from school, but Odelia goes home at 3.00 pm so I give the remains of the cake to her dad so they can sing happy birthday to her again when her mum comes home from work.

After all the kids have gone home and Paolo has gone swimming with the kids from Barnados, I wrap some chocolate and write a birthday card to Josie. She will be 82 on Friday, but I know that I will not have the opportunity to visit her then. When I get there, her friend Jean is doing the same thing. While I am there, I begin to feel uncomfortable, a slight stomach ache. When I think about it I realise that the skin around the stoma has been tender for a few days, I wonder if I have a blockage once more. After spending an hour with Josie, I return home to find that Matteo is home. My phone has been playing up for a few weeks. I can have the phone in my hand and watch the text come up telling me that I have just missed a call even though I know that it hasn't rung. I had been advised to backup and restore it, which I had done, to no avail. I ask Matteo to look at it, within a minute he has diagnosed the problem. "You have got it set to "Do Not Disturb". What! I did not even know it had that setting, how can I have done that? Adam comes out of his bedroom and tells me that he has been to the hospital and they are trying him on a different insulin. I hope it helps. He has been pretty miserable for a while. Diabetes is a horrible illness.

Soon after Paolo arrives home, followed by Jackie and Steve. I light the fire and make coffee and Jackie has me rolling about laughing, showing a video her daughter has taken of her, demonstrating how her latest granddaughter is learning to crawl. While we are chatting, the discomfort in my stomach grows stronger. The natural reaction to pain is to rub it, which I do, but I am embarrassed doing this as I feel people will think I am just drawing attention to the fact I am wearing a stoma bag. I try to ignore it but after a while I cannot stand it any longer and have to get up and walk around. Our friends take their leave and say they will see us on Friday (we are gong to Morecambe to watch a show and spend the week-end in their caravan) and I run myself a bath. The hot water has no effect, the pain is getting unbearable, I take two codeine and get into bed, but I can't find any comfort. Paolo

189

brings me a drink and asks if there is anything he can do, and tries to persuade me to ring the hospital, but I insist that it will get better soon. The memory of sitting in A&E waiting room with Adam for over an hour puts me off. Just as I am thinking of agreeing with Paolo's suggestion, I begin to be sick, I am glad, this is the only way I am going to get any sleep tonight. The pain doesn't go away but the retching has exhausted me and I manage to go to sleep. The next morning I wake up with one leg burning, hard and very painful and I become worried that I might have a blood clot. But the next thing I know, Paolo is waking me up with a cup of tea and my leg is fine. I think I must have been dreaming about the sore leg but the dream had been so realistic. The good thing is that the pains have gone, including the tenderness of the stoma. This is only the third episode of blockages since I had the op. in October. Not bad since I eat anything I fancy.

Wednesday 19ᵗʰ March - I have bought some star charts to try a different method of behaviour management. I tell Isaac that he can have a star if he is nice to his mummy when she arrives to collect him (he usually wants to stay a bit longer, or doesn't want to put on his shoes, or wants to negotiate a trip to buy a new toy). A star if he eats all of his tea, one if he tastes something that he thinks he doesn't like, one if he learns to like something he hasn't previously and one if he hangs up his coat after school. On Monday the plan had worked like a dream, with all the kids eating everything on their plates and being rewarded with stars to stick in the appropriate squares. Today we have parsnips which Isaac adamantly refuses to even put on his fork. Trying a bit of revers psychology, I say "Never mind, you have got plenty of stars up to now, you can give the other kids a chance to catch you up, but that means that you can't have one for finishing your dinner, or for trying something new, or for eating something you don't like!" Isaac is torn, but doesn't give in. He has a drink yoghurt for desert and asks for another one. I refuse as I don't have enough left to give everyone a second one. A little while later Isaac's head appears round the dining room door. "Nanna, you know that yoghurt, well I didn't really like it, but I drank it all up" Yes right Isaac, and I was born yesterday. I laugh and tell him "nice try" but don't give him a sticker.

29 - Sickness Bug

Friday 21st March - All the kids have been collected by 5 pm. A quick tidy up, then wash and change and we are on our way to Morecambe. We arrive at "The Platform" at just gone 7 o'clock, plenty of time before the start of the show (The Manfreds) at 8 pm. Eight of our friends are already there, but waiting for a meal to be served that they had ordered over an hour ago. We go to see if we can save seats, but the venue is already half full and people are streaming in. In the end we all manage to sit close to each other and enjoy the entertainment, singing along to pop songs from our youth. There is an incident where a man objects loudly to Linda and Pat talking quietly while the act is going on and Roy, Linda's other half wanting to punch him. What excitement! and to think I usually spend Friday nights playing sudoku or watching the box. Afterwards we all go back to Linda and Roy's caravan for snacks and drinks and play a quiz game. My general knowledge is pathetic.

Saturday 22nd March - Wake up to realise that the two beds in our room were different lengths due to a cupboard being at the end of one. I had slept in the longest one and Paolo, who is a good foot taller than me had slept in the short one. Happy days. Roy brings us a cup of tea in bed and Linda cooks a Full English Breakfast. I could get used to this. After lazing about for an hour, I offer to take the rubbish to the bin and Paolo comes with me. I say I will see what the other couples have planned for the day. We call on Jackie and Steve and accept their offer of more tea, then somehow settle down to chat and forget that we should go back to the other caravan to our guests. Jackie makes snacks then later dinner and at some point, Linda phones to see where we are and asks if we fancy a ride into Morecambe, but it is cold and wet outside so we go back to our laziness. In the end, apart from a short walk along the beach, we spend the whole day in the caravan, drinking, eating and watching TV in the lovely company of our friends. I can see the appeal of owning a holiday home. Usually on a Saturday, I clean and shop and deal with post. I answer the phone and and deal with any paperwork that needs to be done for the business. Of course if I wagged it every week-end, I would soon find myself living in a pig sty, but we both agree that we should do this much more often.

Sunday 23rd March Morning dawns bright and sunny (but still very cold) and once more Linda cooks a lovely breakfast and I take the rubbish to the bin and stop to say hello to Jackie, Steve, Sue and Phil who are staying with them. But today I don't accept the offer of a cup of tea, but go back. We have a trip to Morecambe market and buy some card for making Mother's Day cards with the kids and an outfit for me because I spot some extra short trousers (I usually have to chop off a couple of inches even when I buy petite. After that we take our leave and drive home. We stop at Botany Bay (the mill, not the town in Australia) and stroll round the stalls and buy hot pancakes and coffee then continue home. What a lovely week-end. Now my batteries are fully recharged and I am ready for another week of childminding.

Thursday 27th March - For a few weeks now people have been asking me how long I have to wear the stoma bag or when am I taking my holidays. I usually just shrug my shoulders and say I don't know, but Paolo needs to go to Italy and Easter would be a good time (no school run). I phone the hospital and leave a message on the answering machine. Soon after the phone call is returned by Mr Hobbiss" secretary apologising that I haven't received a letter, blaming a different department and saying my operation is scheduled for 9th May 2014. My stomach does a somersault and my heart starts to race before I take some deep breaths and answer her.

It's silly that I am frightened, this operation will be much less invasive than the last. Perhaps it is because the last time was a matter of life or death, the operation a lesser fear than a painful death. This time seems almost cosmetic. Now that I know the date of the operation, plans can be made. I whatsApp all the parents, my kids and other childminders to let them know and then post the news on facebook. It is so much easier to give out information like this and then I am less likely to be in the embarrassing position of people not knowing and thinking that I had forgotten to tell them. Paolo books his flights to Italy and phones his mum in Switzerland and arranges to meet her in Padova. It is ridiculous in this day and age that he has to go to another country to sign documents and speak to bank managers when everything could be done through computers.

Saturday 29th March, I wake up and wonder why I haven't booked flights for me to go to Italy with Paolo. For years I have hardly taken a day off work except my scheduled holidays, not wanting to inconvenience the parents and children that I look after. Surely, considering my age and health history, I should be taking a few liberties. I message all the parents and tell them that I am having a week off after my operation (9th May) and that if possible I would also like to take off the week beginning the 5th April (my birthday) to go to Italy.

We go to the photographer in Saddleworth to choose which photos to buy. I was initially disappointed in them, but now that I have chosen the ones I want, I am looking forward to getting them.

I send Helen and Rachael a text to ask if they want to celebrate Mother's Day with dinner at our house and they both reply "Yes please, What time? Paolo's cooking wins every time.

Sunday 30th March - Mother's Day. Paolo brings me breakfast in bed then I have a leisurely morning and go to church. I expected Helen and Rachael to be there but they weren't So I collect their daffodil and call to see them. At 4.00 pm they all arrive for dinner bringing chocolates and flowers and cards, I love being a mum. A couple of hours later, Isaac complains of feeling sick and I so do I. My stoma bag had been filling up quickly all day so I guess I had a bit of a bug. After watching Sandra Bullock and Hugh Grant in a comedy about a lawyer, I think I will have an early night. But just as I am about to get in bed I start being really sick. I am glad of the sickness, it relieves the stomach ache and I go to bed thinking that I can have a good night's sleep and get up better. But I cant sleep, first I can't get warm and then I begin to get painful cramps so all night I am either jumping up to stretch muscles, empty the stoma or make a drink. I feel like I haven't slept all night and can't face the prospects of childminding. I try to phone the stoma team, the nurse from Bolton One and the Doctor. Eventually the doctor rings me back and gives me advice over the phone. Paolo plays with the kids and I go back to bed after taking another loperomide. I just need to sleep. I don't manage to sleep. The doctor had recommended paracetamol to ease the cramps, I take a couple and it does ease it for a while, but I just feel so ill. The stoma nurse returns my call at 2.45 and suggests that I buy some dioralyte and take them at double the strength. After collecting the school children, Paolo makes some vegetable soup which I eat without enjoyment. and then soon after bring it all back up into the toilet. I have another go at ringing the hospital and after a few attempt get to speak to the stoma nurse from Bolton. She says it sounds as if I have a stomach bug and shouldn't be working with children. She advises me to take more dioralyte and also to sip energy drinks or salty drinks such as bovril. She tells me that the veg soup was not a good idea and I would be better with plain pasta or mashed potato. After the children have gone home at 6.30 pm Paolo nips to Tesco to replenish the dioralyte and to buy some sports drinks. It crosses my mind to ask him to buy himself a birthday card for tomorrow, but that would be really taking liberties. I just hope that I am better by tomorrow and can go and buy one. When he comes back, Paolo makes me some pasta soup, I only manage half before I am once more throwing up in the toilet. We have a little Polish boy starting with us tomorrow, his mother phones to remind us. I tell her that I have a sickness bug and it would be better to delay the starting date but she says that she has an interview so I tell her to bring him but then pick him up as soon as possible.

Tuesday 1st April, April Fools Day and Paolo's birthday. I haven't even bought him a card. I am not feeling any better. I take heed of the advice of not having any contact with the children and stay upstairs, sipping Dioralyte and lucozade. At 8.45 a.m. Paolo takes the kids to school, I go down to make myself some breakfast and a cup of tea. At 9.15 I am once more being sick. I go back to bed for a little while and sip more lucozade then decide to have a shower, I'm sure I will feel better then. After the shower I step on the scales, for months my weight has hovered somewhere between 10st 7lb and 11st. Now I am 10st. It almost feels worth being ill. Paolo brings me some tea and toast, which I nibble and sip without enjoyment - I must be ill. Joshua the new little boy arrives, I listen for tears as his mum leaves him, but don't hear any. A few minutes later I do hear him. The crying stops and starts, stops and starts.

Paolo nips upstairs to check on me and asks me "can this child talk?" I don't know, it is months since I arranged for him to start, I am sure I wrote it on the notes but I cant remember off the top of my head. Paolo tells me that he wants everything, the phone, the photo of my grandson the ornaments from the display. Every time Paolo says "no Joshua" he starts screaming. He also wants every toy the other kids are playing with, ignoring all the other toys available and when he gets them he just bangs them as if trying to destroy them. Paolo copes with these four children without once raising his voice (apart from singing Happy Birthday to Jason as they enjoy a birthday party, I am very impressed. The kids enjoy the sunshine in the back garden, play with the play dough, mixing the colours and dropping it on the carpet and still Paolo keeps calm. Thats one of the reasons I love him. When his mum arrives to collect Joshua he doesn't want to go home, she is very upset and says "this is not the reaction I expected". It takes the combined efforts of Paolo and Joshua's mum to fasten him into the buggy and we can still hear him screaming as they turn the corner of the street. I get several phone calls during the day from friends and relatives asking how I am and they get mixed answers. My daughter phones and I tell her I am fine and am sure I am on the mend. My sister phones just after I have been sick again and I tell her that I am thinking of phoning the hospital. Paolo brings me some mashed potato and gravy (without onion) a bit late in the day to start following the rules. I pick at it, forcing it down without enjoyment, I have never in my life "gone off food" In the end my daughter calls with a card and a cake for Paolo and tells me that my decision to phone the after hours doctor after all the kids have gone is not a good one. If you phone the doctor now he might get you in the hospital and on a drip without you having to sit in a hospital waiting area. I phone and speak to his secretary who tells me to sip dioralyte and phone back in the morning to get an appointment. Why did I bother? Five minutes later, she phones me back and says that she has spoken to the doctor and if I can get someone to the surgery before 6 pm they can collect a prescription for an anti-sickness pill. And to make an appointment to see him the next day. Rachael goes to collect the prescription for me and I am a bit worried when I see that the doctor has prescribed three boxes - How long does he think this thing is going to last?

195

Paolo has bought tickets to fly to Italy on Saturday he is contemplating canceling them. I tell him not to be hasty, I have never in my life been ill for a week. The way I am feeling at the moment I can't imagine ever feeling well again but he doesn't need me to help him with his worries.

I take the Metoclopramide tablet issued by the doctor and go to bed, the sickness stops but the cramps come back with a vengeance. I try taking paracetamol to no avail knocking them back with lucozade and electrolade to try to quench my thirst. I get no sleep for another night.

Wednesday 2nd April 8.30 I phone the doctor to make an appointment and am given one for 9.30 am. I phone my sister who has volunteered to drive me as I don't feel capable of walking there and I am frightened that I may cause an accident if I suddenly get a cramp in an arm or leg while driving. Gail drops me off outside the door to the surgery while she finds a parking space (another advantage for having a helpful sister) and I book myself in. I am taking deep breaths to stop myself vomiting as she enters the door so I tell her I am going in the loo to spew (I'm a poet) and to call me when it's my turn. She knocks on the door minutes later and I get to see the doctor. He asks me about my symptoms, takes some blood samples and examines my stomach, at which time I twice demonstrate the spasms as my legs and then an arm cramp robotically. He gives me another prescription for Boscopan Tablets to relieve the cramps and tells me that he will send off the blood samples. He advises me that the surgery is closed for training purposes on Wednesday afternoons but that if the results of the blood samples are not good I will be contacted directly and advised to attend A & E. He also tells me that if I begin to feel worse to phone the out-of-hours doctor for further advice. I go home and am sick once more. I take myself off to bed to be out of the way of the children and try to sleep. Nathan comes to see me and suggests Dioralyte Relief that apparently has the benefit of cooked rice mixed in with it and which had been prescribed for his grandson the week before. He goes out to the chemist and brings me some back. He mixes it, I drink it then I am sick again. I try to ring the out of hours doctor but it is not available until after 6.30 pm Dr Hyams didn't mention that fact. I phone 111 and get some advice,

196

which is to sip dioralyte and water doh!!

Paolo once more begs me to go to A & E and I relent but say I will wait until the kids have all gone home. So 7 o'clock pm sees Paolo driving me to Bolton Hospital. He is worried but relieved that I am seeing sense at last. I am still convinced that the most I will get is a long wait in the waiting room and a prescription for dioralyte. He drops me off outside and parks the car - I could get used to this being chauffeured around. Within about 20 minutes I am assessed by the triage nurse and quickly passed onto a bay and put on a drip, an anti-sickness drug is administered intravenously and am told I will soon feel much better. So far so good. Electrodes are stuck to my skin and I am given an ECG and I am told to sit up straight for 15 minutes before they can give me a stomach X-ray. The time passes very quickly with several different specialists coming to chat to me, ticking boxes, writing notes, making comments. I find myself feeling 10 times better and chatting to a nurse about Paolo's dad disappearing in Switzerland 5 years ago. I make the comment, I feel such a fraud, I don't feel sick at all now. She looked at me with sympathy on her face and said "You are a very sick woman (I've been told that before but with a different meaning of "sick"), your eyes are sunken, your mouth is puckered, its a good job you came in when you did". Well thats what you call socking it to you, I'm glad she didn't have a mirror handy. A doctor tells me that under no circumstances should I be minding children, I tell her that I have been ensconced upstairs away from the children. "That's not good enough, they should not even be in the same house". Another doctor arrives with my blood sample results and his expression tells me he has bad news "I've got the results of you tests" "Not good I'm afraid, you have acute kidney damage". I look across to Paolo and say, "You must still go to Italy" and Paolo bites his lip and shakes his head. The doctor asks when he should be going and tells him not to do anything rashly. "Lets see how things progress shall we" he says gently. He asks me what medication I am taking and I show him the Buscopan and Metoclopramide that the doctor had given me earlier in the day and scrape my brain to think of all the drugs I take. Paracetamol, Gaviscon oh yes and Loperamide to thicken the poo in the stoma bag. He smiles indulgently at me "Is that all you take?" "Yes!

197

What do you take me for - a druggie? He tells me that, in that case the Kidney damage, bad as it is, is probably damaged only by dehydration, in which case it may be capable of mending itself. It is still possible that the damage could be permanent but he is slightly more optimistic now. He tells me that the ECG and X-ray have shown no damage to the other organs, but they would like to admit me to a ward and keep an eye on me overnight. I send Paolo home to sleep. The comments from the doctor about cross-infection to the children has really panicked me, the thought of little kids feeling as bad as I have been for the last few days. I have to wait until a spare bed is made available for me and eventually I am wheeled onto D1, a Medical Assessment Ward and I am given a room to myself with Standard Isolation on the door. As soon as I can, I WhatsApp all my parents and tell them to find alternative care for their kids and keep a close eye on them. The message doesn't send. I have to go into the corridor to find somewhere that the signal to my phone will reach.

I don't sleep very well on Wednesday night, I am cold and uncomfortable and the bag is still filling up too quickly to go all night without emptying. A doctor comes to see me at some ungodly hour and tries to take a blood sample. I am not very generous with giving blood and he asks me if he can try getting it out of my foot. I nod sleepily. I am soon wide awake; I think he is cutting my foot off. He explains that my veins keep shutting down (possibly because of the dehydration) but he quite happily perseveres until he has the required amount. At some point after that a nurse wakes me to test my blood pressure and chats happily to me - it is the middle of the day for her of course.

Thursday 3rd April I am feeling almost completely well and looking forward to breakfast. I am amazed that I am allowed to have milk on my Rice Krispies (The evening before they had advised me only to drink "clear fluids" nothing with milk in.) so I have a cup of tea and some toast - and I do not vomit - result. I don't understand the different uniforms, I'm not sure of the difference between Ward Orderly, Nurse, or Domestic and some of the clerical staff also wear uniform, so I don't know the profession of the beautiful black African girl who is standing outside my room. I am admiring her hair which is a mass of shiny black ringlets. My mum used to put my hair in rags overnight on special occasions such as weddings or whit walks, and it was torture. I am wondering what methods are used by this girl. A Humpty Dumpty white man with a Bolton accent and arms full of paperwork calls to her and says "Ay luv, open't dooer fer me" She replies in an equally broad accent that she doesn't have access. He says 1734 and she promptly gains him access into the medicine room. I laugh at her and say, "Oh good, I'll get my stash tonight when everyone is asleep" She looks at me and says "Oh you like me air, it teks ages). Now I know I sometimes call people by the wrong name but I am sure that I don't ask completely different questions than the ones I am thinking. Am I dreaming the whole thing or could she not hear what I was saying and just guessed from the way I was looking at her? We will never know!

I settle myself down to read "Witness The Dead" a particularly gruesome but well written book that Adam passed on to me. It has its advantages, this being ill, I don't usually get chance to get stuck into a good crime thriller at this time of day. I have a shower in my private en suite (much improved from the shower available when I had my op.) It is slightly disappointing as the shower head is blocked and only about a dozen little squirts of water flow out of a very high shower head, but what hey, it's private and roomy. I change my stoma bag and clean my teeth and brush my hair, I feel like a new woman. I get back into bed and have another little nap while I wait for lunch. This is the life! My lunch arrives, Hot Soup, Corned Beef Hash with spring Vegetables, followed by tangerine segments. I haven't eaten anything for 3 days without vomiting immediately afterwards and I enjoy it more than one of Paolo's lovely meals. As I finish eating, Nathan arrives, followed soon after by Josie. Nathan is telling me about the problems he is having with his daughter (just distracting me from my own problems, you understand) and Josie is telling me how she waited for my promised phone call until 12, when I realise that my stoma bag is full. I had only emptied it just before I started eating. I say "Scuse me you two, let me get to the toilet to empty the bag before it bursts". I swing my legs over the end of the bed and feel wet running down my legs. Oh No! I quickly scoop my nightie up in a vain attempt to stop the flood and run into the toilet, where the bag bursts out all over the place. Nathan goes to alert a cleaner to help me to clean up the mess and goes home to get me another nightie. The cleaner is very efficient, donning apron and gloves, she scoops all the soiled bedding off the bed, bags it up for the wash and remakes it with clean linen as I shower. Then brings me clean hospital nightgowns (designer ones with the sexy split from hem to collar that show off my well washed knickers) I needn't have sent Nathan home. As I walk round the bed, I see that she has not spotted a tiny bit of spillage on the other side of the bed. Josie instructs me to mop it up with some tissue and then tells me to wash my hands again. Yes mam.

By the time Nathan comes back, it is time for him to leave again for an appointment for his grandson's haircut, I am sorry I sent him on the wild goose chase. Josie follows him soon after, having refused a lift from him because she is going to call in Asda to get a loaf. I settle down once more with my Craig Robertson novel. I feel so much better now especially after another meal of spring vegetable pie and a banana and a cup of coffee (the tea is a bit hit and miss).

After my message the night before, alerting the parents to the danger to their children, all the parents bar 2 find alternative care and Paolo finds himself looking after only one little boy the next day and picking up one other after school. He cleans all the washable surfaces of the house and mops the floors and disinfects the sinks and toilets then comes to visit me. He has to drop off one little boy with his dad on the way to the hospital as visiting stops at 7.pm. Just as he arrives at 6 pm, my sister also arrives, she has been helping my brother to move into new accommodation in Stafford, thinking she had until 8.o'clock (as stated on the hospital website) We chat away and Paolo as always sits patiently. I love my sister, but together we sometimes talk too much. Eventually she goes home at way past the 7 oclock deadline and I get to hear about Paolo's day. He tells me that he has stripped the bed and washed all the bedding, on top of amusing the baby and picking up Keith from school and making tea. Then he tells me he loves me and goes home without once saying "I told you so". I love him.

Friday 4th April morning I can hardly rouse myself from sleep

200

when a lovely young geordie nurse comes to take my blood, I sleepily ask her how long she has been a nurse and whether she likes her job (just to be social). She tells me that she loves her job but sometimes has career crisis thoughts when she hankers to retrain as a secondary teacher, she has been inspired by Educating Yorkshire. I easily slip back into dream world until I hear my name being called and asked if I want breakfast. I eat cornflakes and toast and coffee and still I am not completely awake. When Dr Leo comes in for a chat and asks me how I feel, I reply "As if you have given me something to make me sleep" He says it is all the saline that has been dripping into my veins. He tells me that all the tests for eColi and Norovirus have come back negative and that the results from the blood tests have shown that my kidneys are recovering. Relief. He asks me if I want to stay another day for them to keep an eye on me and I tell him I would rather go home. He has obviously read my notes thoroughly because he then says "As for the childminding, you need to rest for a couple of days then you should be able to go back to work" I ask him about the threat to the kids and he says that it is rare for kids to catch things from adults, its usually the other way round. I feel a weight lifting from my shoulders, I would have hated to have put the kids in any danger. He tells me that the nurse will come with the script (didnt know the the word prescription had been shortened so hadn't a clue what he was talking about) and to take the needle out of my arm. I think I might as well have another little nap while I am waiting and slip easily once more into the land of nod.

I was given some "scripts" or at least two sheets of paper with my details and the details of my sickness, treatment and discharge. Here is a sample:

Co-morbidities
Bowel cancer diagnosed May 2010 - ileostomy (this is wrong, it wasn't diagnosed till August)
Investigations Investigation Bloods
Chest x-ray ECG
Faecal samples
Outcome
Abnormal Normal Normal Normal
Result
AKI - urea 25.8, reatinine Nil acute

Sinus tachycardia
Negative for norovirus and C.diff

My sister comes to fetch me an hour or so later and drops me at home, where I eat pasta and chicken prepared for me by the lovely Paolo and then once more lay my head down in my own bed and again drift off to sleep until I am woken by Helen at 4.pm. I have never slept so much in my life. Another day drifts into night and I look for something to put in Paolo's luggage as a little treat for Isaac (Rachael and Isaac are accompanying him to Italy). Each time we go abroad, I seem to forget about the "No liquid in hand luggage" rule), I don't fail this time. Even though I am not going, the treat I slip into Paolo's luggage is a little bottle of blow bubbles!

Saturday, 5th April, my 63rd birthday. Paolo's alarm wakes us at 4.30 a.m. Nathan is coming at 5 to take him to the airport so I make him a cup of coffee and make small talk until it is time to wave them all off and wish them a safe journey, then go back to bed. Paolo gives me a birthday card and wishes me a happy birthday and makes me promise to get myself to the hospital at the first sign of anything amiss and I cross my heart and make the promise, I really have learnt the hard way not to take chances with my health. I make myself some breakfast and go back to bed. I get up for the second time later in the morning, have a shower and get dressed and play on the computer for a while. I post my latest news and read a lot of Happy Birthdays from friends and family. When the post arrives with a letter from the hospital, my first reaction is, "Flipping heck that's quick!" - thinking it is relating to my very recent admittance. But unfortunately it isn't, it is instructing me to report to the hospital at 7.am on 20th May for my operation. Oh no! I had been told it was the 9th May and all my parents have made arrangements to get time off work for that week. I decide not to react until I have had a chance to check with the hospital. I don't want to get all the parents to reschedule their holidays until I am doubly sure. the rest of Saturday is spent very lazily.

Apart from putting some washing on I spend the whole day, either chatting on the phone, or texting various friends. Lesley arrives bearing chocolate and Amaretto. Nathan brings me a card and an orchid. I make a half hearted attempt to find the missing remote control for the TV and then spot it while talking to Lesley. It is under the fire. Good job I hadn't decided to light it. When I tell Paolo later (he had spent the best part of Thursday evening and Friday morning searching for it) he presumed that it must have been put there deliberately, but I think that Jason had probably lobbed over the fire guard and a lucky bounce had catapulted it out of sight. I make bacon butties for Adam and I for lunch and then later overcook fish fingers while pulling the washing out of the washing machine. Have my culinary skills sunk so low that I am incapable of making fish fingers and beans? While watching the TV before bed, I begin to feel sick. I have promised Paolo that I will get back to the hospital at the first sign. Is this the first sign? No you fool its bloody indigestion.

Sunday 6th April, I wake up slowly and lonely. I am amazed that I have slept so soundly once more after spending the majority of the last week in bed. I text Paolo and tell him I love him and am missing him. He tells me something I am not going to share and I answer "You dirty old man" then realise that the quote from Harold Steptoe will be completely lost on him. He laughs anyway (or texts ha ha,- not really the same). I tell him that I have spotted mice in the chicken coop and he thinks I have been up early to clean them out (Its only 5.30 at this point), I would be seriously doubting my sanity if I had. He says he can smell coffee, his mum is already up and probably already preparing the vegetables for lunch. She will be 80 next year and still tends a garden as big as a football pitch, grows and dries herbs, makes jam from fruit she has grown, pickles beans and onions, walks mountain paths to search for wild asparagus and many other skills that I could not possibly hope to achieve. She still knits socks and irons everything she washes. One part of my brain is overawed by her. The other thinks "What a waste of time". Sit down and chill Tecla! Towels dry you better if you don't iron them. Creases drop out of sheets with body heat. The elastic in your knickers doesn't last long if you keep running the iron over it. I can remember my mum doing the same. Growing up in a very damp 2 up, 2-down terraced house, thrown up during the industrial revolution, I watched my mum pile the big

Silver Cross pram with the week's washing and push it down Liverpool Street to the wash house. This was her entertainment time. Sharing gossip with other working class women, helping each other to load machines, fold sheets and offering and accepting advice on how to deal with delinquent children, lazy husbands and how to stretch the meagre housekeeping with cheap cuts of meat. Then she would bring it all home and stand ironing and folding every single item the next morning in between breast feeding the youngest child and taking the older ones to school. Somehow she still sometimes had time to show off how fast she could run, tuck her dress in her knickers and do a hand stand on the wall and buy woollens from jumble sales, unravel them and knit them into new items of clothing. I gave up trying to walk in her shoes years ago. (Although I can still stand on my head).

I am contemplating going to church, but then think I will just look at my emails first. Then Linda "Face Time's" me and Joyce texts me. The next thing it is 10.00am. Too late to have a shower and dry my hair to go to church. Instead I shower and go shopping. As I walk round Tesco, I think to myself that this is the first time I have ever shopped, purely for myself. For the first 20 years or so of my life, I ate whatever my mum put in front of me. Then I married and shopped and cooked for a fussy husband and fussy children. As soon as that relationship was ended, I met Paolo and first of all I shopped and cooked taking his tastes into consideration and gradually he has taken over most of the cooking and a lot of the shopping. I find I cannot choose what to buy. I like everything, but I have got so accustomed to Paolo cooking for me that I don't know how to buy just for me. In the end I buy a cooked chicken and a bloomer so that Adam can have a snack before he goes to work and some food for snacks and meals for the kids this week. I will be kind to myself and make the excuse that it is because my stomach has been off. I'm sure in a few days, I will be shopping for myself with pleasure.

While walking around the supermarket, Robert rings me to offer me dinner and I accept, thinking that maybe it will spark my appetite when lovely hot food is put on the table for me. It does, I have a lovely meal cooked by Robert and I enjoy the company of Helen and the kids Arron, Jamie and Lily and the latest addition to the family, Daisy the dog. After lunch, Lily wants to watch the film Mama Mia and so Helen and I join her on the couch to watch it. I am carrying around this horrible feeling of foreboding. I have promised Paolo and all the rest of the family that I will not take chances with my health but the promise is weighing me down, I am concentrating on how I feel. I am not being sick or having cramps. I have not aches or pains, just a strange feeling. I can't go to the the Dr and say I just feel strange!

On the way home, I begin to think about the way I have brought my kids up. I never had "girlie days" as I see people doing now. Doing each others hair and nails etc. I can't ever remember even going shopping together. Adam has said to me in the past, that he felt pushed out because I used to sit chatting to the girls in the bedroom and he wasn't allowed to join in. I can't remember if that's true. He was the youngest of my original 4. I suppose as the girls got older, I would maybe not include a little brother in the conversation. And when I met Paolo his boys were a similar age to Adam, did I lump them together and spend even less time with him on his own? I didn't know how to make time to do things individually with any of the children. I was too busy, working, keeping house, childminding. But I am really proud of each of my children, so for all my faults, I must have been doing something right. I hope they forgive me for my failings.

As I get home a horrible smell reaches my nose and I see that my trousers have pulled the top of the bag away from my tummy and letting a bit of air out. I go to the loo to empty and change the stoma bag and as I do I little trump escapes from my bum. I had heard that this sometimes happens so didnt worry, but then something else follows through - am I doing a poo? How is this happening? I rack my brains to think of anything that was said to me in the hospital. One of the Xrays was to see if I had a burst bowel, surely that would have been painful and anyway the Xrays were clear. I decide to take no chances and phone up the ward at the hospital. I speak to a girl called Sarah and tell her how I feel and what has happened. She tells me that this sometimes can happen, but hasn't a clue why. She tells me that if I feel unwell to come into A&E otherwise make an appointment to see my GP in the morning. It's at this point that I remember my dad. He had a stroke when he was 54 and retired on health grounds. When he was 62, six months younger than I am now, I left Adam with him while I did a bit of Christmas overtime at work. As I was leaving I thought that he looked a bit peaky. I said "Are you alright Dad?" he answered that he was. I tried again "If you feel unwell, I will not go to work" he said "Don't worry about me, and the lads (Two of my brothers were at home) are here to watch Adam if I feel like a lie down" pacified, I went to work with my dad's words "Seeya cock" ringing in my ears. When I came home four hours later, he had died of a heart attack. What's the matter with me, I have never been this maudlin, I think it must be all this lying down I have been doing in the past week.

I send the "oracle" a text to see if he can shed some light on it. Daren the Bolton 1 Nurse did not answer my last test re the sickness and cramps so I don't really expect a reply. But he does and in his matter of fact northern manner he puts the situation into layman's terms and my mind at rest. He says that the lower bowel, the part of me that is redundant at the moment is very very long and is twisted and curled up to fit inside the body. Little bits of poo settle in these nooks and crannies because the bowel is not being used. Gravity sometimes causes these bits to work their way down slowly and, especially if you have a long wait for the stoma reversal operation, often cause you to need to sit on the toilet to let it out. Yuck!!!

That's all it took to lift my gloomy mood, a chat to Daren and a shower and I am ready to settle down for the night.

Monday 7th April, My first day back at work. Only Keith attends. I take him to visit my friend, also a childminder, who is minding another 6 year old and the two boys enjoy each others company. After lunch I take him shopping and he chooses a gift for his birthday which is on Friday. We play jenga and Connect Four and I listen to him read. The day seems very long.

Tuesday 8th April I have two children today. Keith and Jason. It's freezing cold outside and I am tempted to sit in the lounge and play games with Keith as I did on Monday. But it is difficult with Jason, he is too young to play the games and not at all happy to play by himself while I play a game with the older one. I look at picture books with him and sing some action rhymes while Keith watches TV but I can't allow him to do this all day so I suggest we go to Blackleach to feed the ducks, but Keith is not keen. In the end I pick the childminder friend that lives the furthest away and we wrap up and set out to walk. Dot is glad of the break in routine (I hope). Keith gets to play with two more school children and Jason to squabble with some babies his own age. We have a brew and a gossip and then I walk back. After lunch, I remove Jason's nappy and let him have a practice at going on the toilet. Play with the play dough for a while then I put him in the pram for a nap and give Keith my full attention for an hour. I send Paolo a text saying, "It's freezing, like the middle of winter" he answers "It's lovely here, just like summer" arrgh I should have gone with him. Jason is picked up earlier today and just after he leaves a young Polish couple and their two children arrive. I had had a phone call to see if I could take on the little girl (aged 3), just term time. I explained that I would be taking time off for the operation and also for a week's holiday in the beginning of June and they are fine with that so we start filling in contracts and child detail forms. It's not until I get to the part about fees that I realise that they haven't even asked me how much we charge. I tell them that it is £100 per day if thats all right. And watch their faces as first they realise I am joking and laugh and then think oh dear - How much does she charge? In the end we are all satisfied with arrangements, especially when I say I accept 3 year old funding, so if they can sort it that will pay for two of the five days each week.

Wednesday 9th April - 8 kids today, that's more like it. The rain from yesterday has stopped and the sun is peeking out, not exactly warm, but no longer freezing. I am in my element. It is so much easier to organise children in small groups than to try to entertain them singly. I bribe the three oldest girls (12, 10 and 9 year olds) with money for the sweet shop and they clear the rubbish from the back garden and wash (after a fashion) the outdoor toys. The boys (one aged nearly 7 and two four year old's) join in with enthusiasm. They clean the patio doors with muddy clothes, sweep leaves into the wind so they blow everywhere and chalk crosses over everything. The toddlers, Bobby and Bailey mooch about getting wet and everyone is hungry at lunch time.

The kids are enjoying themselves so much that we forget that we were going to hard boil and decorate some eggs and then have an egg rolling contest. Doesn't matter, we can do that tomorrow. As I am loading the dishwasher after tea, I hear Ashton crying and I look through the window to see his big sister dragging him towards the house. I listen and realise that she has heard him swearing and is bringing him in to be punished. After the usual denials (I'm quite impressed that he doesn't try to get anyone else in trouble), I tell him he had better do some reading so that he can learn new words to use instead of swear words. It shows the affection the boys have for each other, when Oliver and Keith decide to join him to keep him company and the three of them read a "level blue" phonetic book. After a ten minutes or so, they shout in unison that they have read the book and don't need to use swear words again. Yeh right, but a better solution than the soap on the tongue that my mother subscribed to. In the afternoon, Robert brings Jamie and Lily and daisy the dog, which creates a small diversion in which I can sneak a tea break. Nathan comes to pick up Bobby and Bailey and he joins us. Nathan takes his boys home and Lily begs to stay. So I am left with 7 kids. I make beef burgers and mash and carrots and the girls help to set the table and clear away. Life is much easier without the school runs. AT 5.30 I get all the kids to tidy up, Oliver and Keith get picked up and then I take the rest of them home. As I deliver Lily to her house she asks me how many more days does she have off school. I tell her she has another 10. YESSS she says, and then after a little thought "Oh no! In 10 days I will have to have a bath and wash my hair". 6.30 pm the house is relatively tidy and I have finished work for the day. I am not going to do any paperwork (though I should be making files for a couple of new kids). I am going to watch TV and eat chocolate.

Thursday 10th April Maddie does not come, she has got a stomach bug, so her mum keeps her at home. Alise and Shanay bake a birthday cake and biscuits for Keith and decorate them with smarties. After dinner I hard boil some eggs and the kids decorate them then roll them down the slide to see which goes the furthest. The eggs end up splattered all over the lawn and the chickens eat them, (cannibals). I have asked Jason's mum to pick him up early this week while I am on my own. Eleven hours a day is a long time with a two year old who only naps for about 15 minutes each day. She asks me if Paolo will be working from 7 a.m. on 20th May (the day of my op). I say of course not, he will be taking me to the hospital or I will have to leave my car in the car park for however long I am in. It is just a silly thoughtless question, but it opens up a whole lot of grievance. I end off pouring out all my disappointments in her over the last week. I hate doing this, I prefer to write down the things that get to me and read it back to make sure that I am sure of my facts before I start ranting. I tell her I have lost count of how many times she has told me that she is sooooo grateful to me for one thing and another. How many times she has prayed for me, but when I was really in need (i.e. last Thursday when I needed her to keep her child home), she put her job first and me and her child second. I know I will forgive and forget very quickly, but I have said it now and I will have to follow it up.

Friday 11th April I wake up and think it is Saturday, then am disappointed and in a rush when I realise that it is 6.45 - Jason will be here at 7.

We have a lovely day, first going to the Fun House and then to Blackleach country park. We go home for tea (spaghetti hoops on toast, Paolo would be mortified) and then I get all the kids to help clean up before they go home. I have survived a week without Paolo's help. Can't wait to see him tomorrow.

While on the Country Park, Jason's dad phones me to tell me that he is sorry about the misunderstanding and tells me how much they appreciate me. I tell him that I will speak to him at another time face to face.

Saturday 12th April. I get up and do supermarket shop, come home put it away and then go to the airport to pick up the travellers from Italy. I can't remember how long it takes to drive there. Paolo has sent me a text to say that the plane should be landing at 1.pm so I think I will give myself an hour (just in case I take the wrong motorway exit). I arrive at the airport at 12.30, think nothing of it and buy myself a latte and a muffin. They finally trickle through the arrivals gate and we go to pay the car parking £8.26 WHAT???? for 1 hour 6 min. Talk about a rip-off. It's lovely to see them again but next time I will make sure that the plane has landed before I park the car.

Saturday evening, my brother Darren, his wife Sue and daughter Indigo arrive. They have come from Tarvin to watch Scooby Doo at the Lowry. Indigo is going to have a sleepover with Lily her cousin (my granddaughter) but they cannot go until 6 p.m. Helen is working and Robert is sleeping after working a night shift. After they drop Indigo off with Helen, we all go to Witherspoons for tea and beer. This is a very rare occasion when we get to chat to Darren and Sue. Since the birth of Indigo, 7 years ago, they never go anywhere without her. This is nice for them and even better for her, but we look after children from 7 a.m. until nearly 7 p.m. I like to have a bit of adult company and communication in my free time. Its even better when Darren insists on paying for the meals as birthday treats for Paolo and me and Adam (his birthday is on the 28th April, so not far off.)

Sunday 13th April morning I sit down to write a letter to Pat and Peter. I know I will probably see them in church and if not next week when they drop of their son. But there are things I need to say to them. I know when I started talking to Pat, I got too emotional and did not stick to the point. I write that I am disappointed that they brought their son to Paolo to look after when I went in hospital, even though I had sent them a text, I acknowledge that the other parents who have known me longer would know that I don't exaggerate illness and for me to text them so late at night and give them such short notice started alarm bells ringing. I deliver the letter to them, but they have gone to the stations of the Cross at church, so I don't get any feed-back until the next morning. After a few words when she arrived, Pat said she acknowledged the points I had made, agreed with most of what I had said and that Peter would in future pick up Jason before tea. When Peter came later to pick up his son, he told me that he regarded us as family and had taken everything I had written on board. Good Result. I know that if I had merely spoken to Pat on the doorstep, the version that she told her husband would have been distorted by her own thoughts and feelings. I have found in the past that a letter is often more effective than having a row with someone.

Monday 14th April the baby Tahapenes arrives with her mum. I have not seen her in over a week since she kept her away last week. She is obviously still not well. She is miserable and lethargic and just keeps whimpering for me to carry her. I don't really mind, she is such a light little thing, but I hope to God that she is only suffering from teething problems and has not got another bug to infect me with.

Wednesday 16th April I take Niamh, Keith and Tahapenes to church. St Edmunds Children's Mass. I thought it would be more child friendly than it was. Father Leo would have made it short and sweet. He knew most of the children from the school by name and geared his sermons towards them. But he has been moved to a smaller parish on health grounds and Father Michael has taken his place. The school has been rebuilt and doubled in size so I suppose it is unfair for me to expect him to know all of the kids. His heart is in the right place and many of the congregation like him, but he doesn't relate his sermons to the present day, instead harking on about the bible, and his voice is not strong enough to be heard over the odd crying baby. The kids are remarkably well behaved so when we eventually leave the church, I take them into the sweet shop and treat them. After lunch (pasta carbonara) we go to Peel Park, where the Starting Life Well team have organised an Easter Egg hunt day. There are various activities as well as the egg hunt. Face painting, a climbing wall, resources for making Easter Cards, even an inflatable bowel (don't ask!). The sun shines, there are many friendly faces and Keith amazes the volunteers when he scales up the climbing wall without hesitation or fear. We return home with chocolate Easter bunnies, Easter cards, pink cheeks from the sun and wind, and five tired children.

Later in the afternoon, I receive two surprisingly pleasant phone calls. The first from a man trying to sell me life insurance. He goes into his spiel and is in full flow when I tell him that I have just had an operation for bowel cancer and don't think it a good time to change insurance policies, he immediately agrees and then we have a chat about his epilepsy, my cancer and Adams diabetes. The second call was in relation to my Dyson vacuum cleaner. It is making a strange noise and I was about to take it to be repaired when I came across some paperwork reminding me that it has a 5 year warranty. After two unsuccessful attempts to contact them, a man by the name of Henry very efficiently answers my call. without any preamble he asks for my name, the model of the cleaner and then tells me to switch it on so that he can listen to the noise. Then he instructs me on how to dismantle it and between us we diagnose the problem. Then he tells me that the part that is broken is not dispatched separately so he will send me a completely new brush head. Five minutes later I receive an invoice by email telling me that the part costs £65 and that the same £65 is discounted and that the new part is on its way. Thats what I call efficient. Much better than sending a man out, who arrives months later when you have just nipped out and then returns without the part. It just needs to arrive in one piece and I will be a loyal fan of Dyson forever.

Thursday 17th April turns out to be bitter sweet. We have Joshua again and apart from not making eye contact, he is reasonably controllable. He plays happily alongside rather than with the other kids, but this is completely normal. He refuses to hold on to the pram as we walk to the park, but doesn't complain when I loop the strap around his wrist to stop him running into the road. At the park, when I unfasten him, he walks alongside me with no problem. Lily, Niamh and Keith play happily together (usually when three play together, you get two ganging up against the third) Making a birthday cake from sand and water - lots of water. Tahapenes is no longer grizzling with teething problems. All the children eat their dinner and Paolo takes the eldest three to "On Safari". Joshua goes home and I enjoy a brisk walk, pushing the double pram with Jason and Tahapenes. So far so good, but then comes the bad news. Jason's dad, Peter informs me that Jason will no longer be coming to us. Peter has lost a contract and will no longer be earning enough to pay childcare fees. Alfie will also be leaving us as he will be going to a new nursery that has been opened nearer to his house. I am not disappointed about Alfie, he is 4 and a school environment will be better for him than spending his time with younger children. Also I will not be losing contact with him as I will see him when I visit his grandma, who is one of my closest friends. Three of my children will be taking a break from me at the end of this year when their mum goes on maternity leave and two more of the children will be starting full time school in September. Thats the problem with self employed childminders, there are no guarantees how long each child will stay with you. Having less children will also make life easier when I go in to hospital for the stoma bag reversal. We will just have to tighten our belts for a while.

Saturday19th April. Woke up to this lovely sunny Easter Day. I have an email from my friend Lesley: With this joke.

A female CNN journalist heard about a very old Jewish man who had been going to the Western Wall to pray, twice a day, every day, for a long, long time.

So she went to check it out. She went to the Western Wall and there he was, walking slowly up to the holy site.

She watched him pray and after about 45 minutes, when he turned to leave, using a cane and moving very slowly, she approached him for an interview.

"Pardon me, sir, I'm Rebecca Smith from CNN. What's your name?

"Morris Feinberg," he replied.

"Sir, how long have you been coming to the Western Wall and praying?"

"For about 60 years."

"60 years! That's amazing! What do you pray for?"

"I pray for peace between the Christians, Jews and the Muslims."

"I pray for all the wars and all the hatred to stop."

"I pray for all our children to grow up safely as responsible adults and to love their fellow man." "I pray that politicians tell us the truth and put the interests of the people ahead of their own interests."

"How do you feel after doing this for 60 years?"

"Like I'm talking to a f----g brick wall."

It makes me laugh and sad at the same time. Mankind will always be greedy enough to fight and quick to point blame at others, it would be a miracle if ever there were no wars in the world.

I volunteer to clean out the chicken coop. It was my idea to buy chickens, but Paolo has gradually become the main "chicken cleaner-outer". But at the moment he is making a surprisingly good job of block-paving the paths in the front garden, so I might as well clean out the chickens while they are relatively dry. Where the chickens live is the most water logged part of the garden, we really should have bought ducks. Even the smallest amount of rainfall turns the chicken run into a pond. I decide that while it is dry, I will really go to town and throw out all the old sawdust and straw and wash every bit of the inside of the coop. The chickens which have been happily digging up all the plants that Paolo has just planted decide to come and investigate. They peck around my feet and investigate wherever I sweep. They are a blooming nuisance, can't they understand I am trying to make life a bit pleasanter for them. I am rewarded with only one egg - a nice large brown one, but only one. Two of the chickens are slacking, I tell them that I will not make them any more porridge (they love porridge) if they don't start laying. I will give them one more chance.

We have an appointment at 11.a.m to collect the photos. As we leave, I say to Paolo, do you know the way and he says yes. I have no sense of direction and would not be able to find the address, even though we have been there and back twice before. We tear off up the motorway, with Paolo driving like the Ferrari racing driver that he wishes he was. Suddenly we are on the moors. Paolo says "I don't recognise this"! I don't recognise it either. He has been following the directions on "maps" on his phone. I ask him what address he had put on the phone and he says "Saddleworth" What a numbskull. We travel for miles along narrow, one lane dirt tracks, unable to get a signal to get new directions. Finally we see something we recognise and collect the photos, only 35 minutes late. We treat ourselves to a meal at the restaurant that we took the family to after the photo shoot.

I have been feeling a bit sickly since breakfast but decide that it is just wind, or hunger, I am sure that I will feel better after I have eaten. When we get inside the restaurant, Paolo says "Its your turn to buy a meal" I say OK, give me your debit card then" Its just a bit of banter between us, we only have one joint account, but the waitress hears me and finds it very funny. Well I have put a smile on someone's face today. We have bread and olives with balsamic vinegar and olive oil to dip, then I have Lancashire hotpot and Paolo has roast duck and chips. Afterwards, I feel even more sick. I guess its not hunger then. When we get home, Paolo volunteers to go food shopping for Easter Sunday Dinner. I feel so nauseous that

I go to bed and try to sleep. I have promised him and the hospital that I will go straight back if I begin to be sick. I don't want to spend Easter Sunday in the hospital.

Easter Sunday 20th April. I'm up early and get ready for church. The first pair of trousers I put on have come undone at the hem. The next pair wont fasten round my waist, I'll have to wear a skirt. I rarely wear skirts, Paolo gives me a wolf whistle (at least an attempt, I've never met a man with such a pathetic whistle - good job he has other talents). I am looking forward to reading the Mass from my iPad which a friend told me how to download. We'll show these youngsters how technical we can be. When it comes to it though, it bugs me. If we stay on one page for more than a minute, the iPad turns itself off. The friend comes to my rescue and shows me how to go into "settings" and adjust the time, so that now it will stay turned on for up to 15 minutes. It comes in handy because the church is full (free Easter Eggs) and there are not enough Mass sheets to go round.

Helen, Robert and their three kids come for dinner. Rachael and Sofia (her friend's eleven week old baby daughter) arrive. Isaac is in Thailand with his dad. Sofia is a lovely, calm baby, even her cries are quiet, I hope Nicola brings her to me to care for when she goes back to work.

Tuesday22nd April We have two new children. A little boy with signs of autism and a little Polish girl. So much for reducing the number of children we care for until after my operation. Each time I get a phone call about someone wanting childcare, I begin by saying that we are not taking any more children on until after our holiday at the beginning of June, and end off taking the children when the parents say that they can accommodate the week's holiday and also the time needed for my stay in hospital.

30 - The Lodger

Thursday 24th April. Nathan comes to see me to ask if I will allow Shauna to stay with us for one night as she has nowhere to live. She is homeless but is not allowed to live with Nathan and Kathryn because they are fostering Shauna's two little boys (Their grandchildren). I am dubious about allowing her to stay with us since she appears to be associating with some very dubious characters. But one look into Nathan's eyes and I know that I cannot refuse, he is on the brink of collapse with the worry of this wayward daughter.

Shauna becomes my project. I am determined to turn her life around. We sit at the computer, looking for jobs available to her. We write letters of application to all the local restaurants saying that she will be completely flexible if they would only give her a chance to show how she can work and I try to persuade her how life would be so much easier if she would just knuckle down and stop behaving so selfishly.

Surprisingly, she is good company. I have not had much contact with her over the last few years and I am happy to learn that she has turned into an entertaining young woman. She helps to keep the house tidy and does any job that I ask. It's such a pity that she is completely without the work ethic and looks forward to getting her fortnightly benefits as if they were her wages. I point out that Matteo (her uncle, but two months younger that her) has worked all the time he was at college. He has passed his driving test, bought a car and been on several holidays. His girlfriend is a year younger and has also got her own car. I ask Shauna if she wouldn't rather have a boyfriend with a job, who could take her out and buy her nice things, instead of one who hits her and only needs her when she has money? She answers in the affirmative but I know that she is only answering me with what I want to know. I know that she is for whatever reason going to wait around for "the boyfriend" who has a mysterious hold over her. I make several attempts to point out the downfalls of her lifestyle, but it is water off a duck's back, I suspect that as soon she collects her dole, she will disappear for a few days and come back unrepentant and hungry.

Monday 28th April - 31 years since I gave birth to Adam. He was my bonniest baby. He never looked like a new-born, but he was the one who was happiest being a baby. No wonder, perhaps he knew that life was not going to be so kind to him as he grew. He was only seven years old when his dad and I split up. His dad went on to marry a woman with a son who was in a school year below Adam who basically replaced him, as his dad quite quickly disappeared from his life. I married Paolo who also had two sons, slightly younger than Adam, and while they didn't replace him, looking back I can see that I was so desperate to create a "happy family", that I tended to lump the three boys together and so have less one to one time with him. He was the one that, during the first year at high school, developed diabetes, had to undergo an appendectomy and get bitten by the school caretakers dog. He was then bullied by older boys at school as they said he was trying to get the dog "put down" by complaining about the attack. Because of his young age, he was protected from the bitterness of my divorce from his dad, but then became upset in later years because his older brother and sisters had been told more about the split. He has become a bit depressed over the last year or so because he has lost the ability to recognise the signs associated with becoming hypoglycaemic and so has needed the help of me or work colleagues to phone the paramedics to perform first aid. Despite his condition, he never uses it as an excuse to stay away from work, and copes with all the injections and blood monitoring and food measuring, without complaint, I have so much admiration.

Today as I give him his birthday card, and get the kids to sing happy birthday dear Adam, he tells me that he is depressed. I tell him that it is no wonder, but ask him to talk about it instead of shutting himself away in his bedroom. He has an appointment to speak to a diabetic specialist and promises to bring it to her attention.

Wednesday 30th April. As predicted, Shauna goes out and does not come back. But she phones me to say that she is baby-sitting with her boyfriend and will be staying at his mum's house and will come home tomorrow. I don't approve of her boyfriend,

217

but that is out of my hands and I am glad she has had the curtesy to phone.

Thursday 1st May. I drive myself to Bolton 1 for my pre operation assessment and after having blood tests, E.C.G.s blood pressure checks and answering numerous questions I am told that I am fit to face the surgeon on 20th May - yippee!!! I am slightly shaken when one of the nurses tells me that the surgeon will be cutting me open down the scar that he made for the original op. I had been under the impression that the cut would be around the stoma bag. I am relieved when the next nurse tells me that my first presumption was correct. It is still major surgery, but I will not be under aesthetic for as long as I was last October, and the recovery should not take so long. I come home with my arms full of Ensure Plus Juice and my head full of information.

In the evening Shauna arrives home and she tells me that her boyfriends mum had treated them to lunch in a restaurant. She is happy and chatty and I am surprisingly glad to see her. I have a discussion with her about a missed appointment that had come to my notice and I explain how unfair she is being to all these social workers etc who are doing their best to help her, when she doesn't keep appointments. She promises that she will become more reliable and I decide to believe her, there is no point being pessimistic at this point. I will judge her on her behaviour while she is in my house and not on what I have heard about her.

Friday 2nd May I am having a conversation with a parent when Shauna trips downstairs and says something about a solicitor and goes out the front door. Half an hour later Nathan phones asking if I know where she is. I tell him the little I know and he says "What about her access?" I had not realised that she was supposed to see her boys today. Nathan tells me not to phone her as there could be an explanation so I leave them to it. It turns out that she has gone to Manchester with her boyfriend. I am deeply disappointed in her and so angry I feel like throwing her back out into the street. When she returns in the evening I go mad, asking her how she thinks her sons are feeling. She has no idea, she says that she forgot, I say "If they were my children, I would be counting the seconds until I could see them" She has every excuse and I knock back every one. I tell her I am very sad and disappointed. The next morning I ask her where she is going and she answers "Just to meet Tyler to get my phone back" I ask why he has her phone and she tells me that she left it on the bus and he picked it up. I don't believe her for a second, I presume he has talked her into giving it to him so that she has an excuse to see him again. A week later, she is still waiting for him to "in-box" her to arrange to meet to get it back. Silly, silly girl! She is apologetic about the missed access and is grateful when I stop ranting at her and start my usual Saturday morning clean. She grabs a cloth and helps me in silence.

Tuesday 6th May, Shauna is up at 7.30 a.m. and makes tea for everyone. Good start! She has an appointment with the probation and I have been lecturing her about being an adult and keeping appointments. I have told her that I expect her to find out the times of the buses and get herself there each week. She says that she is getting the 9.30 a.m. bus. At 9.10, she is still putting her makeup on and watching the computer screen. I tell her she had better get a move on and she replies that she is waiting for her mum to bring her £4 for the bus fare. I nearly explode. She got her benefits less than a week ago, they are supposed to cover living expenses for a fortnight and she hasn't got a penny left. She explains that she only received £90. I shout, £"90 for doing nothing, thats not £90 spends you know, it is to live on" I give her the £4, send her out of the door and tell her that I am going to phone the Well Woman Clinic (where she goes for probation) to check that she is there at 10.30. For the rest of the week, she doesn't put a foot wrong, willingly doing any chore I ask. I think she has at last realised that I am her last chance. She starts applying for apprenticeships and cleaning jobs. Perhaps there is still hope. In the evening I meet Gail and Kevin in the "Stocks". I am telling them the Shauna Saga, telling them that it is my latest project to get her on the straight and narrow. Kev says that it is a lost cause. He quotes "Give me the boy before he is seven, and I will give you the man". I hope he is wrong, I hope that I can make her rethink some of her ideas.

Friday 9th May I go early morning swimming. I am in training for my operation and trying to do 40 lengths, three times a week instead of 30. When I get back I hang out the washing that I had put on the night before, I always have more energy and "get-up-and-go" when I start the day with a swim. After taking the school children to school, we take the younger kids to the Fun House. It is Odelia's last day for a while as her dad has finished his university course. He is hoping to go back again in September and so is going to apply for agency work. So I might have her again if he gets some temporary work and I might have her again in September, but as far as the situation is at the moment, this is her leaving day. We buy the kids their lunch and I have a fajita chicken wrap with chips and salad. Afterwards I go to the loo and empty my stoma bag. The contents are just the perfect consistency for my health (tooth paste thickness) but the wrong one for flushing down the toilet. I flush it once and wait for the tank to fill up and repeat. The brown sludge is still there, there is no toilet brush to use. I go and wash my hands and then go back and flush for a third time, I am glad that no other person needs to use the toilets. After the fourth flush, I give up and go and tell the reception that someone has left a mess in the toilet. I know I am a coward, I couldn't for the life of me admit that it was me.

Wednesday 14th May. Gail calls, she has been for a walk and is just passing, so dropped in for a brew. I bring her up to speed with the Shauna gossip. After another stint on the internet she has got an interview for an apprenticeship in a hairdressers. One step in the right direction. There seems to be some hope that she may get her furniture back after Nathan put a note through the door. Ive agreed to store her "white goods" in our garage but not indefinitely. This has a knock-on effect because to make room we have to have a clear out. It's surprising how much rubbish we store, just because we have the room to do it. As Gail stands up to leave, she mentions "You haven't for gotten the WITS have you. Of course, once again I have. She reminds me that we are going to watch "Yes Prime Minister" and that it is my turn to drive. I mentally make a note to leave in time to get some cash out on the way.

I am delayed in the evening and when I get to the cash machine it is out of order. I decide to leave it, taking it for granted that Gail will be able to lend me the cash, unfortunately, Gail has barely got enough cash and when we meet Jean in the theatre, neither has she. What a bunch of paupers! The production as usual was brilliantly funny and afterwards we go to the John Gilbert for a drink. (I have coffee as I have decided to abstain until after my operation). We can pay with credit cards in the pub.

Thursday 15th May I drink the prescribed three bottles of Ensure Plus Juice that I have to drink each day from now until 19th May to build up my health. I have a little panic, only 5 more days to go. Isaac is staying the night with us as Rachael is working in London and wont be back until late. Lily begs me to let her stay and I say OK, it is sometimes easier to entertain 2 children than one. I make a resolution to myself that I will get them in bed by eight o'clock but I fail miserably. First my cousin Linda calls around, she is in Little Hulton visiting her mum Josie. Then Helen calls to bring Lily's pyjamas and stays for a brew. I eventually get the kids to bed by 8.30 with a chocolate spread buttie and a cup of milk, watching a DVD. Then I realise that I haven't got anything interesting in for their packed lunches so I nip out to Tesco. When I get back, Paolo informs me that the kids are not asleep and that Lily has spilt the full cup of milk on the bed. Paolo has put a towel on the bed to mop up the spill but Lily is not happy. I open the drawer under the bed to find clean bedding and am aghast at how many single sheets I pull out before a find a double sheet and duvet cover, a clearout and trip to the charity shop is needed.

Friday 16th May. We have two extra children after school for tea. This results in there not being enough sausages for Paolo or me. How sad, Paolo goes to Aldi to buy some steak which we enjoy after the children have all gone home. I decide to have a glass of wine (no self control), it tastes all the better after my week of abstinence. As we enjoy the meal and talk about everything except my up and coming hospital appointment, I feel my stoma spitting food into the bag. Or that is what I presume is happening. In reality, I have my jeans too tight which is blocking half of the stoma bag and so food is being forced up past the seal and coating the inside of my tee shirt. Roll on Tuesday.

Saturday 17th May. It's a glorious day, warm and sunny. Normal people would head for the beach or at least a pub garden. Paolo spends the whole day finishing off the garden and I wash and clean. I even clean all the prams and clean out the chicken

221

coop. Paolo cooks salmon and salad for tea and we sit outside to eat dessert (cornetto). A nice relaxing end to the day.

Sunday 18th May. For no particular reason, I go to Mary the Virgin Church at Ellenbrook. The vicar there is the sister of Lesley, one of my oldest friends. It is Church of England but the Mass is almost identical to the Catholic one. Afterwards I have a little chat to Lesley and Karen (the vicar) and then go to the cemetery to have a chat to my mum. A bit one sided I admit. She could never keep flowers alive and she hasn't lost the knack of killing plants since she has been dead. The first Silver Birch we had planted on her grave died almost immediately and its replacement is a leaning, weak-looking thing. I pull up some grass and straighten the plants and tell her I will come back with some flowers tomorrow. I tell her about my operation. I don't really believe that my mum is there under the mud, but it feels good to talk to her. I leave the cemetery and call on Josie to tell her that we are going to see Pat and Michelle in Sheffield and so won't be cooking dinner. I feel bad that I didn't tell her yesterday so that she could have pulled the chicken out of the freezer sooner. The weather is lovely and we spend time sitting on the grass eating ice cream and listening to the sound of the cricket match with Patrick, (very English). Later we meet Michelle after she finishes her shift and we have very filling Pub Grub for Sunday Dinner. On the way home there are signs asking motorist to slow down as there is a pedestrian on the motorway. The traffic slows down slightly for about ten miles, but we don't see any pedestrians.

Monday 19th May Operation day is speeding towards me. I have diligently drunk 3 Ensure Plus Juice each day for the last 5 days. I have had the first of 3 Pre-load sugar filled drinks which apparently will increase the healing power of my body after the operation and have packed a bag. I feel like Mr Bean trying to decrease my luggage to fit into a smaller bag. When I was admitted in October for my first operation, I took a small carry-on bag. It was too big and in the way, and so I am trying to condense my necessities into a large handbag. I took two of the kids with me to the cemetery to take flowers to my mum's grave, they had great fun watering all the flowers on the other graves. We have beef burgers on barmcakes for tea. Less cooking, less arguments and less washing up. The kids are collected one by one with parents wishing me the best for tomorrow. My heart is racing, I wish it was Wednesday already and this operation was behind me. Two of our friends Jackie and Steve call to wish me well and stop to fill us in with news of other friends. They tell us that Steve is also going in hospital on Friday for a knee operation, but not the same hospital as me so we will not be bumping into each other. Another friend arrives and makes us laugh with tales of her dad's hypochondria. He is in his eighties and quite sick, but he does not believe anything that the medical personnel tell him. He thinks they are conspiring against him. Finally my sister arrives, we drink tea and talk and then she orders me to have an early night and goes home. I have a bowl of cereal and my second pre-load and complete a suduko on the PC. I think I am tired enough to sleep now.

31 - Goodbye Stoma

Tuesday 20th May 2014 I am up early and give Matteo a hug and a kiss before he leaves for work. His shift starts at 6.a.m. I mix the pre-load with water thinking I have to drink it at 6.am but when I check it is 6.30, then nil by mouth.

We leave home at 7a.m. to arrive at 7.10.a.m. Paolo goes to pay for parking and I head for the Main Entrance. I set off in the direction towards the way the car has just entered the car park and notice it says "No Exit for Pedestrians" so I about turn and go through the other gate. Then I stand waiting for Paolo. I can't see him and ring his mobile - it goes straight to answering machine. Seconds later Paolo phones me and I tell him I am at the Main Entrance. Somehow he had managed to pay the parking, lock up the car and get into the hospital and was waiting for me at Ward F6. On this occasion Paolo is not sent home, so we sit in the waiting room. A nurse and an anaesthetist ask me to repeat my details: Name. Date of Birth. Address. Any Medication. I tell him that I am not taking anything long term, he tells me that he has contacted my doctor and been told that I take Loperomide. Oh dear, I didn't even think of this poo thickener as a drug. I tell him that I haven't taken many. He mentions that there has been a re-shuffle of operation times but since my operation was scheduled for 9.a.m., it might not effect me. We are still waiting at 10.30. a.m. A nurse brings me a glass of water and tells me not to eat anything after 11 pm. I tell Paolo to go home, I have run out of conversation and he might as well go home if I am just going to read magazines. At some point later, Mr Hobbis the surgeon in scrubs comes in to apologies to the other woman waiting for her operation. As he turns to leave he sees me and mutters his apologies. I say "Does that mean I will have to come back tomorrow?" He answers "Unfortunately, maybe. I'll just try one more thing!" The next thing I know, a nurse is summoning me and telling me I am next.

My preparation for surgery begins at 2.pm. I have not eaten since 10 pm the night before and the smell of hospital food is making my mouth water.

The preparations seem much simpler this time, no injection in my spine, but I am informed that I will be injected with a local anaesthetic near the site of the stoma as well as a general anaesthetic. Electrodes are struck to my body and I am asked the usual details to ensure that the surgeon operates on the right person. The mask is placed over my mouth and I go to sleep. I remember nothing from that point until I wake up on the ward and see Paolo and Gail waiting by my bedside.

Wednesday 21st May I wake up still groggy, very early in the morning. I need a wee. I try to sit up in bed but it causes too much pain and I lie down again. Slowly I become more aware of where I am. I have white velcro boots on that massage my legs and a saline drip through a cannula in my arm, but I don't have a catheter or a button to press for morphine. It is so much easier to get out of bed and walk around. Before breakfast I have been to the toilet for a wee. After breakfast a nurse takes off the blood pressure monitor, the massaging boots and the saline drip. All I am left with is the oxygen tubes up my nose.

At 2 pm Gail arrives once more, followed by Matteo and Lauren, Josie and Nathan. I am only supposed to have 2 visitors at a time. In the evening I am walking around like Billy No Mates. I phone Paolo in case he thinks visiting time is at 7. He knows that it is 6 - 7.30pm but still has one of the minded children left uncollected. He eventually arrives at 6.30 and it is nice to be able to sit and talk to him knowing that the nightmare is over. I tell him I have been up out of bed and eating as per plan. I have no doubt in my mind that this time, I will be out of hospital in record breaking time and getting on with my life.

Thursday 22nd May Day merges into night in hospital and I am not in the mood to take notes, but I make a few entries on Facebook. As usual, too much, too soon. Straight back from surgery and I am eating 3 course meals. Result sickness and diarrhoea but after a day of liquid only and a good nights sleep, I feel much better.

Friday 23rd May Am awake early and in pain. But just been given some liquid morphine and antisickness. I should feel better soon. Its my brother Perry's birthday. I surface enough to send best wishes to him and then wonder what the hell has happened since Wednesday. Where has all the optimism gone? I Send a Whatsapp to my friends and children.

It's 5 am and I am in pain. Can't wait for my codeine and paracetamol. Just struggled to get out of bed to have a shower then remembered I am still attached to a drip. Can't believe it's Friday.

Just got some Orimorph and anti-sickness. Should start to feel better soon

But I don't feel better soon. My stomach is distended and putting pressure on the already very painful wound. It is also pushing up into my lungs making is difficult to breath and my oxygen saturation levels keep falling too low.

Not a happy bunny. Mr Hobbis has just done his rounds and told me to go back on liquids. I will need a scan again tomorrow to look for the blockage.

The scan that Mr Hobbis recommends, doesn't actually happen until the following Tuesday. I am not sure if this is because of the bank holiday or whether he decided to wait and see a bit longer.

At visiting time Arron my eldest grandchild visits me. He makes me so proud. He is tall and handsome, hardworking and clever, gentle and polite. I moan to him about being in hospital, about my distended stomach about my fears of another operation. What a waste, I could have told him how wonderful he is.

Saturday 24th May If I could have imagined the pain, I would have kept the bag.

On Saturday, Mr Harris, another member of the surgical team comes to see me. He examines my tummy and tells me that it is not unusual for the bowels to be out of synch after major surgery. He recommends that I go back on the saline drip and have only sips of water to give them time to synchronise. At visiting time, Joe arrives with Paolo. Joseph is thinking about going to Australia and tells us about the expense related just to applying to go and visas. I'm tired and embarrassed that I am falling asleep. I suggest they go home early.

After supper, as people are settling themselves down for the night and the nurses are writing up observations and giving out medication; a woman called Wendy who has had a leg amputated at the knee begins to cry hysterically saying that her life is over and that she will never walk or work again. Out of all the patients in the ward and the three nurses, it is a lovely lady called Susan who has had one and a half legs removed, she is the first to offer her comfort.

Saturday 25th May Helen's Birthday The painkillers are spacing me out and not killing the pain. Think I may try to do without them for tonight

After this last text message, I am inundated with messages from friends and family telling me not to do without the painkillers, perhaps they are right.

I am awake early and drag the trolley holding the saline drip to the toilet. I clean my teeth and give myself a wash without removing my nightie and climb back into bed. I send Helen a birthday greeting by text and answer some Facebook comments and email messages via my phone. I finish my book and throw it into the rubbish bin it is too rubbish to pass on to anyone. The breakfast trolley comes round, I don't mind at all that I am "nil by mouth", I am not hungry. I wonder when the scan, recommended by Mr Hobbis is going to be arranged. Another member of the team, Mr Harris I think, comes to see me and suggests that I should have a drain inserted. I have mixed emotions about this. The last time it was attempted, the tube wouldn't go up my nose because it was too painful and I ended up with a nose bleed.

By this point in my hospital stay, my arms are covered in bruises, caused by numerous attempts to find a vein to test my blood or to fit a drip. It has been decided to administer my Paracetamol intravenously to give my stomach one less thing to irritate it. Bev comes to hook me up and realises that I am not "hooked up" She says "Hold on I will fit you another cannula". I lie back resignedly expecting the usual "here it comes, sharp scratch". But she manages it at the first attempt without any pain. She very efficiently and cheerfully attaches the saline and paracetamol and goes about her business as the visitors file in. Gail comes to see me and I have a bit of a moan, but she soon cheers me up and has me laughing until I begin to worry that I will burst out of my stitches. As the visitors leave and the day staff begin to hand over to the night shift, I feel my hand going stiff and when I look it has almost doubled in size. The needle that Bev had inserted so gently has pulled back out of the vein and has been leaking saline into the tissue. I thought it was too good to be true! A new vein has to be found and the canula fitted once more. A nurse is sent to my bed to insert the new one but she can't find a suitable vein she says she will get the sister in charge to do it. By midnight I cannot sleep without pain relief and the nurse gives me two paracetamols. I am very thirsty despite sipping water. Eventually at 1 a.m. the drip is once more connected. The nurse gently wraps a bandage around it in an attempt to keep it attached as it is a very precarious position on the back of my hand. I drag it to the loo then get back into bed. It is too warm, I wish I was back in my own bed. I eventually fall asleep but am awakened to the sound of the two amputees discussing phantom pains and the merits of buttered toast versus jam on toast. I would kill for a piece of toast and a cup of tea. I drag the drip once again to the loo, catch a nurse to give me some morphine and get back in bed, hopeful that I can get some sleep before the morning routine starts, once more at 6.a.m. At some point I am gently aroused from my sleep by a nurse doing observations. I don't ask anything and she doesn't volunteer information as she tests for blood pressure, oxygen saturation and replaces the canula, which despite the bandage has once more become dislodged.

AT 6.30 a.m. a very cheerful voice invites us to choose breakfast. Without opening my eyes fully, I feel my tummy, it is still hard and painful, so reluctantly I shake my head and go back to sleep.

Bev, the lovely sister on the ward brings the equipment to drain my stomach. I am a bit apprehensive but am not going to refuse anything that might help. The tube is quite fine and Bev is very gentle. She lubricates the tube in something that smells of oranges and negotiates it up my nostril. I begin to gag violently so she stops and encourages me to take deep breaths and to swallow sips of water to help the tube go down my throat. The tube reaches my stomach and nothing comes back. Bev gives me a glass of orange to drink and this very quickly rises back up the tube. There is nothing in my stomach! What an anti-climax! The nurse informs the surgical team who send a message to say they will come to see me to review the new situation later. I sit there for a little while but then start to gag violently once more. With each retch it feels like I am being stabbed in my wound. Water is pouring from my eyes and nose Bev hears me and runs up the ward to retract the drain and I find myself sobbing quietly to myself. I am so disappointed, I really thought this would relieve the pain. I will have to wait for the surgical team once more.

Adam and Matteo come to visit and we discuss Matteo's job application and bad working conditions at the hotel where Adam works. I tell them about the book I have read and Adam promises to send me a good one. During the day I have a few promising feelings when it feels as if my bowels are working, but they prove to be false alarms after I have pushed the saline drip to the toilet.

Rachael and Isaac arrive first in the evening and then Paolo and Helen. Once more my visitors are exceeding the recommended maximum number around each bed. I wish Helen a Happy Birthday and promise to treat her when I am out of hospital, she tells me I look brighter. Isaac brings me some giraffe slippers that he chose for me, he says he is learning to swim. After the visitors leave, I lapse into a lovely sleep, feeling too warm but comfortable even as the night staff rouse me to carry out their observations.

Monday 26th May Nathan's Birthday The irony is that last time I spent longer recovering because I was being sick. It seems that not being sick is delaying my recovery now because the bowel is not emptying and so there is too much pressure on the join.

Mr Hobbis arrives early and asks if I am having 40 winks. I tell him that the only time I am without pain is when I am lying still on my back. He tells me he will arrange for a scan tomorrow and the bag may have to be re-attached. I am shocked, that this might be the outcome. How would that solve anything? I become quite despondent at this idea. Before he leaves he give me an enema in the hope that it will jump start the bowels. I lie there waiting for the urge to "go" but it doesn't happen. In the end, I sit on the commode and the liquid from the enema trickles out. Another

229

failure. Later in the day the registrar visits and tells me I am being monitored and that everything might still recover given time. For some reason I decide to be optimistic about this news and convince myself that at some point today I will give a huge fart and all the swelling will go down. While playing on my phone I notice a message from `Josh saying he is bored. I message him to tell him I am in hospital. At lunch time Gail brings me bigger knickers as my usual ones are not comfortable over my swollen belly. My friend Linda arrives late as I have told her I am on F4 when in fact I am on E4 Nathan arrives and I wish him a Happy Birthday, this time 41 years ago I was in Park Hospital, Davyhulme, a new mum. I can't believe how quickly that time has gone and (How I wish I had known then what I know now!) I ask him what he has been given for his birthday and he says "nothing yet", but he has bought a bouncy castle for his grandsons.

Lesley, my friend arrives ready to do fisticuffs with the staff for not looking after me. It was a pleasant interlude and I feel a little more comfortable as they leave. I am convinced that this is the day for the turnaround. As my visitors leave, I take myself off to the toilet, I produce nothing once more and as I rock myself backwards and forwards to encourage something, someone taps on the door to say I have a visitor. It is a lovely surprise to see Josh. An hour late perhaps, but its nice to see him. A surly 17 year old getting off his backside to visit his nanna is appreciated.

Paolo and Shauna arrive for the next visiting session and while he is here I Whatsap all the parents to tell them that I am still in hospital and to contact Paolo if their children will still be attending so that he can arrange extra assistance. My friend Debbie arrives wearing a beautiful scarf to cover her hair. She has married a Syrian Muslim and taken his religion. As with everything she does Debbie gives it one hundred percent, there are no half measures with her. She has taken time out from her very busy life of mother of 4 young children to visit me. I am on an upswing of moods and tell them that I am sure everything will improve soon, and that I intend to snuggle down to sleep as soon as visiting is over. But the optimism is unfounded, I find myself wide awake, and in more pain than ever.

Tuesday 27th May. I wake up early sweating and still in pain. I push the trolley to the toilet to complete my morning ablutions. Not an easy task when your stomach feels like it is falling out. The registrar calls and asks how I am, I tell her my pain is still acute, she says that I will definitely be going for a scan and that she will call back again with Mr Hobbis. Mr Hobbis does come to see me but I have gone walkabout while the domestic changes my bedding. He has to do a return visit. He says that in his opinion my tummy is less tense but he is still worried about my obvious pain. A little while later I am provided with a litre of Gastro Grafin and told to try to drink as much as possible before 1.p.m. I don't find this difficult and almost manage to drink all of it. A whistling porter arrives to take me for the CT Scan and I am relieved that at last they will find the problem. It is so hot on the ward that it is quite refreshing to feel the cool air as we wizz along the corridors, but by the time I am sitting in the wheelchair outside the scanning room, I am feeling quite chilly. Inside I find it very painful to climb on the bed and even worse when told to raise my arms above my head. The scan takes only minutes and then the pain of movement is repeated. the young scanner operator is very sympathetic and puts a blanket around my shoulders to stop me shivering and the porter takes me back to the sauna ward.

It is visiting time as I get back but I am glad I don't have a visitor, I just need some pain relief. Later, the Gastro Gafin seems to have kick started my bowels and I make a couple of painful walks to the loo. Each time I seem to expel a bit of wind and I hope this will relieve the pressure. A little while later the registrar comes to give me the thumbs up but I am confused at what she means. She says the scan has shown there is no problem, just the bowels needing to get working. I have very mixed feelings. On the one hand, I didn't want to go back to surgery, on the other "Why am I in so much pain if there isn't a problem? Mr Hobbis arrives later to tell me that the scan has shown swelling but no obvious problem. I have to accept that I probably brought all this pain on myself by eating too much too soon after surgery. It's a sobering thought. At tea time I eat a small bowl of rice pudding and when the medication trolley comes round I am given a mild laxative, I tentatively start to believe that I am getting better.

231

Wednesday 28th May I've had a couple of futile trips to the toilet during the night but I feel less bloated today. The nurse disconnects the I.V. line and I have a shower and wash my hair. When I get back I eat a small bowl of Rice Krispies and answer a few texts A doctor comes and asks me if I want to go home today or tomorrow. It takes my breath away. I can't go home, I'm still in pain! How soon I have become institutionalised. But I quickly get used to the idea and look forward to going. A nurse comes round to do observations and surprise, surprise, now that I am not hooked up to a saline drip and oxygen mask, my blood pressure is better and oxygen saturation is perfect. Being permanently monitored was keeping me sick. At lunch time I have a small bowl of delicious pea soup, I would murder for a piece of bread to dip but am warned that bread can be quite bloating. Being mobile rather than restricted with the I.V. line encourages me to walk about more, so I am not so tempted to lie down and doze, this has a good effect and strange rumblings keep emerging from inside me. I worry that all the gas will suddenly explode from my bottom and I make more frequent trips to the loo. I have a phone calls from Gail, Nathan, Helen and Paolo but each of them lasts only seconds before contact is lost. I will be glad to be home.

After tea I go into the day room to watch Britains Got Talent and Daren finds me there He tells me I look better, warns me about not wearing the compression stockings and tells me that the scan had shown up "gunge" (a medical term no doubt) around the operation site. I suppose this explains the pain that I am still feeling. I tell him that I still have hopes of a bit of a holiday the next week and he reminds me of the dangers of travel if I am going to be sitting with my legs in one position for any length of time.

Wednesday continues to improve, I eat bread at tea time without any ill effects, and Robert brings me buttered Soreen (which had such magical properties the last time) at the evening visiting which I pick at and enjoy slowly. There are some comings and goings on the wards, saying goodbye to ladies I have shared a ward with for a week is a strange experience and watching the beds being filled within minutes demonstrates how busy this hospital is. The nurses are tireless and cheerful without exception, hardly sitting down except to write out notes. Without the inconvenience of the I.V line

232

and oxygen, I get stuck into the novel that Adam has lent me and I read well into the night by the light of my phone.

Reading into the night does me no good. Afterwards I lie awake, the pain in my side, while not intolerable, just enough to stop me drifting off to sleep. Or perhaps it is withdrawal symptoms from not breathing the oxygen. In the end I ask for more pain relief (who would believe that I hardly ever take so much as an aspirin when I am at home, I worry that I am becoming reliant on the drugs) The busy nurse brings it for me immediately, adding it carefully to my notes and without missing a beat moves on to the next summons to give out TLC. NHS Staff are fabulous.

During the night, a man in the side ward falls out of bed. He is not a doddering, senile old man, but a big man with all his faculties. Instead of buzzing the nurses for help, he had decided to stretch down to the floor to retrieve something and lost his balance. The nurse in charge of the ward, was very upset. The man was not hurt, but from then on a nurse had to be sitting in the ward to keep an eye on him to ensure that he did not fall again. One nurse, 24/7 doing absolutely nothing but watching a stupid arrogant man. One nurse who could be giving out medicine, holding kidney bowls under the chin of a vomiting patient, changing bedding, giving out hugs, listening to worries. Ok that is only my opinion, I do not know the full story, but this book is about my feelings and these were mine at the time.

In the ward was an amazing woman named Sue. She had had one leg amputated just below the knee. And then while she was being fitted for a prosthesis (with her best shoe attached), she had been rushed as an emergency patient and had the other leg taken off completely. She had us in stitches (excuse the pun) telling us that she could feel the amputated foot, saying that she was sure that it had gone through the bed, assuring us that she could feel the floor under the bed. She often told us that her foot was dancing on the floor, giving Michael Flately a run for his money. During the crisis of losing the second leg, the false limb (including shoe) had gone missing. One evening during visiting time, as Sue was manoeuvring herself into a wheelchair so that she could accompany her sister to the cafe, the nurse suddenly remembered

233

"Oh yes Sue, I forgot to mention, your leg has turned up, it had gone to Manchester!" The northern sense of humour kicked in (another pun). "What's it doing in Manchester, has it gone clubbing?" "Is it looking for a sole mate?""Has it gone shopping for shoes?" "Will it be coming home on the Number 8 bus" "Will it hop onto the bus", In the middle of all this hilarity, Sue stretches herself up to her total 4'6" and says "I'm not standing for this (more laughs) You are mocking the afflicted, I am disabled you know!" Then with exaggerated self righteousness she turned around in her wheelchair and once more tried to remember what she needed with her. "Pauline!" she called to her sister, "What am I short of?" without missing a beat her sister answered "Legs"

Friday 30th May I can go home, I send a message on Whatsapp that I am coming home so that no one arranges to visit me and so that one of them can be on standby to bring me home. I send a text to Gail because she hasn't got Whatsapp. Then I go for a shower, and mentally prepare myself for a lazy day in bed waiting for discharge notes, medication and whatever else I need. I don't expect to be home before tea time and am thinking it would be nice if I go home after all the minded children have gone. I stroll down to the cafe which is just outside the ward and buy myself a hot chocolate and a slice of cake. The cake leaves an aftertaste in my mouth and I wonder if my taste buds have changed because of the surgery. I hope not, I love food.

While relaxing there I glance at my phone and see I have a reply from Gail saying she will be there at 11. I text back to say that is too early but she is on the way. I go back to the ward and clear up my cupboard and get dressed. I ask the nurse if she thinks I will be ready to go before dinner. She says it's anyone's guess, but she will take out my stitches if I am in a hurry. I get a text from Gail to say she is in the cafe so I go to meet her there, I try to tell her that it will probably be the afternoon before I am ready but she says she was going to take the lawnmower to her mother-in-law. I begin to feel stressed, then guilty that I am stressed. Gail is so good to me. She is generous with her time, support and on several occasions during my life with financial loans that have got me out of sticky situations. But the balance is wrong. It's all one way, I never have the opportunity to return all this good will. There were several people willing and available to pick me up when I was ready and it would have been half an hour out of their lives. Drive to hospital, pick me up, drop me off. No big deal. A favour I could and would be able to return. But Gail has paid the parking and she is sitting patiently waiting for as long as it takes for me to be ready. I rationalise that as she has just retired from a full-time job, she is probably glad to have something to kill a couple of hours, but in the end, I let her take me home and Paolo goes back later to pick up the medicine.

32 - Home Once More

When we arrive home, Gail comes in for a cup of tea, which Matteo makes for us, and then goes home. I have come home dressed in the clothes I was wearing to go to the hospital which include cropped elasticated waist trousers. The trousers are not comfortable on my swollen waist. I excuse myself, go upstairs to find something more comfortable. The bed is too inviting, I put on a nightie and snuggle down. A little later Paolo rings to say he is taking the kids to McDonalds and do I want anything! No chance, I've had 10 days of hospital food, I need some home cooking. Before the kids go home, I go downstairs and they ask me if the bag has gone? Will the poo come out of my bum again? Does my belly hurt? Will I be better soon? Why am I wearing a dressing gown in the afternoon? When all the questions and answers are out of the way, I sit on our swinging seat and watch them play in the garden. "Watch me Nanna!" "Look what I can do!" No, not like that, watch me again!" The stress of the last ten days slowly leaves my body. The fresh air clears the hospital out of my lungs. What a lovely time of year to convalesce. Later in the evening, after a lovely meal and a small glass of wine, I settle down to watch Britain's Got Talent which Paolo had recorded for me, with a small box of Belgium Chocolates. As the first act begins to perform, I need to go to the toilet. Oh good, the bowels are working fine. Fifteen minutes later I need to go again, not so good. Ten minutes later I need to go again, this time with a bit more urgency. Before we get to the results, I am hardly getting back onto the sofa before I am struggling to get back up again. The pain involved getting from the sitting to the standing position and the soreness of my bottom after numerous wipes are having an effect on me. "Is this what it is going to be like?" Will I always need to stay within a stride from a toilet?" Reluctantly, I go for a shower and get into bed. I take a couple paracetamols and a codeine (codeine makes me sleepy, but it can also make you constipated so have not taken any while in the hospital. Once I am lying down, the need for the toilet diminishes fairly quickly and within half an hour I am once more comfortable and relaxed.

Saturday 31st May dawns early, no squeaking breakfast trolley,

236

no nurses doing observations, no treks to the bathroom. Our chickens are squawking to be fed, the birds are singing in the trees, the sun is streaming through the blinds. The bedroom is cool. Paolo brings me a cup of tea, nice delicious PG Tips, not lukewarm, too strong hospital tea. In ten steps I am in the shower. The pain and the soreness are still the same, but so much easier to bear when I can distract myself. I open post, answer the phone and do bits of housework that do not involve lifting or too much bending. Paolo is bringing the business accounts up to date so that I can fill in the tax returns. I sit at the dining table eating my cereal and look at the flowers that have burst into life while I have been away. At dinner time I make eggs on toast with fresh eggs from our chickens and reward them by letting them free in the back garden. (They thank me by pooing all over the picnic table)

Outside the playroom door we have a large rubber sheet. It has saved hundreds of lumps on heads when toddlers have overbalanced going through the door into the garden. But it is a sponge and holds onto the rain forever and so is constantly wet. Paolo asks me if he should put decking there and I say Ok. Within an hour he is back from B&Q with decking that has the fake grass down the centre. He pushes two wooden pallets up to the door and lays the decking on top and voila! I have lovely decking. It actually takes him the rest of the day to assemble it properly, measuring the gaps and screwing it into place but I have to admit that my husband is fast becoming a DIY expert.

Sunday 1st June 2014 Another lovely sunny day. I settle myself down in the garden with a good book. My peace is shattered when Nathan appears pushing a double pram containing his grandsons and accompanied by Mason, his son. The boys drag toys out and soak themselves playing in water. Initially I was feeling a bit sulky at my shattered peace, but then realised that I was getting all the pleasure of watching grand children without having to do anything of the work. I relaxed and enjoyed their company. At dinner time we had lamb stew with red cabbage and roast potatoes. I took a loperomide (poo thickener) that had been prescribed while I was wearing the stoma. My auntie arrives just as Nathan and co. were leaving, followed soon after by my sister. It was so lovely to get back to a normal Sunday. As we settled down in the evening, I needed the toilet, I went once and then watched TV without any more distractions. I could almost believe that I can draw a line under this whole cancer business.

Monday 2nd June Robert drops off Lily and Isaac, he is taking Jamie fishing. I get out all the paint and we sit at the dining room table having fun with art. Not once did I remind them to rinse the brushes between colours, in fact I dollop white paint into 6 bun trays and they add other colours to make different shades of white. After a picnic lunch, we bake cakes and cookies and then I settle down once again with a book while they play together in the sunshine. What a lovely life I have. In the afternoon, it begins to cloud over so I begin to bring some washing in off the line. As I am doing it Adam shouts me to say that the district nurse is here. I had forgotten about her coming to change the dressing. She takes off the old dressing and says "Oh Wow, it is completely healed, you don't need another" She tells me that she does not need to come back to me as I am young and fit, but to ring if I need anything. It doesn't take much flattery to lift my spirits even higher than they already are. In hindsight, I should have been out of hospital after 3 days not 10. She probably hadn't realised that it had been nearly two weeks since my operation. But it didn't matter, her words had a positive effect on me so that's all that counts. Just as she was leaving, a friend phones to ask how I am. I boast to her about my fast healing skin. Then I copy and paste the message to WhatsApp and Facebook. I love this Social Media for getting messages to everyone you know. Unfortunately, some of my friends are on both facebook and WhatsApp and so they got the message twice and one sent a sarcastic reply. I need honest friends like this to stop me getting carried away with myself.

While on WhatsApp, I jokingly say that I am considering walking round to one of their houses. They take me at my word and are waiting for me to go round. The idea takes hold and I convince myself it is a good idea. Not too far, but a bit of extra exercise and the chance of a catchup of whats been going on in the childminding world for the past two weeks. I think I will just go to the loo first. I go, then have a quick wash, then I need to go again, and again and again. In the end I sit at the computer desk which is about the maximum distance from the toilet that I can manage when the urge takes me. As on Saturday night, the trips become more and more urgent and frequent until finally I don't get there in time. I have a shower and take myself off to bed. Tomorrow I will have to see what is available in adult sized nappies or I shall be stuck inside forever. Once in bed the necessity to go to the toilet goes and I have a good sleep.

Tuesday 3rd June I phone the doctor and Brunlee Surgical Supplies and am directed to Boots chemist. I buy some Tena Ladies (I never realised that they are basically an adult pull up) With the added security we have a ride to Bents Garden Centre where, as usual, we spend too much money. Then to the Moorings for lunch by the side of the canal. We go to price up hiring a canal boat for the day and then set off to visit Jackie and Steve as he has just had a knee replacement. But by this time I am very tired and my belly feels like it is hanging off me. We go home, Paolo to plant the new flowers and me to have a siesta.

Later my bowels start playing up again and I spend an hour or so rushing to the toilet. I am beginning to consider going to bed, but my friend Dot is coming round. As abruptly as they started, my bowels stop. Dot arrives and we spend a pleasant couple of ours chatting and then afterwards I watch a film on TV then go to bed. Things are getting back to normal.

Wednesday 4th June - Paolo goes round to Rachael's house to tidy her garden and I get Shauna to help me to do the housework. In the evening we go to the Chinese Buffet and even later call to see Steve's swollen legs (after his replacement knee operation) I chat to Jackie while Steve and Paolo watch a football game on TV. Just before half time, I start to feel the tell-tale signs that my bowels are getting revved up so we say our goodbyes and go home. But it was a false alarm. My paranoid alter-ego starts to worry that I am now going to be constipated but my rational self enjoys the rest. I watch TV for a while then go to bed and sleep like a baby without any pain relief.

Thursday 5th June We only have Lily and Isaac again this morning. I ask them "Do you fancy walking round to see my friend Joyce? They answer that they do and begin to put their shoes back on. As we walk round Lily obviously think that she has been a bit rash agreeing to this, it would be boring sitting listening to me talk to a friend. She asks me "Does Joyce have grandchildren? I say No, but she is a childminder like me, she has a lot of toys and games to play with" Then Isaac chips in, "She's a childminder but not like you!" I begin to imagine that he is going to say that I am much nicer than Joyce (after all I am his Nanna) He continues "Her hair is smoother" - Thanks Isaac. We drink tea and chat and they explore different games and toys until they are bored. After we pick up Lily's older brother Jamie and go to the cinema to watch Maleficent and then to Frankie and Bennies. After eating a pizza, Paolo orders a chocolate brownie and ice-cream. I'm not a lover of chocolate cake or ice cream and its a bit early in the day really for tea, so I don't have a dessert. Just for something to do while everyone is eating, I pick up a fork and pinch a bit of the brownie. It is like manna from heaven, warm chocolate sponge with bourbon sauce, Paolo is very lucky that I didn't eat it all. But by this time I was feeling bloated and sluggish. I had been supplied with laxative so apparently they had expected me to need it at some point, but I am not ready to admit that my body can't solve this problem with food and exercise. After the kids have been collected, I phone my sister to see if she wants to go out (a pint of Guinness might just be what the doctor ordered). But she is in Manchester.

Then I phone Gary, my brother and sit talking on the phone to him for an hour and a half. By this time it is 9.30p.m. I don't feel like watching TV so I have a bath and go to bed with a book. I don't take the laxative, I will give it one more day.

Friday 6th June I get up and make porridge. Paolo suggests a day or week-end out. I phone the Fat Lamb, a hotel/restaurant in the Lake District that has been recommended. But it is fully booked. Then I think about my brother Perry who lives in Oxford. I have been promising him a visit for ages. I ring him but he is on his way to work and has made arrangements for the weekend. He says his band is playing a gig on Saturday night if I am interested. I don't think I fancy travelling all that way to watch him play and then come home again. I decide to go another weekend when he is not so busy. The sun is shining, do I really want to sit in traffic for an hour or so when I can relax with a book here. And long distance travel is not recommended so soon after surgery as it can encourage blood clots when your legs are kept in one position for any length of time.

Paolo is easy going and has plenty of jobs to keep him busy (Contrary to popular belief, it isn't me that finds these jobs for him to do) I am still feeling bloated, so eventually I give in and take some laxative. I walk round to see a friend to return a pump I borrowed and to see my auntie. Then return home, hang washing out, put another wash in and settle down with a John Grisham novel. Perfect convalescence, a bit of exercise and lots of rest and fresh air.

Saturday 7th June The laxatives have worked - back to the loose stools - lovely! I wear Stena Ladies and we have a ride to IKEA to replace a bathroom mirror that Shauna accidentally smashed. When we get back she is still in her bedroom. I ask her what she is going to do today and she says she hasn't decided. Paolo and I go back out to do food shopping and I buy birthday cards for Bobby who will be 2 on Monday and some water toys. And a card for my brother who will be 61 on Thursday. When we get back Shauna is out, there is no message and she doesn't return home until Sunday evening.

Sunday 8th June 2014 I very bravely go to church wearing normal underwear on the assumption that up to now my loose poos have been in the evening. I don't stay for coffee morning thought, that would be pushing my luck.

Paolo cooks braised steak for dinner with lots of delicious veggies, and huge Yorkshire puddings and disappointing dumplings (suffice to say, the dumplings were my only contribution). Never mind, he didn't marry me for my culinary skills. In the afternoon Nathan phones to ask if I know where Shauna is. I tell him that I am disappointed in her. She is 20 years old, if she wants to stay out all night she is entitled to, but she is also part of this household and as such if would be courteous to say when she is going out, shout a greeting on her way in and let me know if she is staying out the night. The day passes as usual with my sister and auntie spending a few hours here. Shauna comes in and goes to her bedroom without a word.

Monday 9th June, I wake Shauna at 7.a.m. I tell her that we had a deal when she moved in. I would provide a room, pay for the gas electricity, water and food and her part of the deal was to eat three meals a day, keep her appointment, try to get a job and not do anything to jeopardise getting her boys back. She also agreed to do one hour's housework a day. She hardly looks me in the eye, makes excuses about broken phones and gets really shirty when I suggest that she cares about no one but herself. I tell her I want an apology and a change of attitude or she must find somewhere else to live. Later she sends me a text apologising and promising to change her attitude. I think this has been instigated by her mum and dad who would not want the hassle of finding her somewhere else to live. I accept her apology and say I will speak to her later.

Tuesday 10th June. Another glorious day. Childminding is so much easier when the weather is good. We have a little boy in our care at the moment who doesn't show much emotion with facial features. Paolo brings out drinks and fruit for snack and shouts to the kids "Snack Time" They all respond except this one child who carries on playing in the sand. I go to get him and say "Come on Josh" but he doesn't acknowledge me so I get hold of his hand and say again "Come on Josh, snack time" and run across the garden pulling him with me. His face lights up into a big grin and he starts squealing with pleasure, so I continue round and round the garden until I am exhausted (he rarely seems to get out of breath). In the afternoon his mum comes to collect him and I tell her about it. As he is ignoring her I take hold of his hand once more and run around the garden until again he squeals in pleasure. She is pleased about her son but aghast at me. "Would your surgeon approve of you running like that?" she says. I admit that he probably wouldn't.

Wednesday 11th June I have stomach ache. Possibly from the inadvisable running or maybe from my bowels starting to process food properly. Whatever the reason it is quite uncomfortable. We have 5 little ones today and they paint and play with water, watering the plants and soaking themselves in the process. I do a lot of sitting down watching, rubbing my belly to try to relieve the discomfort. In the afternoon I ask Paolo to help with the school runs. Today we have to pick up at three schools, one of them twice to accommodate two children in after school clubs. Paolo goes to pick up at Wharton Primary at 3 pm and then goes to St Pauls Primary at 3.30. I Walk to Dukesgate Primary for 3.15 pm, pushing the double buggy and calling at the butchers for bacon on the way. The walking believe it or not, is easier on my tummy than driving. On the way back I realise that I have not brought my keys out with me but I don't worry about it. By the time we have walked home, Paolo should be arriving in the car. We get home and I check to see if I have left the garage door open but of course Paolo has locked it before he left. I sit patiently on the bench in the front garden while the kids run around kicking the ornamental stones so lovingly laid by Paolo. By 3.50 p.m. I am getting seriously worried, I have to return to Wharton by 4 o'clock and drop off a baby with her granddad. At 3.57 p.m. The car carrying Paolo and 6 kids turns into the street. He had been delayed by one conscientious teacher who didn't recognise him and insisted on checking up on him before allowing the child to go. (She was a "new" child, only having been with us a week, so the teacher was doing her job properly.) We swap places in the car and Paolo takes the kids inside and starts making tea (spaghetti carbonara, a favourite with all the kids except Isaac, who insists on removing every last piece of bacon before he eats it). I needn't have worried about the time, as I arrive at school, the children are only just leaving and Alise is chatting to a friend and not in the least bit of a hurry. When I take the baby to her granddad, he is painting a play house for her and hadn't even realised the time.

Thursday 12th June The pains in my tummy are worse, I should really have taken a parecetamol or other pain relief, but I am quite stubborn and convince myself that if I keep walking I will eventually get better. We have 4 kids and take them with a picnic to Victoria park in Swinton. But by lunch time, the sun is so hot that I worry about these little blonde babies and so we go to the Fun House. It was a good choice because it is nearly empty so the kids have the place almost to themselves. We buy the kids dinner and Paolo and I have warm baggets. It is a mistake since the pains in my stomach become much more persistent. I'm not sure if the pains are being caused by the warm bread, the cheesy chips that I pinch from the kid's plates, or by the running around that I had done with the children yesterday. I have arranged to meet my sister in Wetherspoons and invited my brother Kevin along since it is birthday. At 7 p.m. the cramps are so bad that I am lying on my bed trying to find a comfortable position but by 8.15, I am washed and dressed and ready to go out. Paolo knows better than to suggest that I don't go, but very kindly offers to run me there in case I urgently need the toilet while I am walking. My sister phones to say that she doesn't mind if I would rather stay at home. I tell her that an evening in the pub is just what the doctor ordered. If I feel too bad after a drink, I can easily come home again. By 8.30 I am in the pub with my sister and drinking a pint of Guinness and blackcurrant . A few minutes later my brother arrives and later still his girlfriend Diane. While drinking the Guinness, my pains start to subside and I don't need to rush to the loo. By the second one we are laughing and joking and I feel better than I have done all week. By the time Kev drops me off at home, I am tired and relaxed. I say hello and then goodnight to Paolo, get into my pyjamas and am asleep in minutes and don't awaken until 8 o'clock the next morning. Sometimes the best way to deal with a problem is to ignore it and hope it goes away. p.s. Paolo is not excluded from these pub nights but it is not his "thing" he prefers to get on with his gardening, watch TV or fall asleep in a chair, but unlike my ex-husband he is not jealous that I want to go out and does not worry that I might be cheating on him (I'm probably not the "catch" I once was)

Friday 13th June - Paolo does the morning school run and takes two babies with him. He then puts petrol in the car and does some shopping, while I clear away the breakfast dishes. I send a couple of photos via email to one of the parents who can't receive photos on her phone. Then I take over the childcare while Paolo cuts the grass. After dinner the youngest child goes to sleep and the other two settle down in front of the TV. Joyce has got some children's chairs and is selling them for £2.50 each. I have ordered four. When I go to pay her for them, I offer to take chairs to Wendy and Dot as they don't have a car at their disposal. While I am talking to Wendy, her house phone begins to ring, but she lets it go to answer machine. Then her mobile rings and once more she ignores it. When it rings for a second time, I ask her "Don't you think you should look who is calling you, it might be an emergency. She

244

looks at the screen and says "Oh its your Paolo" I take the phone from her and Paolo says "Where is your phone? (in the car) What are you doing about Jamie?" OH SHIT!!! I am supposed to have picked up my grandson at his primary school at 11.45 am and dropped him at St James High for a taster day. I rush out of Wendy's house without even saying goodbye and do a U-Turn in the road. I pick him up at 12.20 and get him there at half twelve. I rush into the reception ready to beg and plead for them to let him join in the taster even though he is late. I needn't have worried, as we walk into the reception, I woman (teacher I presume) says "Hi Jamie, just come and sign my list so that we know you are in the building" Then turns to the rest of the group sitting waiting patiently and says "only two more to come and then we can get on with it". I am glad I forgot, it saved Jamie having to wait there. Later in the week, Helen tells me that she had told me the wrong time, he should have got there at 12.30. Serendipity!

Saturday 14th June, Rachael has suggested that we have a World Cup Football party so that they can all have company while cheering on England. This is not unanimous Paolo of course supports Italy. The England v Italy match is not on until 11 p.m. they will probably all be tipsy on wine or beer by then and Paolo will probably be asleep, sunshine and wine soon get to him.

Helen and her two youngest children Lily and Jamie arrive first, this in itself is reason for celebration. Helen never arrives early for anything. Nathan and his son Mason come next and then Rachael. Adam and his girlfriend Valda, Matteo and my sister Gail complete the party. Paolo makes a delicious lasagna, some garlic bread and pizza. Lily practises riding a bike without stabilizers for hours until she has mastered it. Mason and Jamie play football and then make elastic bracelets and everyone else helps themselves to food and drink and we chat and watch football matches until the England/Italy match comes on. Just before half-time, my bowels began to make themselves heard. Not wanting to gas everyone, I feign tiredness and go to bed with a book. I am not a big football fan, the best part of the day i.e. having the family together, has been lovely.

Sunday 15th June, I woke up early, the sun was streaming through the blinds, Paolo seemingly sleeping peacefully. I asked "Who won?" obviously not in such a deep sleep, but still with his eyes shut, he did a little victory dance with his hands. It was Father's Day. I went downstairs and made breakfast for us and also made a start on the mess from the evening before. A little later I hear noses in the kitchen. I knew it would be Rachael cleaning up so I went downstairs to help her. A couple of minutes later Adam and Valda also appeared and she said to him "Help your mum" and he did and so did she. Many hands make light work. The kitchen was soon sparkling like a new pin, Rachael had gone home, Adam and girlfriend went out and I went back to bed to read my Jeffrey Deaver novel.

I can easily lose hours when reading a good book so I am not sure what time it is when my friend Lesley calls to see me. I answer the door in my pyjamas and we drink coffee and catch up with each other's news. When she leaves, I think "I had better get dressed". Still not looking at the time, I wash and dress, only as I put my watch on do I realise that it is 1.23 pm. For a minute I try to remember what I had had planned for today. Then I remember, I had promised Lily that I would go to church to see her walk with Rainbows. I am out of the door in minutes and soon joining in the Whit celebrations. The band and banners. It was a little sad watching the tiny procession! Apart from the band and church leaders and Brownies and Rainbows, there were only about 50 other walkers, mainly elderly men and women. When I was Lily's age, the processions (Catholics on Good Friday and Anglicans on Whit Monday) took hours to pass. Rain or shine thousand of people came to walk or to cheer on the walkers, celebrating their love of God and showing off their best clothes.

In the afternoon, Paolo receives Father's Day cards and gifts from our children. I don't cook Sunday dinner, (It would be a crime to let me loose on a roast lamb) but I do help with the vegetable preparation and do all the cleaning/washing up afterwards. I give him a card from me and tell him I have bought him a present. He says "I thought we agreed that we wouldn't buy presents for each other (the Astra was a joint present for us for our birthdays, both in April, Mothers Day and Fathers Day), but then he laughs when he sees that I have just replaced his toothbrush which had run out of batteries.

In the evening Paolo cheers as Switzerland win, Monday I wake up early and go to the loo. For the first time since the operation there are no stains on the pads in my pants (I know! too much information) Another box ticked on the road to recovery. I am quite pleased how quickly things seem to be improving. Before the first op. I was warned, that I might have to wear a bag for the rest of my life, or that I might never completely regain control. Well the bag is off and control is galloping forward.

The weather is sunny and we spend the majority of time childminding outdoors, either in the garden or in the park feeding the ducks. I am sure that this is helping with my recovery. I am not attempting to go swimming yet, it could be a bit embarrassing, though I did consider wearing my Tena Ladies on the outside of my costume like superman. (Is it a whale?, is it an octopus? - No its Tena Lady). To make up for this I am doing more walking and this is having the advantage of keeping my weight down to the couple of pounds lighter that resulted from all that "Nil By Mouth" rubbish. Helen has registered to do the 5K Run For Life at Heaton Park. Rachael asks me if I fancy doing a walking half marathon. I say "Ok, go on then, when is it?", "It's in July" I was thinking she was talking about next year. Well I guess I have committed myself now. It will give me a chance to give something back to Bolton Hospital and Cancer Research for saving my life.

Wednesday 18th June.. Another lovely day. I am waiting in for a plumber to sort out the leak in the shower and a man from Lancashire Iron to give me a price for fitting a gate to the side of my front garden. Neither of them arrive. We have 2 three year olds, 3 two year olds and a 1 year old. The youngest has discovered that she can undo her nappy. I think that maybe she is trying to tell me that she is ready for potty training, but no, she wont sit on the potty or toilet. Oh well its no hardship, if she "goes" in the garden it can easily be cleaned up and it might be an early lesson if she realises what she is doing. Bobby brings me a plastic kangaroo. He shows me and says "kangaroo" I say "Yes, it's got big strong legs to jump very far". In his other hand is a very politically correct figure of a man wearing callipers. Bobby says

247

"Man jump very far?" I answer, "No, he's got poorly legs, look at the callipers". Bobby says "Kiss him better?" With that he gives the man's legs a kiss and then launches him up the garden. "Man can jump very far now!" Bailey is playing with a wooden crocodile out of a very old Noah's Arc, floating it in the water. Nathan arrives to take him home and says, "Bailey don't put that in the water, it is wooden" Bailey says "No its a crocodile" Nathan says "its a wooden crocodile, put it back in the Arc, put the elephant in the water (plastic elephant). "No!" I can't" says Bailey, "The crocodile will eat it"

As I stand outside St Paul's Primary waiting for Keith, Millie and Charlotte, my bottom goes into hyperdrive. I am trumpeting like an elephant and the smell is awful. Usually, I pretend that I am an innocent party and don't acknowledge that I have smelt anything. Today is different, it is perfectly obvious where the noise and smell is coming from. I notice a couple of mothers giving each other knowing smiles and then turning their backs on me to hide their giggles. I have to change my tack before they begin to point me out to the rest of the population waiting to pick up the children. I say out loud "I am soooo sorry about the smell, I have just had surgery for bowel cancer and I was warned that this would cause this problem for a few months". At once the women stop giggling and look at me with embarrassment. Then one of them says, "Are you cured then now?" and when I answer in the affirmative, she congratulates me and says, don't worry about farting, mine are much louder than that and I don't even have an excuse" I pick up the kids from school and Paolo makes Meat Balls and Pasta for tea. He has also repositioned the swings and the concrete is not dry. There isn't a cat in hell's chance that all the kids will remember to keep off the swings, so after tea, I take them all to the park. Isaac practices riding a two wheel bike, doesn't quite manage it, Charlotte rides around with her new skill (she has just mastered riding a two-wheeler) and Keith nearly knocks everyone over, riding fast and using only one hand. We set off for home just as several of the parents come looking for us. When we get home, Paolo has cleared away all the tea pots, and also most of the toys. Summer is so much easier.

248

33 - Barbecue

Friday 20th June 2014 - As we watch TV in the evening, the weather forecaster reminds me that it is "the longest day of the year tomorrow" and also that the weekend is going to be warm and dry. Why didn't I arrange for a barbecue? I have been meaning to organise one with the parents of the children we look after, partly to celebrate my recovery and to thank them for their co-operation and support over the last 8 months, since my first hospital appointment. I mention it to Paolo and he just says "Invite everyone now then, if they have other commitments they can say no and if they can come, they will" So I do, I WhatsApp all the parents.

Saturday 21st June 2014 - I wake up and remember that I once more have forgotten Jackie's Birthday. She is one of my closest friends, I have known her for 40 years and yet I still forget her birthday. It upsets me that I do this, I do not have a good memory but I am particularly good at remembering family birthdays (and there are a lot to remember) and last Thursday when we were celebrating Kevin's birthday in Wetherspoons, I remember thinking that I must remember to get a card for Jackie. I know that she will forgive me, she always does but the brain is a strange thing, and I wish I could just insert a new memory stick into it to remind me of such things.

I check my phone and have received two replies from the message I sent yesterday. One to say No, they are away and another to say Yes Please. I hope I receive more replies. By tea time, we have a sufficient number of people to throw a party - 16 Adults and 16 kids - what are we thinking of, kids ransacking my house on a week-end. We must be mad.

I get a text from Shauna saying that she is staying at her mum and dad's house tonight, that she has got an offer of a flat and would I write her a reference. She has also got an appointment for a job interview. I have mixed feelings about all this. I am glad she is going to get her independence back but there has been such an improvement in her behaviour since she has lived here, I really want to have more input. I worry that without the structure of a normal household she will revert to her old ways of partying through the night and not getting up for work in the morning. Still it is not my decision, so I write a reference and email it to the housing department.

Sunday 22nd June dawns bright and sunny. After a lazy morning, Paolo begins to cook. He cooks the ham joint that I had originally bought for Sunday dinner along with some new potatoes and of course his speciality lasagna. He also prepares several salads, beetroot and mayonnaise, coleslaw, orange and fennel and green beans in a delicious dressing.

Paolo is Italian but was brought up in Switzerland. He is a happy man. Being brought up with a mixture of languages, Paolo does not have a recognizable accent, no-one would guess he was Italian. But he has little foibles. When cold callers ring, he will answer them saying "sorry I am not interesting" and although his English is very good, he still confuses the sound i as in ink and ee as in sheep. This, as you can imagine can change the whole meaning of a sentence. Heap hip, sheep ship, been bin, heat hit, leave live, fit feet, etc. He is like a child learning to put on their shoes. The law of averages would mean that sometimes they get them on the correct feet. You would think that Paolo would sometimes get the correct pronunciation but he rarely does.

His mispronunciation of ee and i nearly cause a problem. As I am grating carrots and arranging the drinks etc, he points to a pan of liquid and says "this is for the bin when it is cold", I carry on with the grating and then test the liquid and yes it is cold. I am just about to tip the contents of the pan down the sink when Paolo spots me and shouts "STOP! What are you doing". I tell him that I cannot just pour it into the bin, so I am pouring it down the sink. He says, "But that is the dressing for the beans, not the bin" As I mentioned earlier, his english is very good but it still confuses. At the eleventh hour, I decide that I should have bought bread for the sausage and beef burgers that Adam is going to barbecue, I send Matteo to Tesco. Just as he leaves, Adam asks me where I have hidden the charcoal for the barbecue, I tell him that if it is not with the barbecue then he had better phone Matteo to pick some up.

The party is a success. Of course it would have been better if I had arranged it earlier, but it was good enough. The kids painted the Wendy House and then left red hand prints everywhere they touched until they had each been caught and had their hands washed. Adam lit the barbecue but then everyone had had their fill with the lasagna and ham etc so there was no need to cook sausages and beef-burgers (and no need for me to send Matteo to Tesco) The kids skewered marsh mallows and melted them over the hot coals so it wasn't a complete waste. The sun stayed shining, everyone was complementary about the food, the kids enjoyed themselves without making too much mess and I hardly trumped or had to rush to the toilet all afternoon.

Later, I discover that by chopping and changing my mind about the barbecue, I had nearly caused Adam to go hypo. When I first asked him to cook the sausages and beef-burgers, he injected his insulin, so that he would not have to leave the fire unattended while the kids were running around. Of course, I then told him to delay cooking the sausage etc as everyone seemed to be having their fill of lasagna. I fret and worry about him, but then at other times forget his condition altogether.

Tuesday 24th June - As I drop some jumble off at the charity shop, I notice a readers digest book for sale (Like new, who would believe that anyone would buy a book from readers digest and not read it!) The Title is Managing Pain - the natural way. I flick through it in the evening and think that I may send it to my brother. But then I think, "Will he find ways of relieving his pain, or will he discover more conditions to be affected by". I decide to send it. I can be a bit of a hypochondriac, I am sure that I would discover that I am suffering from several illnesses once I learn the symptoms.

Rachael tells us that to encourage Isaac to practice learning to ride his bike without stabilizers she has promised him the latest "Ben Ten" toy once he has mastered it. But Isaac didn't want to wait for it and was pestering her. Being awkward and uncooperative with all her plans for the week-end. She said to him"Isaac, you might as well forget about the toy if you are going to pull your face all day" to which he replied, "I wouldn't be pulling my face if you just bought the toy, I would be very happy"

251

If he can argue with such good reasoning now, aged 5, God help us when he is 15.

Lily has just pulled out her first milk tooth. How she didn't lose it I will never know. It was the tiniest tooth I have ever seen (or maybe my eyesight is worse than I thought it was). It was wrapped in a piece of kitchen roll and every time a parent came to pick up their child, they were treated to a showing. When her dad came to pick her up, she was giddy with anticipation of going to bed and putting the tooth under the pillow for the fairies. It is lovely to watch children before they get wise and stop believing and it reminded me of an incident I had when Matteo was younger. I can't remember how old he was. Going into his bedroom, while he was at school, I noticed two milk teeth on his window sill. I was surprised that they were there as I didn't think he would have any more milk teeth to lose. I was quite sad that he no longer believed in the fairies as they were not under his pillow. I decided to play a game and replaced them with 50p's. When he came home, I said, a little tongue in cheek, "the fairies saw your teeth on the window sill and left you some money!" He replied "Those fairies must have been short-sighted, they were not teeth, they were Rice Krispies" He didn't return the £1 though.

Thursday 26th June. I was looking forward to my usual night out with my sister. She phoned to say that she would be late and so I agreed to meet her at 9 pm. I had been particularly "windy" all day and had made many runs to the toilet, not all of them productive. Paolo offered to run me there, I agreed but said I would walk back. I'm sure the 20 minute walk does not burn off all the calories of two pints of Guinness, but it must burn off more than sitting in a car. The pub was very busy with people taking advantage of the Curry Night and to watch the last stages of the World Cup, but it wasn't too loud for us to hold a conversation. We decided to share a plate of chips and mayo (the walk home definitely would not make an impact on the calorie intake) glancing at the menu, I realised that I could have had a curry, which included a free pint, for only pennies more than what I had paid for the Guinness and chips. As we were discussing the merits of curry v chips, I remarked to Gail that each time I had drunk Guinness since my operation, not only had I slept all night without having to go to the toilet, but the next day, I had also had much less activity of my bowels. The first time it had happened, I had presumed that it was just a co-incidence but this was the third night out, so if it happened again, I was definitely going to believe the old adage "Guinness is Good for You"

Friday 27th June, I wake up after a perfect night's sleep, no trips to the toilet. The day continues in the same vein, I can almost believe that I am completely back to normal. I google Guinness and am informed that Diago, the company that now brews it, reports: "We never make any medical claims for our drinks" But researchers speaking at a meeting of the America Heart Association Orlando, Florida, report that it reduced clotting activity in the blood. I mention it to my son Adam and he offers his wisdom "Well everyone knows that after a night on the beer, you have larger bowel movements the next day" For whatever reason, I choose to believe that Guinness is doing me good and pour myself and Paolo a pint while we watch TV. I will have to keep an eye on my waistline.

Saturday 28th June, Paolo makes a lasagna for Joseph (one of the parents for his daughter's birthday). We have been invited for the party, but are not planning on staying. I love kids, but 5 days a week are sufficient, I like to enjoy adults company at the weekend. In the afternoon we go to St George's closing down party. This is the High School that I attended (it was called a secondary school then). As we drive towards the school, we see that all the roads leading towards it are full of parked cars on each side. I say to Paolo, "Just drive to Jackie's house, the space in front of her drive will be free" And I am right and feel quite clever. Jackie and Steve live directly opposite the main entrance. There are several cars parked on their drive but the house is empty so we go in search of them in the school. The assembly hall is full of bodies, looking at old photographs and it is stifling, We spot Steve (he also went to this school) and chat to him, then Jackie. I tell them that I am going outside as it is too warm for me. On the way out I catch sight of Zoe, their daughter and I wave to her. She waves back, then I see a thought dawn on her. "Is that your people carrier blocking my mum's drive?" She asks, "We have been Tannoying you to move your car so we can get out" Whoops!!

I was hoping to catch sight of pupils of my year. The school and grounds were heaving and accept for a few faces that I have seen around for the past 50 years, I don't see anyone else that I recognise of my age. But as I look around at the crowds, old and young, I think that I could be looking at someone from my year and not even know who they are, I am 63, I am sure I look a bit different from when I was 16 and so wouldn't they. I should have worn a t-shirt with my name and leaving date emblazoned across it. In the end we go back to our friend's house and drink coffee. Jackie asks what we are having for tea and I say "Liver, why?" "Oh I just didn't fancy cooking, I thought you might be eating out, I was going to suggest that we join you" I ask Paolo if the liver will stretch to four meals and he says it will so I invite them to join us. Steve is incredulous and laughs at his wife. "Jackie, How cheeky are you?, you can't make someone a cup of coffee and then ask them to make your tea for you". Jackie of course had no intention of inviting herself for tea, but she becomes embarrassed and laughs at herself. I say "If you can't invite yourself to tea with friends you have known for 40 years then when can you?

We have a lovely evening hardly mentioning my recovering bowels or Steve's new knee joint. It's been four weeks - old news.

34 - Friday 4th July

American Independence Day and the day I got engaged to my first love eons ago. It didn't last. A few months later my gran died, the first time that I had lost someone close and things that seemed important, no longer were. (What was the point of anything if you just died at the end of it?)I split up with Tom and started going out with Ken. He also was not "Mr Right" but his grandad had just died and he didn't mind me going on about my Gran. We had a holiday in Greece, traveling in a mini bus and sleeping in tents and me throwing up all the way there, much to the annoyance of the other 10 travellers. For all the wrong reasons (getting pregnant was one) we got married. Borrowed wedding dress, reception in my mum's kitchen, and a weekend in rainy Southport. We were not good together, but out of it came the most amazing four children. (2 boys and 2 girls, just as I had always planned as I read Enid Blyton's Bobbsy Twins). I was determined to make it a good marriage, like the good Catholic girl that I was, but after 20 years together, I threw in the towel. I decided that I could bring up my children better alone, that marriage had no advantages for women. I was going to go back to college, run a marathon, have a career; after all I was only 39. On my 40th birthday I met Paolo and the rest as they say is history. It has not been a bed of roses, debt, ex-partners, step children, cancer have all tried our strength. Paolo is 6 years younger than me so his Italian parents were not happy. But we have survived, grown and conquered everything that life has thrown at us and now are blessed with a wonderful family.

Saturday 5th July On the way to look for a new microwave, we call at the tip to dump the broken microwave and a buggy that had become unsafe. As we pull into a bay, I notice a man about to throw a children's slide into the skip. Before Paolo knows what I am doing, I jump out of the car and ask the man if I can have the slide. We already have three in our garden, but I hate seeing things that are not broken being discarded and I imagined that I could push it up against the trampoline to provide steps. Paolo laughs at me and then we treat everyone to a comedy scene as we try to fit it into the car. However, when we get back home, it is too high to use with the trampoline so I give it to Nathan for his grandsons.

255

Sunday 6th July - Another example of my"Womble" side occurs to me when I wake up. I had been at my brother's house on one occasion when he told me he had a bed to throw out. There was nothing wrong with it, just taking up space in a spare bedroom where he wanted to install exercise equipment. I immediately offered to take it off his hands, it was in better condition than the one in my spare bedroom. Kev said "Ok I will put it in the garage, I never lock it so just take it whenever you want". That was before I discovered I had cancer so possibly about a year ago. I no longer want to replace the bed that is in our spare bedroom because it is a metal framed one and has lots of storage space underneath, but I feel obliged to do something about it and phone around everyone that I can think of who might make use of it. My brother's partner, Shelley says that their daughter could do with a new bed, so we go to collect it. When we get there (with my brother Carl chunnering about dragging him out when he could be marinating his chicken) they decide that Holly's bed is more "girlie" and so will repair the one she has already. Carl offers to take the bed to the tip, so at least Kevin has room in his garage once more. But if I hadn't interfered in the first place, the bed would perhaps have gone to a charity.

Paolo cooks duck and pork for dinner, followed by a shop bought Italian dessert. My auntie Josie comes for dinner as usual and Gail comes to pick at the vegetable and drink tea. We sit in the back garden in the glorious sunshine and plan a night out and Rachael phones to say that she has booked us up for the 5k run for life that takes place next Sunday 13th July. When she had suggested that we take part, I didn't realise that she meant this year, but never mind. I enjoy walking, I don't think I could manage to run far, so there is no need to train. After they leave I stack the dishwasher and clean the kitchen (my side of the bargain since Paolo cooks) then as Paolo watches the Grand Prix on TV, I read emails and play sudoko on the computer. I download a book onto my Kindle called Playing, Laughing and Learning with Children on the Autistic Spectrum". We are looking after a child who is possibly autistic. Gradually I become aware of my tummy rumbling and take the Kindle into the toilet with me. I have the most awful diarrhea that seems to last forever. Have I picked up a bug, should I go to the hospital or is this just another symptom of my bowels playing me up? I decide to wait and see. I go back to reading the book, but don't go too far away from toilet just in case.

Monday 7th July morning I awake to find that I have stopped needing to rush to the toilet, my bowels are back to "normal"

Saturday, 12th July. Paolo wakes me with a cup of tea, I am still tired. After eating a curry before bed, I have been suffering with indigestion all night and not had much sleep. Joyce phones me and asks "Who's been shot on your street?" I tell her that I haven't a clue, that I have been awake most of the night and had not heard anything. I phone another friend who lives at the other end of our street she quickly tells me that no-one has been shot. A couple were having a fight in the street and the police were called. The man then threatened a police officer with a gun, but the girl was fine and had been seen this morning. One of my minded children is having a splash party for his 5th birthday and I volunteer to take Lily and Isaac. With a pair of black knickers under a black swimming costume, I'm hoping that any small accidents will be contained until I get to the toilet. On the way, I pass the house where the incident with the gun occurred. In the street are 4 rapid response vans, two police cars and what seems to be the whole of the police force for the north west. I was under the impression that I was living in a rough area, perhaps I am mistaken, if all these resources can be deployed, 12 hours after the incident. The party is a success, for the birthday boy and for me. I have not needed the toilet for the full hour. The way is open for me to resume my early-morning swims.

Matteo has helped me to create an "event" on Facebook to advertise the fact that we are doing the Run For Life tomorrow and also to invite everyone to our house for a celebration party. I have told Paolo that there will probably be about 20 people but when I check on the computer, there are already 30 people plus children who have replied. Paolo asks me how many I have invited and I have to admit, about 100, quickly adding that a lot of people have already replied that they will not be coming for one reason or another. I hope I am not being too optimistic in thinking that I can complete this 5K race and still be fit enough to play hostess to so many guests. By 10 pm on Saturday, I have only just stopped.

257

Apart from the kid's party, I have cleaned the house, washed clothes, shopped for food for tomorrow and for a present for the birthday boy. Paolo settles down to watch TV and I am tempted to join him, but then remind myself that I have not had enough sleep last night and really need to sleep tonight if I intend to get up early and complete a sponsored walk.

Sunday 13th July dawns. The weather is a bit overcast so I pull on a shirt over my pink tee shirt. Rachael picks me up and then Gail. Isaac despite having been cooperative for his mum all morning has now decided that he doesn't want to do it. Helen, Robert and Lily are travelling separately so Rachael tells Isaac that he can stay with Robert and Jamie. When we eventually meet up in the middle of the thousands of runners (mobile phones are a godsend) Jamie is not with them, he has had a sleep-over with his friend. Isaac starts playing with Lily and forgets for the moment that he doesn't want to take part. The sun comes out, we join the competitors further back and it is lovely walking and chatting. The 1K marker is slow coming. As we reach it and take photos of each other Isaac says, does that mean we only have 1K to go. Rachael tells him that we have another 4K and he has a hissy fit. "Thats why I told you I didn't want to do it." Helen gives him her phone and tells him to take photos and I give mine to Lily. I must have about 50 pictures of the floor or trees or strangers but it has the desired effect and the kids don't complain again. As we reach the finishing line we all hold hands and go across together, except Isaac, who wants to get his medal first!

When Rachael drops me off at home, I find that it has been decorated with streamers and balloons and Paolo has bought me flowers. We have a lovely day with family and friends enjoying the sunshine and Paolo's food. I am not tired at this point although at the end of the day I wish for the stragglers to go home, but they are watching the world cup and since it goes into extra time, it is midnight before I go to bed and I haven't even attempted to clean up the mess. We are still recycling bottles and cardboard when the first of the minded children arrive but there are enough left over treats to keep them happy for a short while. I do not suffer cramped legs the following day, I must be regaining my fitness.

35 - Goodbye Pat

18th July - My eldest grandson's 18th Birthday. It would have been my mum's 87th. This is the first year I think that we have not got together to have a family meal in remembrance, it makes me sad that she is slipping further away. Silly really, she has been dead for 10 years, I make a note to gather the clan together soon. When she died, she left a note (written I suspect a few years earlier during a moment of melancholy) to say that she loved us all and was proud of us. She asked that we look after each other. It is difficult sometimes, with a sister and 6 brothers and families to keep track. The letter was particularly heart wrenching since I can't remember her ever saying she loved me to my face. She was a tough northern woman who rarely gave out praise, but you always knew she would be there for you and she would never give up on any of us. Arron is not having a party and doesn't ask for anything in particular, so Helen and Robert book rooms and a meal in the Midland Hotel in Manchester. Afterwards he goes out with his friends and doesn't need to worry about taxi fares home. We have Jamie, Lily and Daisy the dog for the night and despite my fears have no problems i.e. dogs or children waking me in the night.

During the evening, our friend Linda phones to tell us that Pat has been admitted to hospital and is having tests for suspected cancer. I am not surprised! When we went to Morecombe with them last August, after I had just been diagnosed, Pat was having problems then. She was having pains and needed to go to the toilet frequently but as she put it "only runny stuff was coming out, as if there were a blockage and the bulk of the poo couldn't get past". I advised her to get help immediately but she told me that she had already been to the doctor who had just prescribed laxatives. Apparently after that she had visited the doctor several times and even been to A&E but because in the past she has suffered with diverticulitis they had just put it down to that. So I was worried but relieved that she was at last being taken seriously. I told Linda that I would visit her in hospital over the weekend. On Saturday morning, the sore throat that had started the day before is much worse. I gargle with salt water, have a teaspoon of honey and take a couple of parecetamol, then I phone Pat to tell her that I will not be visiting today as I don't want to bring tonsillitis into the hospital. I ask her if they have reduced her pain and she explains that they have put a stoma bag on her (which had very quickly filled up with green gunk) to relieve the pressure and given her morphine and paracetamol so she was feeling much more comfortable. She had been for a scan but had not got the results back. She was worried about problems with a house. Years ago, Pat and Terry had moved to Spain. Before she went, she had sold her house and she had bought her mother-in-law's council house using the right-to-buy. She assumed that when the mother-in-law died, they would have a house to come back to. Unfortunately the move to Spain was not successful and they came back home and moved into a very small, one bedroomed council bungalow. At the time of the holiday in Morecombe, she told me that her and Terry were planning to move in with the old lady as she was now in her 90s and frail. Unfortunately the rest of Terry's siblings objected to them moving in, also unfortunately, Pat had never officially had the house put in her name. She was planning to see a solicitor about it. As I spoke to her in her hospital bed, I asked her about it and she told me that the old lady had since died and she had an appointment with a solicitor on Monday to sort out the deeds of the house and change her will. Terry has been suffering with dementia for a couple of years and she wanted to make sure that he would be taken care of if anything should happen to her. I suggested that I ask the solicitor should visit her in hospital but she said that she would just make another appointment when she got out. Later in the day, Jackie, another friend phoned her but she said that Pat seemed "spaced out" and was not making sense. We both planned to visit her on Sunday.

Sunday 20th July. Linda phoned me to tell me that Pat had only hours to live. She had organ failure due to overuse of paracetamol. The news hit me like a punch in the face. She told me that she had been at the hospital since the early hours. Pat was in a coma and her daughter and grandson, two aunties and several friends were around her bedside. I decide not to go, my throat is still very sore and I feel weak and lethargic. I phone Jackie and Steve and they rush to the hospital. Later Jackie reports that Pat had looked like a little old lady, gulping for breath. She was on a drip with a paracetamol antidote running into her veins. I send Linda a text and ask "does that mean that Pat is in with a chance, being on the drip" she replies "No darlin, they have taken all the drips away from her, its just a matter of time" The next phone call I receive tells me that Pat has passed away at 8.00 p.m. I am so angry, all that money raised for cancer research is useless if doctors don't listen when people tell them that they are ill and fob them off with laxatives, painkillers or antidepressants. Pat was the life and soul of the party, she was full of energy. She had a hard job looking after Terry but never complained.

Now the house she had paid for would not go to her daughter as she had planned and her family would grieve for her, years earlier than necessary. Selfishly, I once more counted my blessings for my early diagnosis and recovery.

36 - More Drama

Monday 21st July I don't hear the tap on the door at 5 am, but I am woken by Paolo jumping up and answering the knock with "Yes, what is it". Lauren has come to say that Matteo in lying on the bed in pain, he cannot move his neck. Paolo goes to see him and I look for some painkiller, I presume that he has overdone the exercise at the gym. But Paolo comes back to our room worried, Matteo has told him that on getting out of the shower he had heard a crack and a pain had shot down his back. I decide to phone 111 and ask for advice. The operator asks the usual questions, I expect him to tell him to take some pain relief and to rest, but instead he says that an ambulance is on its way. The paramedics are here within minutes and Lauren says she will go with him in the ambulance. I follow in my car to bring them back. At the A&E Matteo is still in pain but feeling a bit sheepish. He says he feels a fraud, even though he is still in a lot of pain and cannot move his head which is turned to look right. The triage nurse assesses him and gives him paracetamol and tells him to wait to see the doctor who will give him some muscle relaxant. I get him a snack from the machine and go home for a wash and to do the school run. I tell him to phone me when he is discharged.

Life is easier with sons when there is a girlfriend. I am reminded of this when I get home, still only 7 a.m. and Adam's girlfriend, Valda, is leaving for work. She doesn't speak to me as she is late for her bus, but sends me a text asking me to keep an eye on Adam because he is very tired, which was how she felt just before she had been ill with a very nasty bug the week before. I promise her that I will make him test his blood sugar levels before he leaves for work. In reality, I can't make Adam do anything, but I will suggest it to him. I'm beginning to rethink my last remark. I worry less about Adam when he is out with Valda, or for that matter when he is in the house with her, I no longer worry about him becoming ill during the night. But in reality, I don't worry about him 24/7, I have many other people and situations that need my concern, in fact sometimes I even forget about his diabetes, but with his girlfriend worrying about him and texting me to see if he is OK, I am reminded of it more often.

Matteo rings at 8.30 a.m. Paolo goes to get him and is still back in time to take Keith to school. The hospital were going to give Matteo a prescription for parecetamol and ibuprofen but told him it would be cheaper to buy them himself. They told him that he did right going to the hospital and to go back immediately if any other part of his body starts to go numb or painful. He has a day in bed, enjoying his first ever day off sick. He has made arrangements to go to Thorpe Park on Tuesday, staying over with some friends he made at Uni and then going to the fun park on Wednesday. He is worried that flinging his neck around on the rides might jolt it back into a painful stiffness again. I tell him to sleep on it, the decision will be easier after a night's sleep.

Tuesday 22nd July. Matteo gets up and goes to work, his neck is recovering. In the evening Lauren comes to the house and he sets off for Thorpe Park. I have an appointment to attend Mr. Hobbiss's Clinic at 10.40, I'm expected to be kept waiting and not expecting to actually see Mr Hobbiss in person. The first assumption was correct, but the second was a surprise. I waited around for over an hour but I didn't mind, this time I had remembered to bring a book. A nurse weighed me and then after a while I was ushered into another room. I didn't even take off my reading glasses as I presumed that I would have to sit waiting in the next room but, I was wrong. Mr Hobbiss along with a student were waiting to see me. Mr Hobbiss asked if "Things had returned to normal with the bowels" I answered that I had forgotten what normal is, but that I was managing and that I was sure that sooner or later things would get back to how they were. He reminded me that he had cut a large proportion of the bowel away, and that I may never regain full control. He asked me if I was making notes of how different foods affected me and I answered no, and I have no intention of doing so. I prefer to eat and drink whatever I fancy and deal with the consequences. Sooner or later, I am sure, my body with adjust to the loss of bowel. I do not want to be a victim in any way to this cancer. Up to now I have made the minimum of concessions and it has worked out well.

In the evening we picked up Jackie and Steve and went to visit Linda and Roy for an evening of remembrance for Pat. We reminisced about the way she would be a regular visitor to the

Labour Club. Always fashionable in the shortest of mini skirts (when she was younger and minis were in fashion) and a handbag full of babycham (so that she did not have to pay pub prices). I learned the name of her first husband and realised that he had gone to school with my brother and had actually saved him from drowning on a school trip. Small world. We got angry together about her treatment from her doctor and the hospital. Linda told us that Pat's daughter was planning a no-expense spared funeral but Linda reminded her that her mum was not like that and would be annoyed if she went into debt to bury her. A compromise seems likely. We talked about Terry, her husband who you wouldn't guess had dementia on first meeting him. At 70, he still has an eye for the ladies. One minute he remembers that Pat is dead, the next minute he is asking where she is. It's ironic that after her looking after him for so long, and lately wondering if she would be able to manage if his condition deteriorated, it is no longer her problem, the caring has been passed on to her daughter.

Friday 25th July 2014

Dear Mrs. Scotton
I am pleased to say that your CEA blood test, taken when you came to clinic yesterday, has been reported as entirely normal. We will see you in the clinic as planned.
Yours sincerely
Dictated not signed
J H Hobbiss MD FRCS Consultant Colorectal and General Surgeon

Saturday 26th July 2014

Dear Mrs Scotton
I am writing to inform you that your appointment to attend the Royal Bolton Hospital has been arranged.
Your appointment is with Miss G Faulkner Clinic and will be on:
Friday 23rd January 2015 at 930 am in General outpatients. Access to reception is through F Block Outpatients Ground Floor.

So that's it. The end of my journey. I will need to attend the clinic every 6 months for 5 years, which I am sure will be reassuring. It's a sobering thought though, that almost 12 months ago, as I added my sample to the screening cards and popped them in the post, Pat was just beginning to suffer the symptoms of bowel cancer. How different were the paths we took. RIP Pat xxx

In Hindsight

Would I have done things differently? Possibly I could have gone to Italy in August 2013. I don't think it would have made any difference to the outcome. Paolo could have done all his trips to the banks, post offices, solicitors and councillors that seem to be necessary since his dad's disappearance. We could have spent time with his mum and I would have had time to build myself up for an operation. But this would have necessitated waiting for appointments and for C.T. scans etc which would have given me more time to worry and stress and would have been very inconvenient for the families we service. The time between discovering the tumour and the operation would have been more drawn out and so given me and family and friends more time to worry. And more time for the tumour to grow and spread. I make many decisions in my life spontaneously, not giving myself time for self doubt. Sometimes I regret my decisions (especially when it involves confronting people without having the full facts of the situation), but on the whole I have no regrets and I am happy with the decisions I have made. So not going to Italy, telling family and friends immediately that I have a tumour rather giving myself time to get used to the idea myself, the choice of hospital, eating everything without checking recommended food and finally getting out of bed and back to work as soon as possible (with lots of support from my lovely husband primarily and all my other lovely family and friends.) It worked for me.

I am grateful for my life, my husband, children and grandchildren. I am thankful that I am still around and able to help out wherever I can. I love to listen to children's take on the world and to watch them grow. I have no hunger to travel the world though I wouldn't say no to holidays abroad, I have everything around me to make me happy. Thank you God!

Epilogue

This diary began as a way for me to remember the details and emotions I was living through. The humour is the way I cope with life I suppose. Because of the nature of the disease, it was difficult to write without using words that I wouldn't normally use day to day.

Early on in the treatment, I related to my doctor the incident of blocking up the shower, causing the bathroom flood. He was laughing so much and said I should write it down because there are thousands of cancer sufferers who would benefit from a bit of lightheartedness.

I suppose I wanted to show that life can carry on around the treatment. Also for my children, I wanted them to remember, If the treatment hadn't been successful, that my life during this treatment had still contained lighter moments and happiness. At the same time, I didn't want people to underestimate how low my mood was at times and to know this is normal but not permanent.

Other SWit'CH Publications

My Life and Other Misadventures

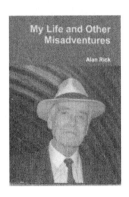

ISBN 978-1-326-60665-7
By Alan Rick

A collection of humorous and poignant nostalgic reminiscences covering Alan's early school years in the war to national service in Egypt. Alan looks askance at the society of the day with a wry, knowing, smile.

The Big Switch

ISBN : 9798644090433

Iin large print format 'The Big Switch' is a compilation of extracts from some of the group's previously published works. It is designed for easy reading with a font design developed by RNIB.

Peterloo People
ISBN 978-0-244-18472-8

A potpourri of passions gives the reader the chance to walk in those shoes to the peaceful protest, the actions on the day and shameful reaction afterwards. But the focus is not only on the victims; the perspectives of the authorities and militia are treated with sympathy and criticism in due turn – and there's even a wry tale of hope and salvation for a government spy.

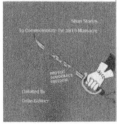

Switch On, Write On, Read On

ISBN 978-1-326-73048-2

Approx. 200 page the first showcase of the group's creativity. Containing nearly sixty humorous, whimsical, thought-provoking, ironic, and eclectic writing.

268

A Write Good Read

ISBN 978-0-244-73623-1

Tales from Swinton and Salford; the Wigan train and around the world drawing on the experiences and interests of the group. Modern telecoms and IT feature, so do the Ten Commandments and seven dwarfs. Historical pieces range from the industrial revolution to individual childhood memories.

The Taste of Teardrops

ISBN 978-0-244-26569-4
Novel by Judith Barrie.

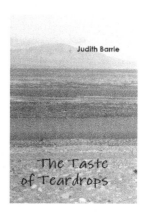

A gripping psychological thriller set in a sleepy seaside town on The Solway Firth. It's 1981 and a young woman settles into her cosy new home believing that she had found peace and tranquillity after a painful break-up.
But there are mysteries. Who is the woman upstairs? And who is the irresistibly attractive man who visits her? Susan is unaware of the nightmare she will drawn into, driving her to the very edge of her sanity.

Memories Unlocked

ISBN: 9798570919617

Childhood recollections were gradually teased out; the memory of one triggering recall in another. Mainly set in the North West the groups' horizons were broadened as new members brought insights of being raised in Italy, Switzerland, the Caribbean and Pacific Islands. Nature notes, plane crashes, sex education, walking home after dancing, vanished places make up the mischief, mayhem and misadventures of our young lives.

Printed in Great Britain
by Amazon

55951737R00159